A Text Book Of

FUNDAMENTALS OF BOTANY
PLANT DIVERSITY AND INDUSTRIAL BOTANY

For
F.Y.B.Sc. Botany, Term I : Paper – I & II
As Per New Revised Syllabus of Pune University, June 2013

Dr. K. N. Dhumal
Professor of Botany (Retd.), Dept. of Botany,
University of Pune,
Pune – 411 007.

Dr. T. N. More
Principal, MAEER'S Arts,
Commerce and Science College,
Pune - 411 038.

Dr. H. S. Patil
Asso. Prof. & Head, Dept. of Botany,
Vidya Pratishthan's Arts, Science
and Commerce College, Baramati.

Dr. B. N. Zaware
Principal, PDEA's
Anantrao Pawar College,
Pirangut, Dist. Pune.

Dr. S. S. Gadekar
Asso. Prof. & Head, Dept. of Botany,
N. Wadia College, Pune - 411 001.

Dr. A. D. More
Asso. Prof., Dept. of Botany,
Fergusson College, Pune – 411 004.

Dr. B. P. Shinde
Asso. Prof. Fergusson College,
Pune 411 004.

Dr. K. S. Bhosale
Asso. Prof. N. Wadia College,
Pune 411 004.

Advancement of knowledge

F.Y.B.SC. TERM-I : FUNDAMENTALS OF BOTANY (PAPER I & II) ISBN 978-93-83073-76-4
First Edition : July 2013
© : **Authors**

The text of this publication, or any part thereof, should not be reproduced or transmitted in any form or stored in any computer storage system or device for distribution including photocopy, recording, taping or information retrieval system or reproduced on any disc, tape, perforated media or other information storage device etc., without the written permission of Authors with whom the rights are reserved. Breach of this condition is liable for legal action.

Every effort has been made to avoid errors or omissions in this publication. In spite of this, errors may have crept in. Any mistake, error or discrepancy so noted and shall be brought to our notice shall be taken care of in the next edition. It is notified that neither the publisher nor the authors or seller shall be responsible for any damage or loss of action to any one, of any kind, in any manner, therefrom.

Published By :
NIRALI PRAKASHAN
Abhyudaya Pragati, 1312, Shivaji Nagar,
Off J.M. Road, PUNE – 411005
Tel - (020) 25512336/37/39, Fax - (020) 25511379
Email : niralipune@pragationline.com

Printed at
Repro Knowledgecast Limited
Thane

DISTRIBUTION CENTRES
PUNE

Nirali Prakashan
119, Budhwar Peth, Jogeshwari Mandir Lane
Pune 411002, Maharashtra
Tel : (020) 2445 2044, 66022708, Fax : (020) 2445 1538
Email : bookorder@pragationline.com

Nirali Prakashan
S. No. 28/27, Dhyari,
Near Pari Company, Pune 411041
Tel : (022) 24690371
Email : dhyari@pragationline.com
bookorder@pragationline.com

MUMBAI
Nirali Prakashan
385, S.V.P. Road, Rasdhara Co-op. Hsg. Society Ltd.,
Girgaum, Mumbai 400004, Maharashtra
Tel : (022) 2385 6339 / 2386 9976, Fax : (022) 2386 9976
Email : niralimumbai@pragationline.com

DISTRIBUTION BRANCHES

NAGPUR
Pratibha Book Distributors
Above Maratha Mandir, Shop No. 3, First Floor,
Rani Jhanshi Square, Sitabuldi, Nagpur 440012,
Maharashtra, Tel : (0712) 254 7129

JALGAON
Nirali Prakashan
34, V. V. Golani Market, Navi Peth, Jalgaon 425001,
Maharashtra, Tel : (0257) 222 0395
Mob : 94234 91860

BENGALURU
Pragati Book House
House No. 1, Sanjeevappa Lane, Avenue Road Cross,
Opp. Rice Church, Bengaluru – 560002.
Tel : (080) 64513344, 64513355,
Mob : 9880582331, 9845021552
Email:bharatsavla@yahoo.com

KOLHAPUR
Nirali Prakashan
New Mahadvar Road,
Kedar Plaza, 1st Floor Opp. IDBI Bank
Kolhapur 416 012, Maharashtra. Mob : 9855046155

CHENNAI
Pragati Books
9/1, Montieth Road, Behind Taas Mahal, Egmore,
Chennai 600008 Tamil Nadu, Tel : (044) 6518 3535,
Mob : 94440 01782 / 98450 21552 / 98805 82331, Email : bharatsavla@yahoo.com

RETAIL OUTLETS
PUNE

Pragati Book Centre
157, Budhwar Peth, Opp. Ratan Talkies,
Pune 411002, Maharashtra
Tel : (020) 2445 8887 / 6602 2707, Fax : (020) 2445 8887

Pragati Book Centre
Amber Chamber, 28/A, Budhwar Peth,
Appa Balwant Chowk, Pune - 411002, Maharashtra,
Tel : (020) 20240335 / 66281669
Email : pbcpune@pragationline.com

Pragati Book Centre
676/B, Budhwar Peth, Opp. Jogeshwari Mandir,
Pune 411002, Maharashtra
Tel : (020) 6601 7784 / 6602 0855

PBC Book Sellers & Stationers
152, Budhwar Peth, Pune 411002, Maharashtra
Tel : (020) 2445 2254 / 6609 2463

MUMBAI
Pragati Book Corner
Indira Niwas, 111 - A, Bhavani Shankar Road, Dadar (W), Mumbai 400028, Maharashtra
Tel : (022) 2422 3526 / 6662 5254, Email : pbcmumbai@pragationline.com

Preface ...

The subject of Botany is gaining ground and has come into limelight because of the globalisation. Plant resources have become crucial for the sustainable development of any country, hence indepth basic and applied knowledge of this subject is of prime importance.

We, the authors, are therefore pleased to publish this Botany text book for F.Y. B.Sc. students. This text book is written according to new syllabus of **F.Y.B.Sc. Botany**, University of Pune for the academic year 2013-2014. It includes 1st Term of Paper I and Paper II. The title of **Paper I** is **Fundamentals of Botany (Plant Diversity)** and **Paper II** is **Industrial Botany**. We are thankful to all the students and teachers from affiliated colleges of Pune University for giving an overwhelming response to our previous text books of Botany.

The contents of this book will also satisfy the quest of knowledge of a layman for plant diversity and industrial botany. Both these papers will help our students and teachers to strive for excellence. This book is very illustrative and useful for all students. Plant diversity includes topics like Introduction, General Characters, and Outline Classification of Algae, Fungi, Lichens, Bryophytes, Pteridophytes, Gymnosperms and Angiosperms. The most important facet of this book is points to remember and exercises given at the end of each chapter. It will be most useful and popular amongst students and teachers.

Industrial Botany includes topics such as introduction to various industries like Floriculture, Plant Nursery, Plant Tissue Culture, Agriculture and Mushroom. The authors have taken great efforts to justify the topics included in this paper. We have also duly acknowledged the literature referred to. We are grateful to our most popular publisher Shri Dineshbhai Furia of Nirali Prakashan. We are also thankful to Mr. Jignesh Furia for providing us this opportunity. We would also like to thank the supporting staff which includes Rama Raghu, Sarita Soman, Prachi Sawant, Neha Deshpande of Nirali Prakashan for their timely help. Some valuable suggestions and comments for the enhancement and improvement of the text will be highly appreciated.

Pune　　　　　　　　　　　　　　　　　　　　　　　　**On behalf of all Authors**
　　　　　　　　　　　　　　　　　　　　　　　　　　　　　　　K. N. Dhumal

Syllabus ...

PAPER – I

FUNDAMENTALS OF BOTANY

Term – I: Plant Diversity (36 Lectures)

1. **Introduction :** General outline of plant kingdom, Introduction to plant diversity with reference to following groups: Cryptogams: Thallophyta (Algae, Fungi, Lichens, and Bacteria), Bryophyta and Pteridophyta, Phanerogams: Gymnosperms & Angiosperms. **3L**

2. **Algae :** General characters, Outline classification according to G.M. Smith (1955) up to classes with reasons. Life cycle of Spirogyra. **6L**

3. **Fungi :** General characters, Outline classification according to G.M. Smith (1955) up to classes with reasons. Life cycle of Cystopus (Albugo). **5L**

4. **Lichens :** General characters, Nature of Association, Types of Lichens on the basis of thallus morphology, Economic importance of lichens. **3L**

5. **Bryophytes :** General characters, Outline classification according to G.M. Smith (1955) up to classes with reasons. Life cycle of Riccia. **5L**

6. **Pteridophytes :** General characters, Outline classification according to G.M. Smith (1955) up to classes with reasons. Life cycle of Nephrolepis. **6L**

7. **Gymnosperms :** General characters, Outline classification according to Chamberlain (1934) up to classes with reasons. Life cycle of Cycas. **5L**

8. **Angiosperms :** General characters, Causes of evolutionary success of Angiosperms, comparative account of monocotyledons and dicotyledons. **3L**

(Note: Development of sex organs not expected, for all the above mentioned life cycles)

PAPER- II

Term I – INDUSTRIAL BOTANY (36 Lectures)

1. **Introduction to Industrial Botany** **2L**

    1.1 Concept of Industrial Botany.

    1.2 Plant resources and industries: Food, fodder, fibers, medicines, timber, dyes, gum, tannins. (Two examples of each resource and the relevant industries with which they are associated).

2. **Floriculture Industry** 8L

   2.1 Introduction to floriculture.

   2.2 Important floricultural crops, open cultivation practices, harvesting and marketing of Tuberose.

   2.3 Greenhouse technology: Concept, advantages and limitations.

   2.4 Cultivation practices (greenhouse technology), harvesting and marketing of Rose and Gerbera.

3. **Plant Nursery Industry** 8L

   3.1 Concept and types of nurseries: ornamental plant nursery, fruit plant nursery, medicinal plant nursery, vegetable plant nursery, orchid nursery, forest nursery (with reference to infrastructure required, outputs, commercial applications and profitability).

   3.2 Propagation methods: Seed propagation, natural vegetative propagation and artificial vegetative propagation (Cutting: Stem, Layering: Air layering, Grafting: Stone grafting and Approach grafting, Budding : T- budding).

4. **Plant Tissue Culture Industry** 6L

   4.1 Concept of tissue culture.

   4.2 Culture techniques: Types of explants, preparation of media, methods of sterilization, inoculation techniques, incubation and hardening.

   4.3 Commercial significance

5. **Agri Industries** 8L

   5.1 Organic Farming: Concept, need of organic farming, types of organic fertilizers, advantages and limitations.

   5.2 Seed industries: Importance of seed industries, seed production, seed processing and seed marketing with reference to cotton. Major seed industries and corporations of India.

6. **Mushroom Industries** 4L

   Mushroom cultivation: Plant resources, cultivation practices of oyster mushroom, uses of mushrooms, value added products, commercial significance.

Contents ...

PAPER I : PLANT DIVERSITY

1.	Introduction	1.1 - 1.18
2.	Algae	2.1 - 2.10
3.	Fungi	3.1 - 3.18
4.	Lichen Diversity	4.1 - 4.6
5.	Bryophytes	5.1 – 5.18
6.	Pteridophytes	6.1 – 6.20
7.	Gymnosperms	7.1 – 7.20
8.	Angiosperms	8.1 – 8.6

PAPER II : INDUSTRIAL BOTANY

1.	Introduction to Industrial Botany	1.1 – 1.8
2.	Floriculture Industry	2.1 – 2.28
3.	Plant Nursery Industry	3.1 - 3.34
4.	Plant Tissue Culture Industry	4.1 - 4.12
5.	Agri Industries	5.1 – 5.12
6.	Mushroom Industries and Cultivation	6.1 – 6.18
*	Bibliography	B.1 – B.2

Paper - I Term - I

Chapter 1...
Introduction

Contents ...
1.1 Introduction
1.2 General Outline of Plant Kingdom
1.3 Cryptogams and Phanerogams
  Points to Remember
  Exercises

1.1 Introduction

"Biological diversity is the variety of life forms ... at all levels of biological systems (i.e., molecular, organismic, population, species and ecosystem). The 1992, United Nations Earth Summit defined "biological diversity" as *"the variability among living organisms from all sources, including, 'inter alia', terrestrial, marine, and other aquatic ecosystems, and the ecological complexes of which they are part: this includes diversity within species, between species and of ecosystems.* This definition is used in the United Nations Convention on Biological Diversity. The textbook definition is *"variation of life at all levels of biological organization.* Genetically, biodiversity can be defined as *"the diversity of alleles, genes, and organisms and the study of processes such as mutation and gene transfer that drive evolution"*.

Measuring diversity at one level in a group of organisms may not precisely correspond to diversity at other levels.

"Biodiversity" is most commonly used to replace the more clearly defined and long established terms, species diversity and species richness. Biologists most often define biodiversity as the "totality of genes, species, and ecosystems of a region". An advantage of this definition is that it seems to describe most circumstances and presents a unified view of the traditional three levels at which biological variety has been identified:

o species diversity
o ecosystem diversity
o genetic diversity

The concept of biodiversity breaks down into three major factors, all of which are interwoven: First is the concept of genetic diversity. This refers to the variation of genes within a single species and can be further broken down into two components: genetic variations within distinct populations of the same species, and genetic variations within a population.

Next is the concept of species diversity. We consider the varieties of species within a region. There are two main measures to assess this: the first is species "richness" or the number of species, both plant and animal, that inhabit an area; the second is the more precise "taxonomic diversity," which takes into account the relationships between species in addition to their numbers.

The third factor, and the overarching one, is ecosystem diversity. Since the boundaries between various biological communities are highly fluid, this is the most difficult factor to measure accurately, yet it may very well be the most important, since this is where changes that affect all life occur. Climate change, often caused by things like global warming, is among the greatest threats to ecosystem diversity.

Biological diversity includes the variety of ecosystems, and their patterns. It also includes their linkages across regional landscapes. There is a hierarchy of the parts and processes of biological diversity that is, admittedly, artificial. This hierarchy also has a distinct human context (i.e., things are seen in the context of how useful they are to humans). Still, it provides a focus for the concept of biodiversity, which is so infinitely varied that any lens taken to it must be narrowly focused compared to the full spectrum of both the topic and human needs.

Table 1.1: Diversity of major groups of plants and microorganisms in India

Sr. No.	Plant groups	Number of species described in World	Number of species described in India	Percentage of India to the world	Number of endemic species	%
1.	Virus/Bacteria	8,050	850	10.6	-	-
2.	Algae	40,000	7,175	17.9	1925	26.8
3.	Fungi	72,000	14.500	20.1	3500	24.0
4.	Lichens	13,500	2223	16.4	527	23.7
5.	Bryophytes	14,500	2.500	17.2	629	25.1
6.	Pteridophytes	10,000	1,200	12.0	193	16.0
7.	Gymnosperms	650	67	10.3	7	14.9
8.	Angiosperms	2.50,000	17,527	7.0	6200	35.3

Understanding the concept of biodiversity should be a high priority for everyone, since we cannot preserve it if we don't understand it, and not preserving it will ultimately affect the lives of all of us. One of the best ways of understanding the very broad concept of biodiversity is reading the various definitions used by scientists, philosophers, environmentalists, and others.

In terms of plant diversity, India ranks tenth in the world and fourth in Asia. With over 45,500 plant species, India represents nearly 11% of the world's known floral diversity. As elsewhere in the world, many organisms especially in lower groups such as bacteria, fungi, algae, lichens and bryophytes are yet to be described and remote geographical areas are to be comprehensively explored. The richness of Indian plant species as compared to the world is shown in Table 1.1.

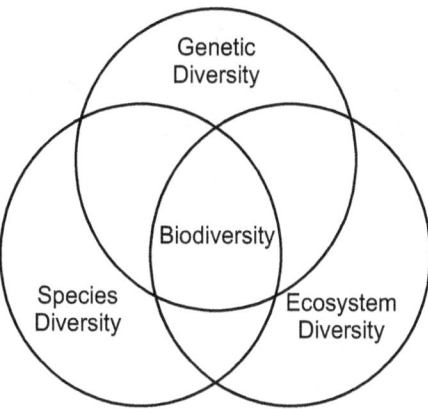

Fig. 1.1: Biodiversity

Algae are represented by over 7,175 species in 666 genera. They are found in a variety of habitats ranging from aquatic (both fresh water and marine) to terrestrial. Chlorophyceae with 4,495 species is the largest family followed by Cyanophyceae (1,453 species) and Bacillariophyceae (516 species).

India has 14,500 species of fungi in 2,300 genera and 250 families with maximum diversity in the Western Ghats followed by the Eastern Himalayas and the Western Himalayas. Deuteromycetes with 900 genera and 6000 species (40 %) is the largest group of Indian mycoflora, followed by Ascomycetes [680 genera / 3500 species (25 %)] and Basidiomycetes [520 genera/3400 species (23 %)]. *Cercospora* with 707 species is the largest genus of Indian fungi followed by *Puccinia* (328 species) and *Phyllosticta* (280 species). About 3500 species are endemic to the country.

Lichens representing symbiotic association of fungi and algae, constitute a dominant component of epiphytic and saxicolous vegetation (growing on or among rocks), and comprise 2,223 species in 283 genera and 72 families. Western Ghats are the richest region with 800 species (38%) followed by Eastern Himalayas with 759 species (37%) and Western

Himalayas with 550 species (27%). Families such as - Parmeliaceae, Graphidaceae, Physciaceae, Usneaceae, Cladoniaceae, and genera like *Parmelia, Graphina, Usnea, Graphis* and *Lecanora* are among the dominant families and genera of Indian lichens. About 23% species, mainly belonging to genera *Graphina, Trypethelium, Graphis* and *Poring*, are endemic to India. Andaman and Nicobar Islands (24%), Western Ghats (20%) and Eastern Himalayas (18%) show high percentage of endemic species.

Bryophytes represented by 2500 species are the second largest group of green plants in India distributed largely in Eastern Himalayas, North-eastern India, Western Himalayas and the Western Ghats. Mosses constitute the major component of Indian bryoflora with 1576 species followed by liverworts and hornworts (924 species). Lejeuneaceae (155 species) is the largest family followed by Pottiaceae (129), Dicranaceae (119), Bryaceae (98) and Sematophyllaceae (92 species). *Fissidens* (67 species) is the largest genus followed by *Plagiochila* (65) and *Frullania* (63). Nineteen genera and 629 species are endemic to India.

India has about 1200 species of pteridophytes under 204 genera. While species of *Marsilea, Azolla* and *Salvinia* grow in aquatic habitats, those of *Acrostichum* occur in mangrove ecosystems. The north-eastern region (including Eastern Himalayas) is rich in pteridophytic diversity with about 845 species, followed by South India (including Eastern and Western Ghats) with 345 species and north India (including Western Himalayas) with 340 species. About 17% of the species are endemic to India. The families such as Polypodiaceae (137 species), Dryopteridaceae (125 species), Athyriaceae (97 species), Thelypteridaceae (83 species), Selaginellaceae (62 species), and genera like *Selaginella* (62 species), *Asplenium* (45 species) and *Polystichum* (45 species) are some of the dominant families and genera of the pteridophytic flora of Indian region.

India has about 17,527 species of angiosperms or flowering plants (more than 7% of the world's known flowering plants) in 247 families and 2984 genera. The dominant families with more than 500 species are Poaceae-1291; Orchidaceae-1229; Leguminosae-1225; Asteraceae-892; Rubiaceae-616; Cyperaceae-545; Euphorbiaceae-527; and Acanthaceae-510.

Gymnosperms are represented by about 67 species. Pinaceae (6 genera and 15 species) is the largest family, followed by Cupressaceae (13 genera and 13 species), Ephedraceae (1 genus, 7 species) and Gnetaceae (1 genus and 5 species). The species of *Gnetum* and *Cycas* are mostly confined to North Eastern region.

1.2 General Outline of Plant Kingdom

The Kingdom Plantae includes all chlorophyllous organisms. They have a distinct cellulosic cell wall. Plant body may be microscopic or large. The plant body of higher plants is well developed and is differentiated into root, stem and leaves. It shows various tissue systems. Sexual reproductive organs are well developed. On the basis of thallus structure or plant body, mode of nutrition and nature of reproduction, kingdom Plantae is divided into two divisions i.e. Cryptogams and Phanerogams. The outline of the classification of kingdom Plantae is as follows.

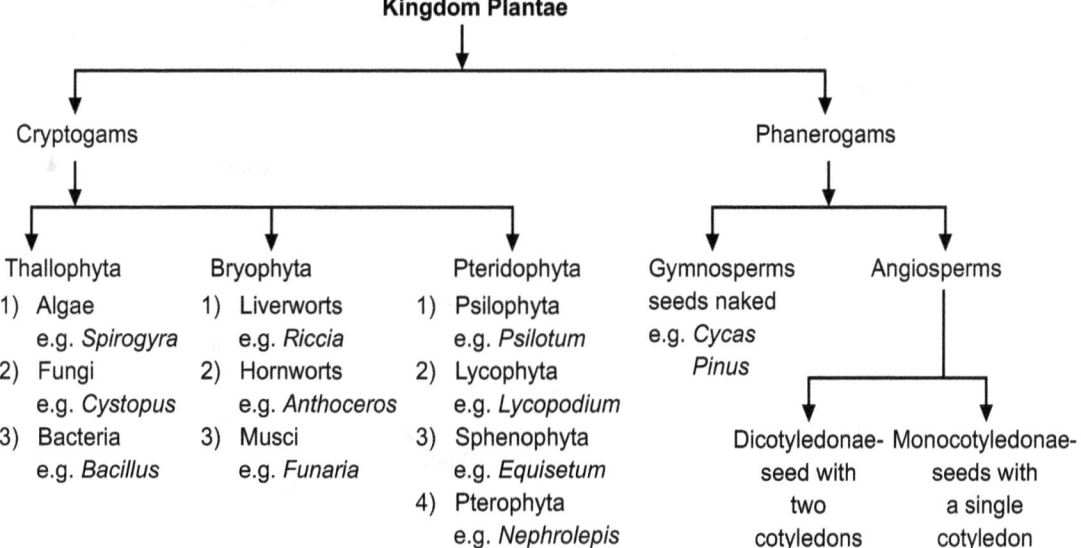

Five Kingdom System

A more recent and well accepted system of classification of living organisms is proposed by Whittaker (1969). He classified living organisms into five kingdoms based on

1) The complexity of cell structure i.e. prokaryote or eukaryote.
2) The complexity of thallus, i.e. unicellular or multi-cellular
3) The mode of nutrition i.e. autotrophs or heterotrophs.

The five kingdoms of the living world are Monera, Protista, Plantae, Fungi and Animalia according to evolutionary sequence.

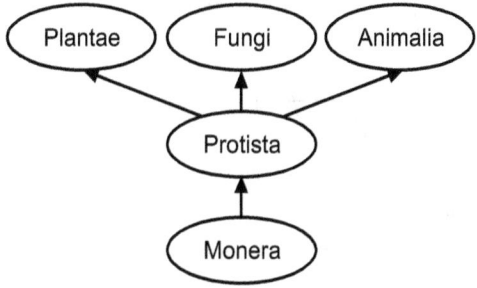

Fig. 1.2: Five kingdom classification

Key for five kingdoms of the living world.

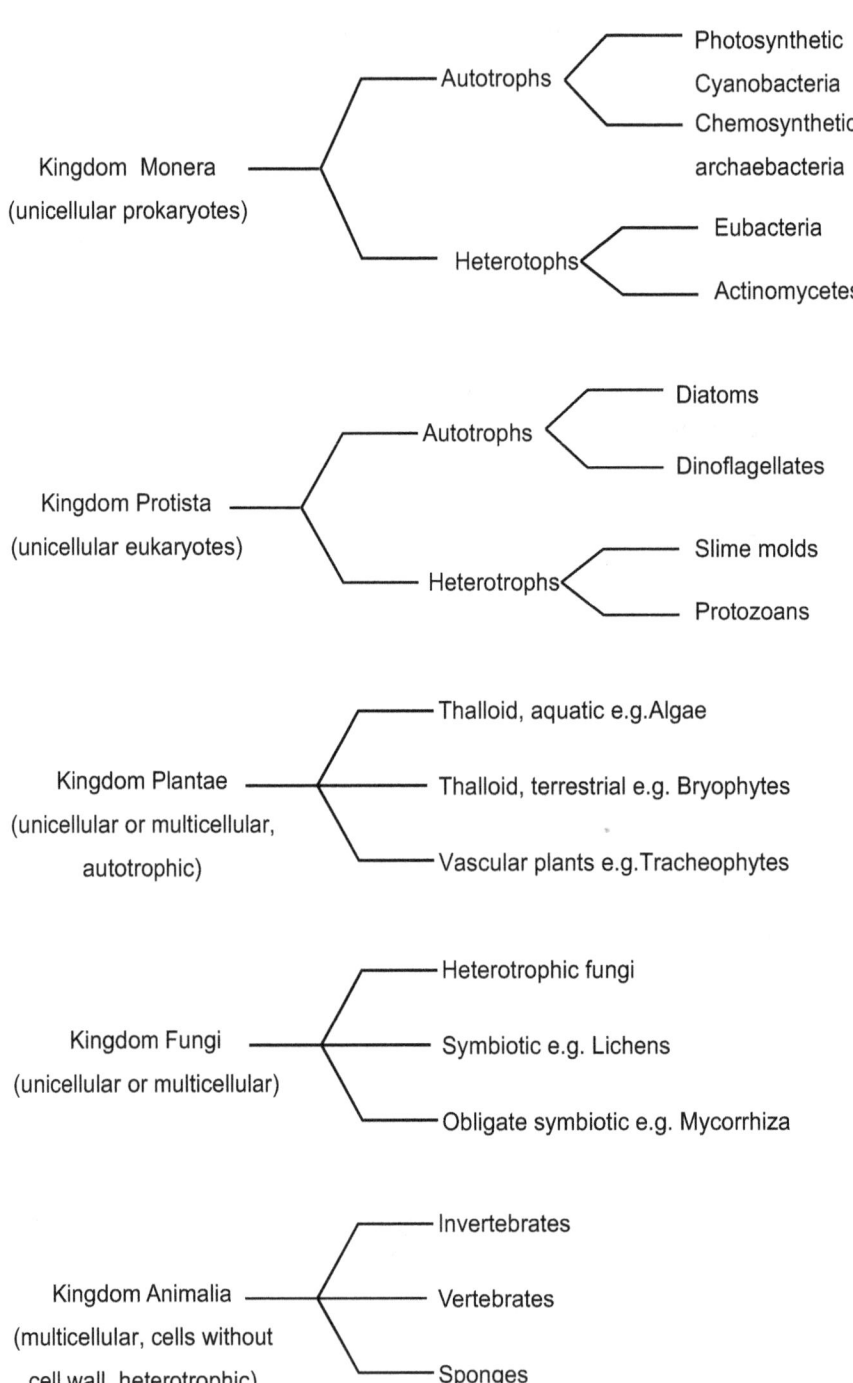

1.3 Cryptogams and Phanerogams

A) CRYPTOGAMS

I) Thallophyta

a. Algae

1. The members of algae are prokaryotic or eukaryotic, chlorophyllous, thalloid organisms.
2. They mostly grow in an aquatic habitat (fresh and marine) or on moist soil.
3. Plant body is known as thallus.

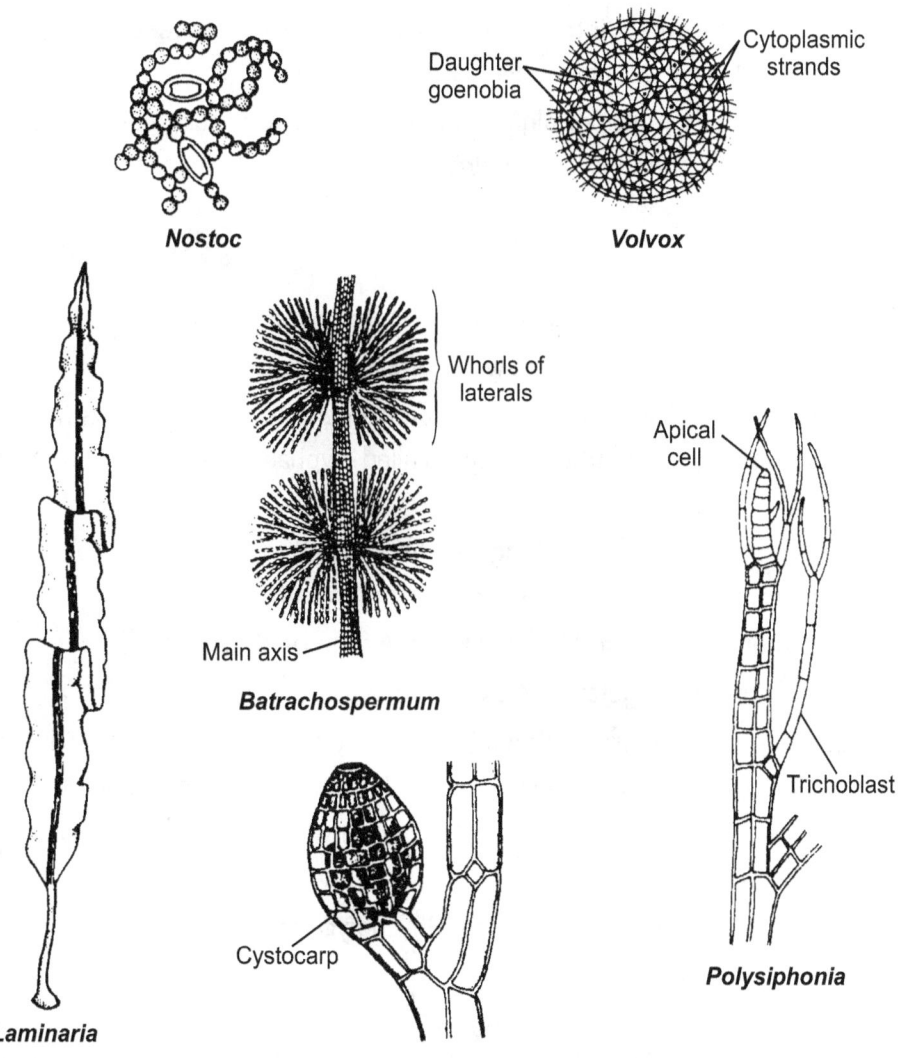

Fig. 1.3: Algae

4. The thallus is unicellular, colonial, motile or non-motile, filamentous, branched or unbranched and multicellular.
5. The mode of nutrition in algae is autotrophic.
6. They store food material in form of starch.
7. Algae reproduce by means of vegetative, asexual and sexual methods.
8. Asexual reproduction occurs by various types of spores like aplanospores, (immobile flagellae spores) zoospores (mobile pores that move with the help of flagella) and akinates (thick walled).
9. Sexual reproduction in algae is isogamous, anisogamous and oogamous.
10. They are divided into Cyanophyceae, Chlorophycaea, Xanthophyceae, Bacillariophyceae, Phaeophyceae and Rhodophyceae.
11. Some common examples of algae are *Spirogyra, Chlamydomonas, Chlorella, Volvox, Hydrodictyon, Cladophora, Sargassum, Fucus, Nostoc, Anabaena, Batrachospermum, Chara* and *Nitella*.

b. Fungi

1. Fungi are eukaryotic, achlorophyllous, heterotrophic organisms.
2. They are commonly found in soil, water or cause diseases to other plants.
3. The plant body or mycelium is unicellular, filamentous or multicellular. Mycelium is composed of a web of tiny filaments called hyphae. The hyphae are septate or aseptate.
4. The mode of nutrition in fungi is heterotrophic. They commonly grow as saprophytes, parasites, or even as symbiotic organisms.
5. The stored or reserved food in fungi is in the form of glycogen.
6. Fungi reproduce by vegetative, asexual and sexual methods.
7. In true fungi, sexual reproduction takes place by means of sex organs. The male sex organ is antheridium and female sex organ is oogonium or ascogonium.
8. Zygote divides meiotically to produce sexual spores or meiospores which are called ascospores or basidiospores.
9. Fungi are classified into Myxomycetes, Phycomycetes, Ascomycetes, Basidiomycetes and Deuteromycetes.
10. Some common examples of fungi are *Stemonites, Pythium, Rhizopus, Mucor, Penicillium, Aspergillus, Morchella, Agaricus, Puccinia, Ustilago, Alternaria* and *Fusarium*.

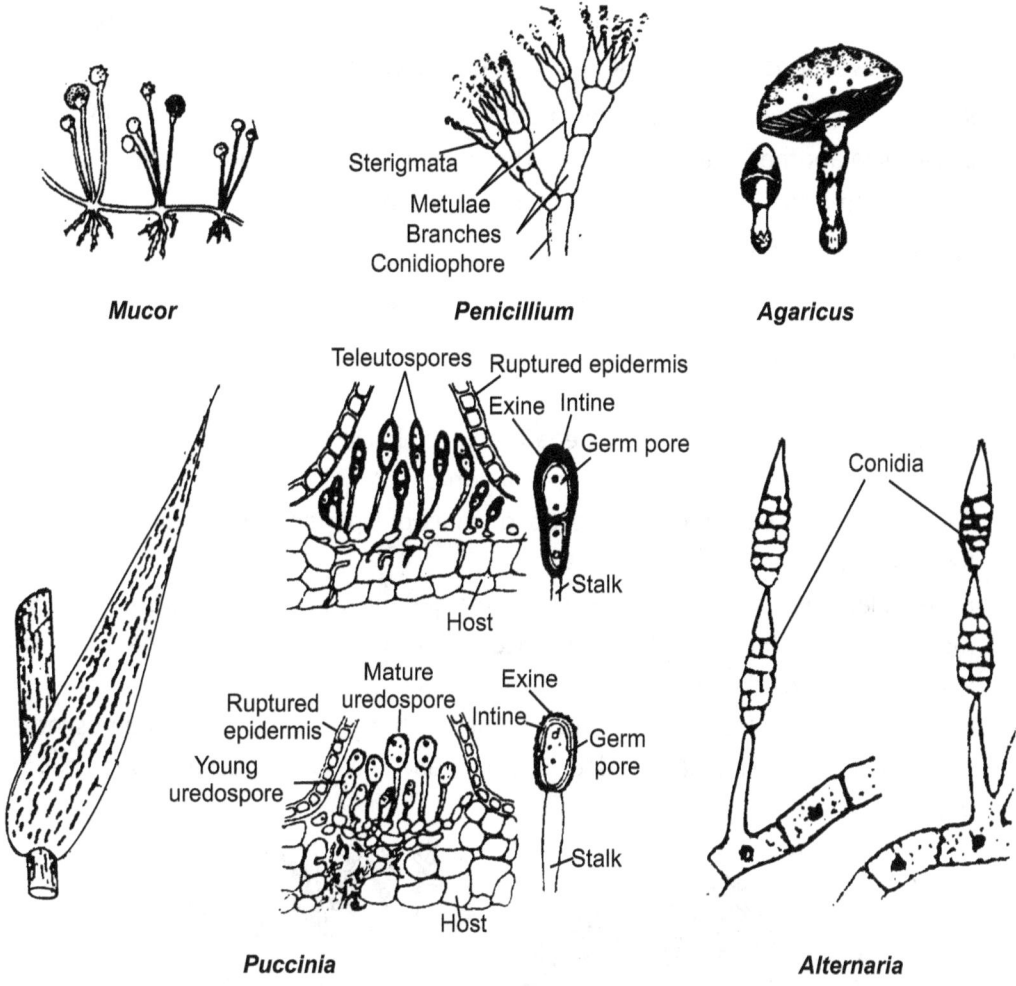

Fig. 1.4: Fungi

c. **Lichens**

1. Lichens are composite organisms consisting of a fungus living in intimate association with an alga.
2. The mycobiont belongs to Ascomycotina, Basidiomycotina or Deuteromycotina
3. Algal members are unicellular and belong to Chlorophyceae or Cyanophyceae.
4. Morphologically, lichens are classified into three types, crustose, foliose and fruticose.
5. Lichens reproduce by vegetative, asexual and sexual methods.
6. Vegetative reproduction in lichens occurs by fragmentation of thallus and by formation of vegetative propagules like soredia and isidia.
7. Asexual reproduction in lichens takes place by pycnidiospores produced in pycnidia.

8. Sexual reproduction takes place in fungal partner of lichens only. Most of the lichens have fungal partner belonging to Ascomycetes and Basidiomycetes.
9. In Ascolichens the ascospores are produced in asci which are produced in fruiting bodies like apothecia and perithecia. The male and female reproductive organs are called spermogonium and carpogonium respectively.
10. In basiodiolichens, basidiospores are produced on basidia.

d. Bacteria

1. Bacteria are smallest living organisms rarely exceeding 5 microns. They are present in air, water and soil.
2. The common forms of most bacteria are cocci, bacilli and spirilli. A few species are filamentous. The bacterial cells are prokaryotic.
3. The cell wall of bacteria is made up of mucopolypeptide. Many of them possess flagella for locomotion.
4. Bacteria lack well organised nucleus, possess genetic material in the form of a ring.
5. Mesosomes are the projections produced from the plasma membrane which bring about terminal oxidation.
6. Some bacteria are autotrophic, either photosynthetic or chemosynthetic. Chemosynthetic bacteria include sulphur bacteria, iron bacteria and nitrifying bacteria.

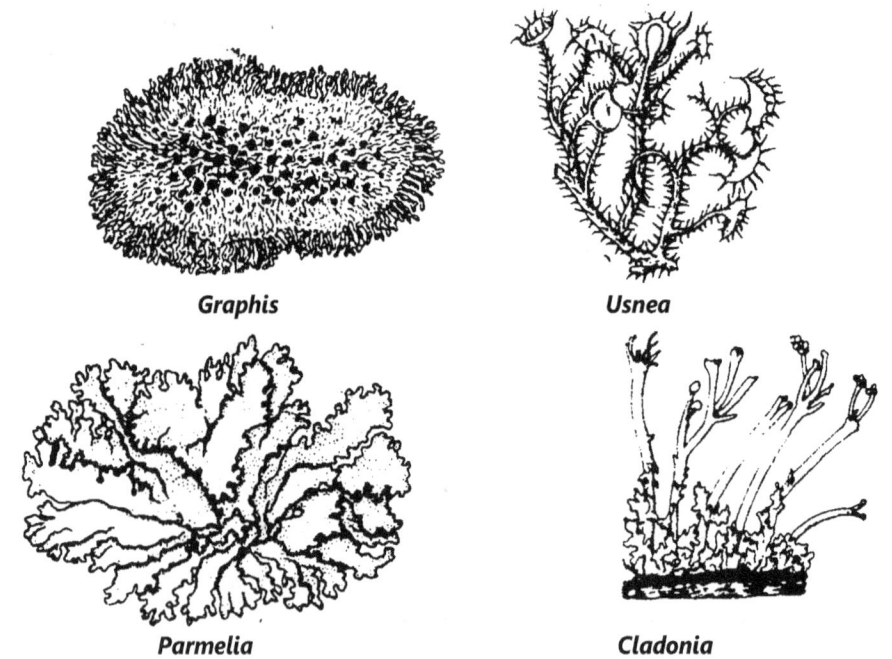

Graphis *Usnea*

Parmelia *Cladonia*

Fig. 1.5: Lichens

7. Heterotrophic bacteria are of two types, parasites and saprophytes. Obligate parasites live only in parasitic fashion, facultative members are either parasites or saprophytes.
8. Bacteria are either aerobic or anaerobic.
9. The common method of reproduction is fission. Usually, under unfavourable conditions, some bacteria produce spores.
10. Sexual reproduction occurs by conjugation.

II) Bryophyta

1. These are commonly known as plant amphibians which are found in water and on moist soil.
2. Plant body is thalloid, dorsiventral in hepaticopsida and differentiated into root like, stem like and leaf like structures in musci.
3. Plant body is gametophytic, bears multicellular sex organs. The male sex organ is called antheridium and female sex organ is called archegonium.
4. Vascular tissues are absent. They are commonly known as non vascular cryptogams.
5. The mode of nutrition is autotrophic.
6. Water is necessary for fertilisation.
7. Sporophyte develops on gametophyte; it is made up of foot, seta and capsule.

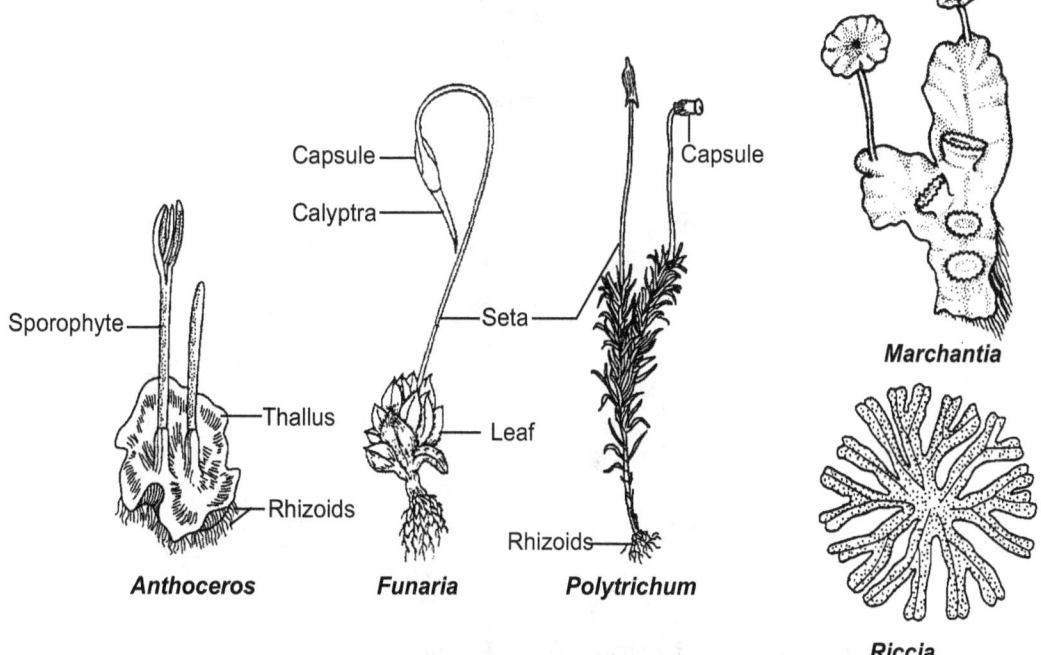

Fig. 1.6: Bryophyta

8. The life cycle shows alternation of generations. The gametophytic generation is dominant over sporophytic generation.
9. They are divided into three classes-Hepaticopsida, Anthocerotopsida and Bryopsida.
10. Common examples of bryophytes are *Riccia, Marchantia, Plagiochasma, Anthoceros, Funaria* and *Polytrichum*.

III) Pteridophyta

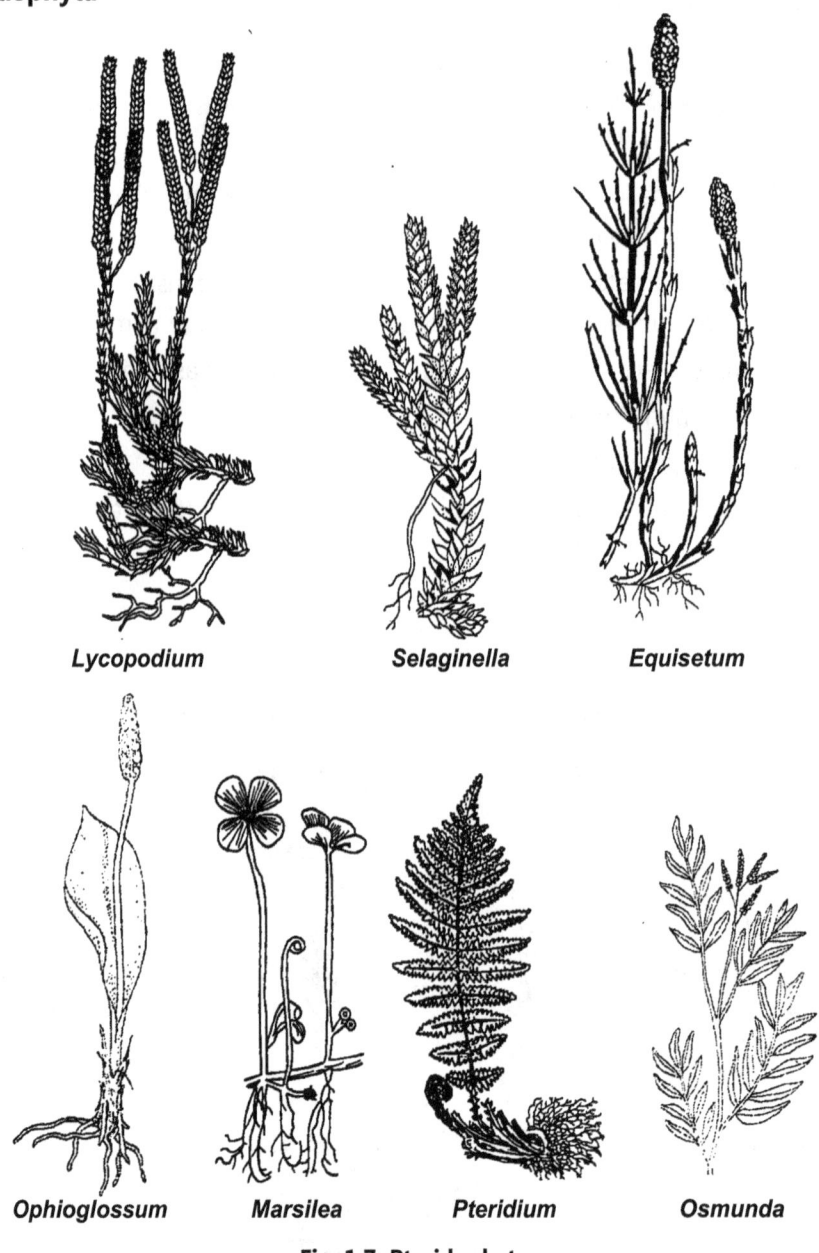

Fig. 1.7: Pteridophyta

1. The plant body is differentiated into true roots, stem and leaves.
2. Plant body is sporophytic, posses well developed vascular tissues.
3. Sporophyte produces asexual reproductive structures known as spores. The spores are produced in sporangia. The sporangia develop on sporophylls.
4. The plants may be homosporous or heterosporous.
5. The spores germinate and produce gametophytes.
6. The gametophytic thallus is green and with rhizoids. The gametophyte develops antheridia and archegonia on male and female gametophytes respectively
7. Antherozoids are multiflagellate, water is necessary for fertilisation.
8. Zygote remains in gametophyte which further develops into a simple embryo. The embryo develops into the sporophytic plant.
9. There is distinct alternation of generations in life cycle of Pteridophytes. The sporophytic generation is dominant over gametophytic generation.
10. They are divided into four classes- Psilopsida, Lycopsida, Sphenopsida and Pteropsida.
11. Common examples of Pteridophytes are *Psilotum, Lycopodium, Selaginella, Marsilea, Equisetum, Pteris, Adiantum, Nephrolepis* and *Cyathea*.

B) PHANEROGAMS

1. Plants are well adapted to the land habit and they are herbs, shrubs or trees.
2. These are seed bearing vascular plants, so called as spermatophytes.
3. Seeds are naked or enclosed inside fruits.
4. The plant body is sporophytic which produces spores within the special organs such as microsporangia (pollen sacs) and megasporangia (ovules).
5. The gametophyte is very much reduced and completes its life on the sporophyte.
6. Plants are heterosporous; pollens or microspores are produced in microsporangia while megaspores are produced inside the megasporangia.
7. Sexual reproduction is siphonogamous.
8. Zygote develops into an embryo and embryo is protected inside the seed.
9. Seed after germination develops into the sporophytic plant.
10. Plant possesses well developed vascular tissues.
11. Phanerogams are further divided into two divisions viz. Gymnosperms and Angiosperms.

a) **Gymnosperms**

Most of the gymnosperms are trees. There are about 500 species of conifers, 100 species of cycades and 71 species of gnetales. *Ginkgo biloba is* called as a living fossil. It is endemic to China. Conifers occur worldwide but predominantly in the temperature and alpine regions of the tropics. The Gnetales consist of three living genera, *Gnetum, Ephedra* and *Welwitschia.*

1. These are the spermatophytes with naked seeds (Gymnos-naked, sperms-seed).
2. Plant body is sporophytic. They are woody shrubs or trees.
3. Plants are heterosporous which produce microspores (pollens) in the pollen sacs. Pollen sacs or microsporangia develop on microsporophylls which are grouped in the male cone.
4. The ovules are naked and develop on megasporophylls which are grouped in the female cone.
5. Plants are wind pollinated (anemophily)
6. Ovules are orthotropus, with three layers of integuments.
7. Fertilisation is in three steps, siphonogamy, zooidogamy and syngamy.
8. Zygote develops into an embryo after fertilisation. Endosperm of the seed is haploid.
9. Vascular tissue is with xylem and phloem, xylem lacks vessels and phloem lacks companion cells except in members of gnetales.
10. There is distinct alternation of generations in life cycle of gymnosperms. The sporophytic generation is dominant over gametophytic generation.

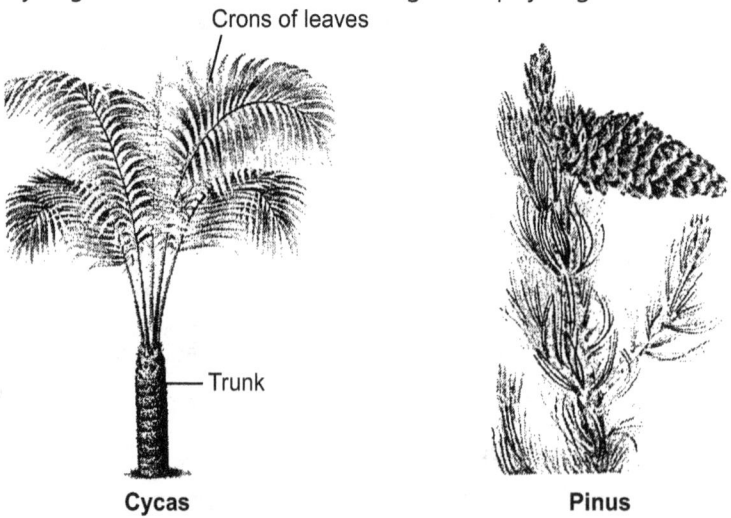

Fig. 1.8: Gymnosperms

11. They are divided into three classes- Cycadopsida, Coniferopsida and Gnetopsida.
12. The common examples of Gymnosperms are *Cycas, Zamia, Pinus, Cedrus, Thuja, Juniperus, Cupressus, Gnetum, Ephedra* and *Ginkgo*.

b) Angiosperms

The angiosperms constitute an extremely diverse group of vascular plants. There are about 2,35,000 to 3,00,000 species. Angiosperms are the most recent group of plants. Most of the food and other requirements of human come from angiosperms. The plants range in size from 1 mm across (*Wolffia* species) to over 100 meters tall (*Eucalyptus*).

These are the most advanced and dominant members of the plant kingdom. They have following characters.

1. Plants have well developed flowers and produce fruits. The floral parts are calyx, corolla, androecium and gynoecium.
2. Seeds are enclosed inside fruit. The fruit develops from the ovary and seeds develop from ovules.
3. Plant body is sporophytic; they may be herbs, shrubs, trees or climbers.
4. They have well developed vascular tissues.
5. Female gametophyte is reduced. It is generally seven celled with eight nuclei.
6. They show double fertilisation and triple fusion. Endosperm is triploid.
7. Ovule has two integuments.

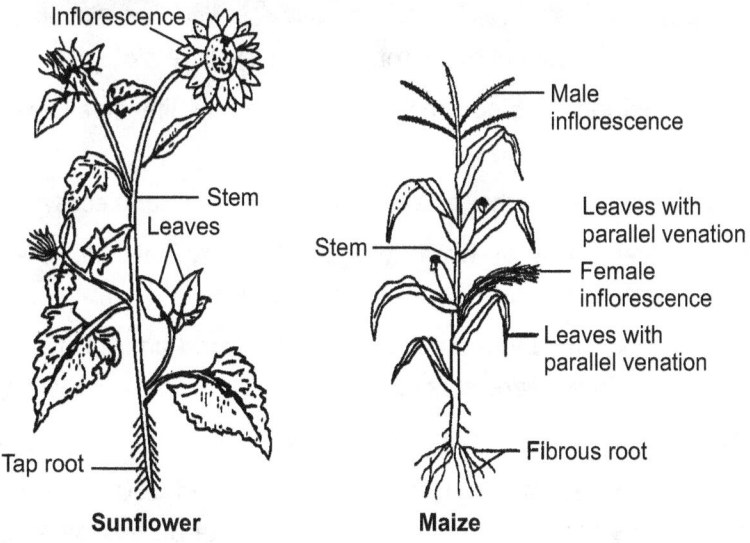

Fig. 1.9: Angiosperms

8. Pollination is anemophilous, entamophilous or hydrophyllous in angiosperms.
9. They are divided into two classes- Monocotyledonae and Dicotyledonae.
10. Common examples of angiosperms are maize, jowar, rice, wheat, coconut (monocots) sunflower, mango, pea and beans (dicots).

i) Monocotyledonae

1. Plants are mostly herbs or rarely trees.
2. Plants possess fibrous or adventitious root system, stem with distinct nodes and internodes and leaves with parallel veination.
3. Flowers are trimerous, seeds possess embryo with single cotyledon.
4. Seed germination is generally hypogeal.
5. Secondary growth is absent.
6. Stem shows scattered vascular bundles, which are without cambium.

ii) Dicotyledonae

1. Plants are herbs, shrubs trees or climbers.
2. Plants posses tap root system, stem is branched, leaves show reticulate venation.
3. Flowers are generally pentamerous, seeds possess embryo with two cotyledons.
4. Secondary growth is present.
5. Vascular bundles are arranged in a ring in stem, which are with cambium.

Points to Remember

- Biological diversity is the variety of life forms...at all levels of biological systems.
- The textbook definition of biodiversity is "variation of life at all levels of biological organization.
- Biodiversity is also defined as the "totality of genes, species, and ecosystems of a region".
- The three traditional levels at which biological variety have been identified include species diversity, ecosystem diversity and genetic diversity.
- In terms of plant diversity, India ranks tenth in the world and fourth in Asia. With over 45,500 plant species, India represents nearly 11% of the world's known floral diversity.
- Algae are represented by over 7,175 species in 666 genera.
- India has 14,500 species of fungi in 2,300 genera and 250 families with maximum diversity in the Western Ghats followed by the eastern Himalayas and the western Himalayas.

- Lichens representing symbiotic association of fungi and algae, constitute a dominant component of epiphytic and saxicolous vegetation, and comprise 2,223 species in 283 genera and 72 families.
- Bryophytes represented by 2500 species are the second largest group of green plants in India distributed largely in the Eastern Himalayas, North-Eastern India, Western Himalayas and the Western Ghats.
- India has about 1200 species of Pteridophytes under 204 genera. India has about 17,527 species of flowering plants (more than 7% of the world's known flowering plants) in 247 families and 2984 genera. Gymnosperms are represented by about 67 species.
- The members of algae are prokaryotic or eukaryotic, chlorophyllous, thalloid organisms.
- Fungi are eukaryotic, achlorophyllous, heterotrophic organisms.
- Lichens are composite organisms consisting of a fungus living in intimate association with an alga. Bryophytes are commonly known as plant amphibians which are found in water and on moist soil. Plant body of bryophytes is thalloid, dorsiventral in hepaticopsida and differentiated into root like, stem like and leaf like structures in musci.
- The plant body in Pteridophytes is differentiated into true roots, stem and leaves. It is sporophytic, possesses well developed vascular tissues.
- Plants are well adapted to the land habit and they are herbs, shrubs or trees in Phanerogams. They are seed bearing vascular plants, so also called as spermatophytes. Phanerogams are further divided into two divisions viz. Gymnosperms and Angiosperms. Gymnosperms are the spermatophytes with naked seeds.
- Plants body is sporophytic. They are woody shrubs or trees.
- The angiosperms constitute extremely diverse group of vascular plants. Plants are with well developed flowers and produce fruits.
- The flowers show calyx, corolla, androecium and gynoecium.
- Seeds are enclosed inside fruit. They are divided into two classes- Monocotyledonae and Dicotyledonae.
- Dicot plants posses tap root system, branched stem and leaves with reticulate venation. Flowers are generally pentamerous, seeds possess embryo with two cotyledons.
- Monocot plants possesses fibrous or adventitious root system, stem with distinct nodes and internodes and leaves with parallel veination. Flowers are trimerous, seeds possess embryo with single cotyledon.

Exercises

Short Answer Questions
1. Define the following terms
   a) Plant Diversity
   b) Biodiversity
   c) Biological diversity
2. Give an account of five kingdom system.
3. Comment on plant kingdom.
4. Give an outline of plant kingdom.
5. Discuss importance of study of plant diversity.

Long Answer Questions
1. Describe plant diversity in Cryptogams.
2. Describe plant diversity in Phanerogams.
3. Comment on biodiversity of following plant groups
   a) Algae
   b) Fungi
   c) Lichens
   d) Bryophytes
   e) Pteridophytes
   f) Gymnosperms
   g) Angiosperms
4. Enlist different levels of biodiversity.
5. Write a short note on plant biodiversity.

Chapter 2...

Algae

Contents ...

2.1 Introduction
2.2 General Characters
2.3 Outline Classification According to G.M. Smith (1955)
2.4 Life Cycle of Spirogyra
    2.4.1 Plant body
    2.4.2 Occurrence
    2.4.3 Cell Structure
    2.4.4 Reproduction
    Points to Remember
    Exercises

2.1 Introduction

The term algae (Latin - seaweeds) was first introduced by Linnaeus in 1753. Algae comprise of a large heterogeneous assemblage of plants which are diverse in habitat, size, organisation, physiology, biochemistry, and reproduction. It is an important group of **Thallophyta** (Gr. *Thallos* - a sprout; *phyton* - a plant), the primitive and simplest division of the plant kingdom. The orderly systemic study of algae is called **Phycology** *(Gr.phycos - seaweeds; logos - study or discourse)*. The algae are chlorophyll-containing primitive plants, both prokaryotic and eukaryotic, with a wide range of thalli ranging from unicellular to multicellular organisations. They are typically autotrophic organisms having thalloid plant bodies like Bryophytes.

The definitions of algae as given by some phycologists are

Fritsch F.E. (1935) defined algae as the holophytic organisms (as well as their numerous colourless derivatives) that fail to reach the higher level of differentiation, characteristic of the archegoniate plants.

Smith G. M. (1955) defined algae as simple plants with an autotrophic mode of nutrition. **Chapman V. J. (1962)** defined algae (seaweeds of the seashore and green skum in stagnant fresh water, ponds and pools) as among the simplest in the plant kingdom.

Singh, R. N. (1974) defined that the algae are by and large simple plants which display a spectrum of photosynthetic pigments and evolve oxygen during the process of photosynthesis.

2.2 General Characters

1. Algae have chlorophyll-bearing, autotrophic, thalloid plant body.
2. Algae are of two types prokaryotic (blue green algae) and eukaryotic.
3. Prokaryotic algae do not show sexual reproduction, they reproduce only by vegetative and asexual means.
4. Vegetative reproduction occurs by means of fragmentation, fission, formation of hormogonia, intercalary heterocyst, by separating discs, etc.
5. Asexual reproduction also occurs by means of spore formation e.g. Zoospores, aplanospores, autospores etc.
6. Eukaryotic algae reproduce by asexual, sexual and vegetative methods.
7. Thallus shows little differentiation in tissues.
8. Almost all algae are aquatic.
9. The plant body may range from being unicellular to large robust multicellular structure.
10. The multicellular complex thalli lack vascular tissue.
11. The sex organs are generally unicellular but, when multicellular, all cells are fertile and in most cases the entire structure does not have any protection jacket.
12. There is no embryo formation after gametic union.
13. The zygote undergoes further development either by mitosis or meiosis, but not through embryo formation.
14. Both the generations when represented in life cycle are independent.

2.3 Outline Classification According to G. M. Smith

G. M. Smith (1955) proposed the classification of algae, based on the physiological characters of vegetative cells and the morphology of motile reproductive cells. He divided the algae into seven divisions and then related classes were included in each division. According to him, the number of divisions necessary for complete classification of algae is less than the number of classes as the classes that show close affinity should be placed in the same division. e.g. Xanthophyceae, Chrysophyceae and Bacillariophyceae show certain resemblances in the structure and composition of the cell wall, flagella and nature of food reserves and despite differences in their pigments there is enough ground for placing them together in the same division, Chrysophyta. The outline of this classification system is as under.

Division: Chlorophyta
- Dominant pigments are chlorophyll a and b carotene and xanthophylls.
- The reserved food material is starch.
- Motile reproductive cells are bi or quadriflagellate, flagella are equal, whiplash type.

Class-Chlorophyceae (Grass green algae)

e.g. *Volvox, Oedogonium.*

Class-Charophyceae (Stoneworts)

e.g. *Chara.*

Division: Euglenophyta
- Dominant pigments are chlorophyll and β carotene.
- The reserved food material is paramylum and fats.
- Motile reproductive cells are uni, bi or triflagellate, flagella anterior.

Class-Euglenophyceae (Euglenoids)

e.g. *Euglena, Colacium.*

Division: Pyrrophyta
- Dominant pigments are chlorophyll a, c, carotene and xanthophylls.
- The reserved food material is starch/ oil.
- The cell wall is cellulosic.
- Sexual reproduction is rarely absent.

Class-Desmophyceae (Dinophysids)

e.g. *Exuviaella.*

Class-Dinophyceae (Dinoflagellates)

e.g. *Dinastridium* .

Division: Chrysophyta
- Dominant pigments are carotene and xanthophylls.
- The reserved food material is leucosin and oil.
- The cell wall is usually composed of two overlaping cilicified halves.
- Sexual reproduction isogamous, anisogamous or oogamous.

Class-Chrysophyceae (golden brown algae). e.g. *Chromulina, Chrysoclonium.*

Class-Xanthophyceae (yellow-green algae) e.g. *Botrydium.*

Class-Bacillariophyceae (diatom) e.g. *Pinnularia, Cyclotella.*

Division: Phaeophyta (brown algae)
- Dominant pigment is fucoxanthin.
- The reserved food material is laminarin and mannitol.
- Cell wall is cellulosic with fusinic and alginic acid.
- Motile reproductive cells are pyriform with two laterally inserted flagella one of which is tinsel.
- Sexual reproduction isogamous, anisogamous or oogamous.

Class-Isogeneratae e.g. *Dictyota, Ectocarpus.*

Class- Heterogeneratae e.g. *Laminaria,Myrionema.*

Division: Cyanophyta (blue-green algae)
- Dominant pigments are chlorophyll a, b, c phycocyanin and c phycoerythrin.
- The reserved food material is cyanophycean starch.
- Sexual reproduction is absent.
- Aesxual reproduction by hormogonia, fragmentation and akinets.

Class-Cyanophyceae or Myxophyceae.

e.g. *Nostoc, Anabaena, Gloeocapsa, Gloeotrichia.*

Division: Rhodophyta (red algae)
- Dominant pigment is r- phycoerythrin.
- The reserved food material is Floridean starch.
- Sexual reproduction is oogamous
- Motile reproductive cells are not found.

Class-Rhodophyceae. e.g. *Polysiphonia,Batrachospermum.*

2.4 Life Cycle of *Spirogyra*

2.4.1 Plant Body

Spirogyra is one of the commonest green alga. The plant body is a multicellular, unbranched filament which is slimy to touch because it is covered with a mucilaginous sheath of pectose. There is no distinction of base and apex and all the cells are alike throughout the filament. Within the stratified cell wall of the cylindrical cells that make up the filaments, there is the primordial utricle. Embedded in this are one or more spirally arranged ribbon-like chloroplasts with undulating edges, which form the most striking feature of the plant. (Fig. 2.1 (a) and (b)).

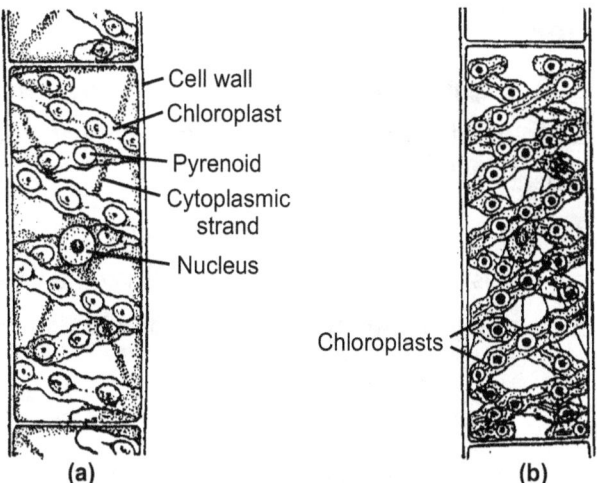

Fig. 2.1: *Spirogyra* cell

2.4.2 Occurrence

It occurs mainly in ponds, pools, ditches, and similar other places. It prefers stagnant, rather than running water and is one of the free-floating algae known as 'pond scum'. It exists mostly in large quantities.

2.4.3 Cell Structure

The most prominent feature of a *Spirogyra* cell are the ribbon like, spirally arranged chloroplasts. Each chloroplast is studded at intervals with several pyrenoids. In every cell there is one nucleus Fig. 2.1 (a) which is, either suspended in the centre by means of cytoplasmic strands, or embedded in the primordial utricle. The nucleus contains a large nucleolus. The cross walls of the filaments are essentially of five types, for example, plane, replicate, semi replicate, colligate and unduliseptate (Fig. 2.1 (b), (c), (d). In some species the middle lamella of the cross wall develops ring-like ingrowths on either sides to which the subsequent apposition layers are deposited. Such a septum is known as replicate septum.

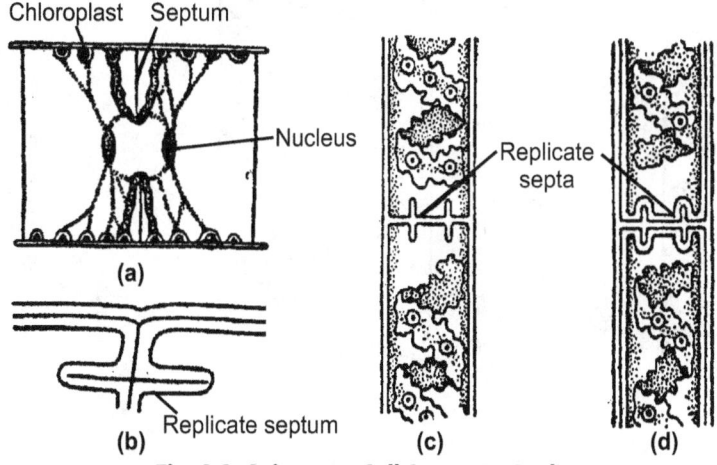

Fig. 2.2: *Spirogyra*: Cell Structure (a-d)

2.4.4 Reproduction

Spirogyra is an aquatic alga; it produces neither zoospores, nor flagellate gametes. Except for the occasional breaking up of a filament into its constituent parts, *Spirogyra* possesses no asexual means of propagation.

Its normal reproduction is always sexual, and is accomplished by conjugation - an aplanogametic isogamy. In this process, two vegetative cells combine their contents to form a zygote. Conjugation is mainly of two types (1) Scaliform or ladder like and (2) Lateral conjugation.

Scalariform Conjugation

Usually, conjugation takes place between the cells of two different filaments, but it may also take place between adjacent cells of the same filament. In scalariform conjugation, the cells in two filaments which are in contact, form protrusions which lie opposite one another and as they elongate, the filaments are pushed apart (Fig. 2.3 (a)). Finally, the walls separating the protrusions of the conjugating cells are dissolved resulting in an opening called as the conjugation tube. Meanwhile, the contents of the two participating cells contract. Fusion of the contracted cell contents takes place within one of the two conjugating cells. This type of conjugation is known as **scalariform conjugation** (Fig. 2.3 (b) & (c)). The active gamete i.e. the cell whose contents pass through the conjugation tube may be designated as a male gamete and the cell where fusion occurs is known as the female gamete though they are morphologically similar.

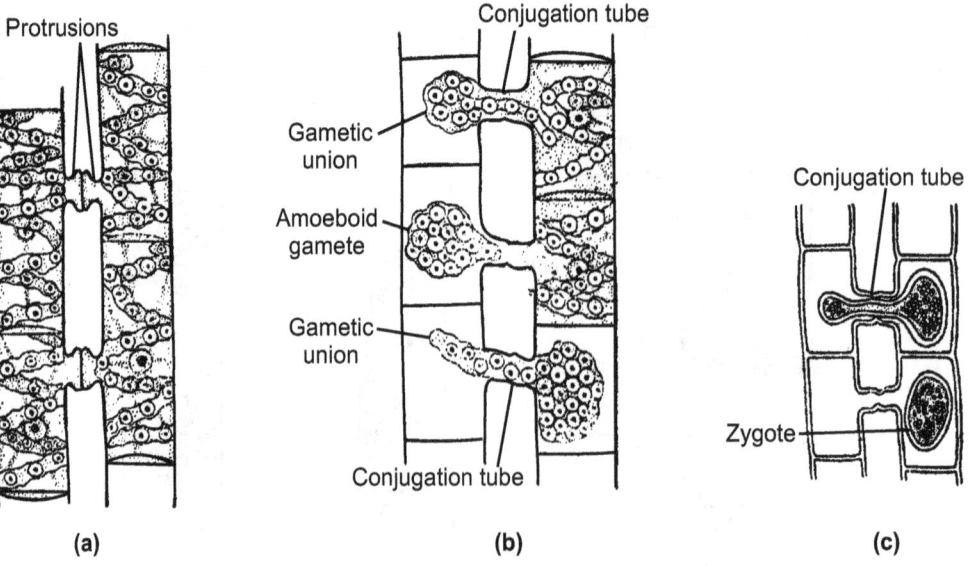

Fig. 2.3: *Spirogyra* : Scaliform Conjugation

Lateral Conjugation

In a few species, conjugation occurs between the adjacent cells of the same filament. Small protrusions arise as a result of the growth of the lateral wall on either side of the cross-wall of the participating cells. With the growth of the protrusions the cross-wall also becomes stretched (Fig. 2.4 (a), (b), (c), (d)). Finally, as the cross wall cannot keep pace with the growth of the 'protrusions, the latter losees its contact with the former, a side link is thus established between the two cells; through which the protoplast of one cell migrates into the other fusing to form a zygote (Fig. 2.4 (e) and (f)). This is called as **lateral conjugation.**

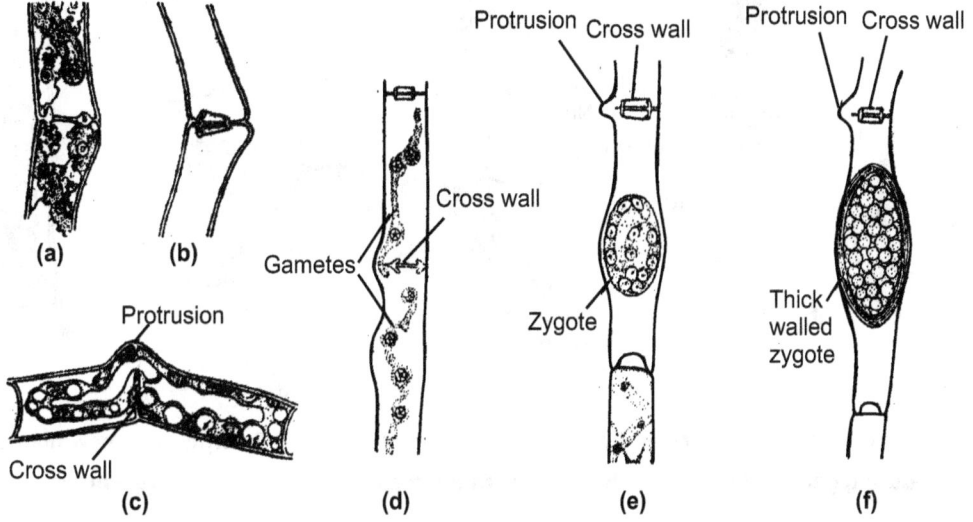

Fig. 2.4: *Spirogyra* : Lateral Conjugation

The fusion product of conjugation is a zygospore which develops three-layered thick wall and is highly resistant to extreme cold and drought (Fig. 2.5 (a), (b), (c), (d)). The zygospore generally sinks to the bottom of the pool where it germinates after a period of rest. During germination, the two outer layers burst open, the innermost cellulose wall elongates forming a cylindrical germ tube which divides transversely to form a new filament. Meiosis usually occurs during germination of the zygospore and thus the new filament is haploid (Fig. 2.5 (e) and (f)). Three of the four haploid nuclei formed in meiosis degenerate, so that each filament is derived from a haploid uninucleate cell. Sometimes the contents of certain cells of a filament round up and secrete walls to become spores parthenogenetically without any sexual fusion. Such spores are known as **parthenospores or azygospores** (Fig. 2.5 (g) and (h)).

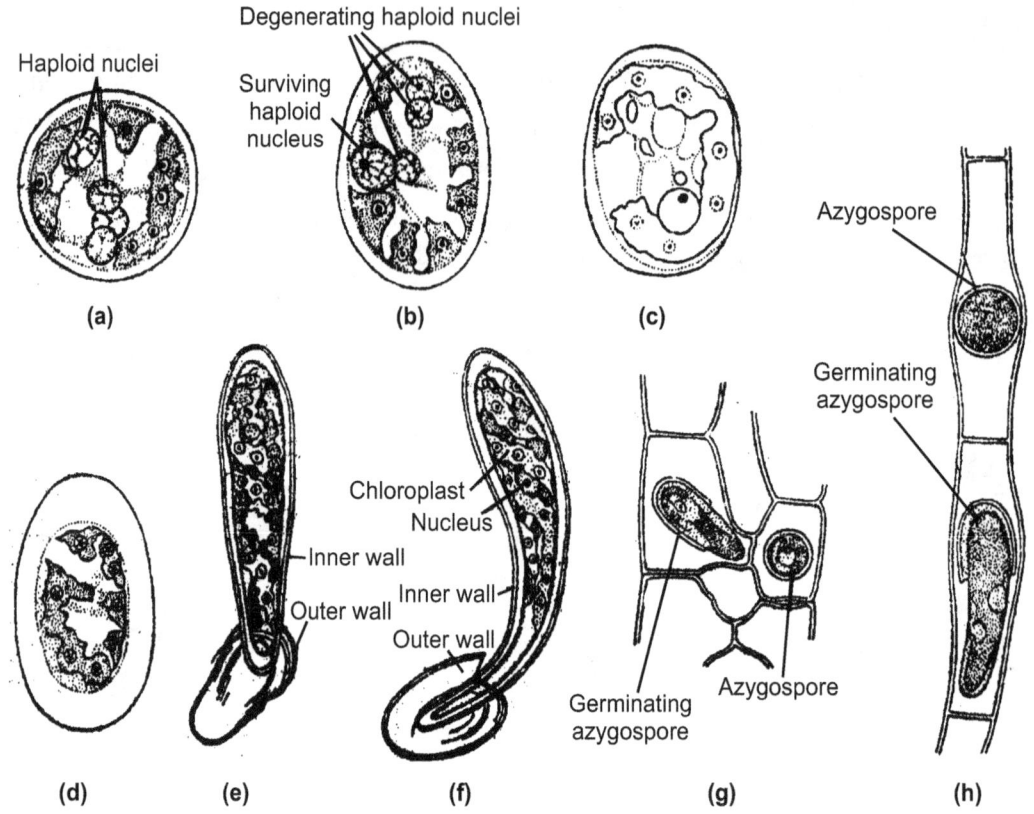

Fig. 2.5: *Spirogyra* (a-d) : Nuclear division during germination, (e-f) Emergence of new filament during germination of zygote, (g-f) : Formation and germination of a zygospores

The amoeboid gametes involved in the sexual process do not exhibit any morphological differences. Species in which only scalariform conjugation occurs are no doubt in part dioecious with genotypic sex determination. The morphologically similar gametes exhibit difference only in their behaviour. A situation where one of the fusing gametes is active and moves to the other awaiting gamete, indicates a case of physiological heterogamy. From the behaviour, the active gamete may be known as male and the passive as female. This differentiation of sex between the gametes is also accompanied by sexual differentiation between the filaments. The filaments bearing cells which produce active gametes behave as male and those having cells with passive gametes act as female. Thus such filaments are **unisexual** and the species having filaments of this nature as dioecious.

Sex Differentiation

The conjugating cells of the filaments of *Spirogyra* behave as gametangia since the entire content of each cell metamorphoses into a gamete. The gametes produced are morphologically similar and are thus isogametes, but they exhibit differences in their behaviour. One of them is active and moves from the cell of the filament where it is developed to another, where its fusing partner awaits for fusion with it. This situation may be defined as primitive anisogamy or physiological heterogamy. The active gamete thus behaves as male and the passive as female. The filament whose cells produce active gametes are sexually distinct from that whose cells produce passive gametes. Both the filaments are thus unisexual. In spite of such sex differentiation, the sexual reproduction in *Spirogyra* is isogamous since there is no other visible difference between the fusing gametes.

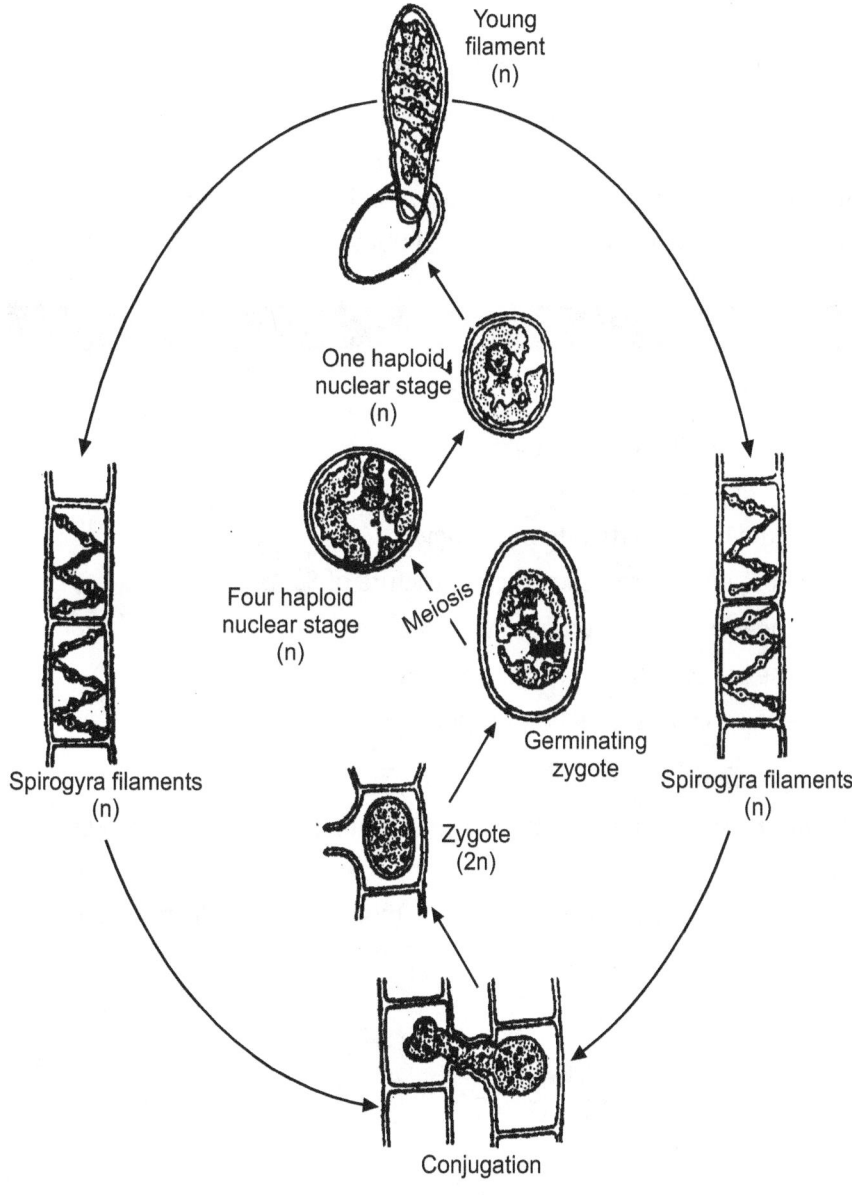

Fig. 2.6: Life cycle of *Spirogyra*

Points to Remember

1. *Spirogyra* that has filamentous unbranched plant body, without being differentiated into base and apex.
2. Basal cell is called as hold fast, it attaches the filament to the substratum
3. It is characterised by the presence of replicate septum.
4. Presence of spiral chloroplast.
5. Absence of flagellate gametes.
6. Sexual reproduction by conjugation, morphological isogamy, but physiological heterogamy.
7. Conjugation both lateral and scalariform.
8. Conjugating cells of filaments of *Spirogyra* behave as gametangia.
9. Sexual reproduction is *Spirogyra* is isogamous.

Exercises

Short Answer Questions

1. Write a note on pigments in algae.
2. Enlist the general characters of algae.
3. Describe the thallus structure of *Spirogyra*.
4. Write a note on occurrence and cell structure of *Spirogyra*.
5. Explain the process of lateral conjugation.
6. Explain the process of scalariform conjugation.
7. Describe the sex differentiation in *Spirogyra*.

Long Answer Questions

1. Describe the vegetative structure of the thallus and mode of scalariform conjugation in *Spirogyra*.
2. Give an account on thallus structure, mode of reproduction and life history of *Spirogyra*.

Chapter 3...

Fungi

Contents ...

3.1 History and Introduction
3.2 General Characteristics of Fungi
3.3 Outline Classification of Fungi Proposed by G.M. Smith
3.4 Life Cycle of *Albugo* (*Cystopus*)
   Points to Remember
   Exercises

3.1 History and Introduction

History

Man's interest in fungi started with the observation of beautiful mushrooms and toadstools growing on damp soil forming "fairy rings". Etymologically, mycology means the study of mushrooms (Gr. Mykes = mushroom, logos = discourse). Man discovered that these mushrooms were edible. Since then mushrooms have become a part of man's main diet.

The discoverer of bacteria, Leeuwenhoek also observed yeasts under his simple microscope. But the first illustrations of microfungi were made by Robert Hooke. **Anton De Bary (1931 – 88)** is called the founder of modern mycology. His mycological interests were more biological than taxonomic.

Alexander Fleming noticed that the fungus **Penicillium notatum** prevented the growth of many other pathogenic bacteria. It was Alexander Fleming who first reported the production of the antibiotic penicillin by the fungus **Penicillium notatum**.

Introduction

Fungi are the non-chlorophyllous thalloid plants with very simple organisation. This group is represented by approximately 1,00,000 species having diversity in their organisation, mode of nutrition and reproduction. They are cosmopolitian in distribution and inhabit all possible habitats. Fungi have attracted the attention of human beings due to their useful as well as harmful activities. The forms of fungi ranging from macroscopic to microscopic show varied life cycle patterns.

Fungi are classified into two divisions
1. Myxomycophyta
2. Eumycophyta

Myxomycophyta have a vegetative plant body called as plasmodium.

The plasmodia are generally found creeping over moist decaying vegetable matter including rotting logs, old wood piles and decaying leaves. A plasmodium is differentiated into an inner granular portion containing many nuclei and an outer hyaline portion without nuclei. Some plasmodia are colourless while others are coloured. The colour is generally due to a pigment produced by the plasmodium; but it may be due to pigments from organisms ingested by the plasmodium.

The **Eumycophyta** include all fungi with a definite cell wall throughout the stages of vegetative development. Most genera have the branching filamentous type of thallus known as a mycelium. A single filament is known as hypha. Mycelium may be septate or aseptate (coenocytic). There are no phytosynthetic pigments and the mycelium is either a saprophyte or a parasite.

3.2 General Characteristics of Fungi

1. The fungi are without chlorophyll.
2. Plant body is thalloid and known as mycelium.
3. Mycelium on or in the substratum is plasmodial, amoeboid or pseudoplasmodial.
4. Mycelium may be septate or non-septate.
5. Mycelium may be unicellular, multicellular or filamentous.
6. Mycelium is non-motile, but zoospore is the motile state in the life cycle of some lower fungi.
7. Plant body is very simple and made up of hyphal fragments called mycelium.
8. True fungi (Eumycophyta), have a well-defined cell wall made up of chitin (cellulose in oomycetes).
9. Fungi are heterotrophic in nutrition.
10. Their mode of nutrition is absorptive as against photosynthetic mode of nutrition in plants and ingestive mode of nutrition as in animals.
11. Under heterotrophic mode of nutrition, they may be saprophytes or parasites.
12. Fungi which can survive both as saprobes or parasites under different circumstances, are called facultative saprobes (or facultiative parasites)
13. Reserve food material is in the form of glycogen, lipid globules and oil drops.

14. Asexual reproduction takes place by means of (1) Fragmentation, (2) Budding, (3) Fission and (4) Spores.
15. Asexual spores are conidia, aplanospores, chlamydospores, arthrospores etc.
16. Sporangiospores are formed within a sac-like structure called sporangia.
17. Conidia are formed externally on hyphae or on morphologically differentiated conidiophores.
18. The motile sporangiospores are called **zoospores** and the non-motile sporangiospores are called as **aplanospores**.
19. Sexual reproduction involves: **plasmogamy**, **karyogamy** and **meiosis** occurring in a cyclic manner.
20. Plasmogamy consists of five basic modes of union of sexual elements.
    (i) Planogametic copulation : Isogamy, anisogamy and oogamy.
    (ii) Gametangial contact
    (iii) Gametangial copulation
    (iv) Spermatisation
    (v) Somatogamy
21. **Karyogamy:** The two compatible nuclei undergo fusion to give rise to dipole (2n) nucleus.
22. **Meiosis:** The diploid nucleus in the zygote may undergo meiosis.

3.3 Outline Classification of Fungi proposed by G. M. Smith

According to Gilbert M. Smith (1955) the fungi are classified into 2 divisions and 7 classes.

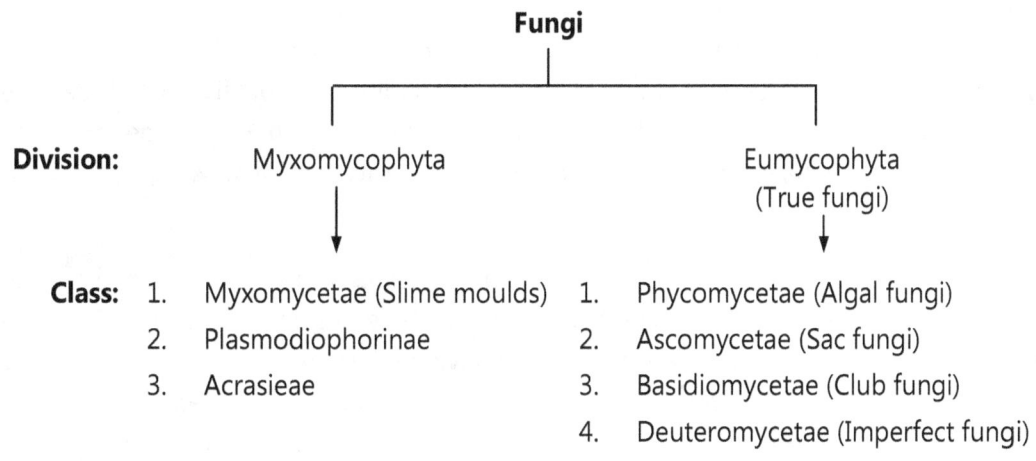

I. Myxomycophyta

The members of myxomycophyta known as slime molds, resemble true fungi (Eumycophyta) in their lack of photosynthetic pigments and in their food reserves. They differ from Eumycophyta in that the plant body is a naked protoplast throughout all stages of vegetative development. They show amoeboid movement. Reproduction of myxomycophyta is by a formation of small uninucleate spores, each with a distinct wall. Members of myxomycophyta are free living, diploid and holocarpic. It includes three classes.

1. Myxomycetae
2. Plasmodiophorinae
3. Acrasieae

1. Myxomycetae

The vegetative phase of members of this class is naked, amoeboid, multinucleate, free-living plasmodium that may be upto several centimeters in diameter. At the time of fruiting, a plasmodium heaps up to form one or more sessile or stalked sporangia that generally have a wall like layer (peridium) on the outside. The protoplast of a sporangium becomes divided into a large number of spores, each surrounded by a definite wall. There are about 60 genera and 400 species. These are divided into two subclasses, Endosporeae and the Exosporeae. E.g. *Physarum, Stemonitis*.

2. Class: Plasmodiophornae

The plasmodiophoreae have a naked, multinucleate, plasmodial type of thallus in which all vegetative development takes place within living tissues of a host plant. The spores, each with definite wall may be regularly or irregularly arranged. Spores germinate and give rise to a biflagellate swarmer. e.g. *Plasmodiophora*.

3. Class: Acrasieae

Members of Acrasieae resemble the Myxomycetae in being free living and differ in that there is a development of a multinucleate plasmodium or of flagellated swarmers. Reproduction is by aggregation of large numbers of uninucleate myxamoebae into a mass, the pseudoplasmodium, in which each myxamoeba retains its individuality. e.g. *Dictyostelium*.

II. Eumycophyta

Fungi with a definite cell wall throughout all stages of vegetative development come under Eumycophyta. Thallus is known as mycelium. There are approximately 3,700 genera and 36,000 species. Eumycophyta have been divided into four classes. These are the Phycomycetae, the Ascomycetae, the Bisidiomycetae, and the Deuteromycetae (Fungi imperfecti).

1. **Class: Phycomycetae**
   (i) It mostly includes lower fungi.
   (ii) Majority of the members of these genera are aquatic.
   (iii) Mycelium of most genera are unicellular and multinucleate.
   (iv) Mycelium is aseptate i.e. coenocytic.
   (v) Asexual reproduction takes place by means of zoospores, aplanospores or conidia.
   (vi) Zoospores are without walls and are motile.
   (vii) Sexual reproduction is isogamous, ansogamous and oogamous. e.g. *Albugo, Plasmopara, Pythium, Mucor* etc.

2. **Class: Ascomycetae**
   (i) The thallus of an ascomycetae is of a mycelial type except for yeasts and a few other forms.
   (ii) Mycelium is multicellular, septate with a central pore.
   (iii) Motile cells absent.
   (iv) Asexual reproduction is by conidia which are exogenous.
   (v) Separate male and female sex organs are formed.
   (vi) Ascospores are the sexual spores produced in a sac like structure called as ascus. e.g. Yeast, *Penicillium* etc.

3. **Class: Basidiomycetae**
   (i) Basidiomycetae include the mushrooms and their allies, the jelly fungi, the smuts and the rusts.
   (ii) Presence of primary and secondary mycelium.
   (iii) Asexual reproduction is by spores.
   (iv) Sexual spores are basidiospores produced exogenously on club shaped structure basidia. e.g. *Agaricus, Puccinia* etc.

4. **Class: Deuteromycetae**
   (i) The Deuteromycetae (the imperfect fungi) include those fungi which do not form zygotes, ascospores or basidiospores at any known stage of development.
   (ii) They are the fungi in which the perfect stage i.e. zygote, ascus or basidium has not been discovered or is lacking.
   (iii) The Deuteromycetae also include certain fungi that never form spores.
   (iv) Mycelium is septate.
   (v) Method of asexual reproduction is by conidia. e.g. *Alternaria, Curvularia* etc.

3.4 Life Cycle of *Albugo (Cystopus)*

Introduction

The genus *Cystopus* is an important representative of phycomycetous fungi. *Albugo* is the only genus of the family Albuginaceae and is represented by 25 species, distributed all over the world, out of which 10 have been reported from India. *Albugo* is a pathogenic fungus which causes "White Rust" disease.

Occurrence : The fungus occurs in higher plants as an obligate endoparasite and causes the well-known "White Rust" disease. *Albugo* is the name derived from Latin word, *albus* meaning white and it refers to the white colour of the diseased host. Many plants belonging to families like Cruciferae, Capparidaceae, Convolvulaceae, Portulaceae and Asteraceae are susceptible to infection by *Albugo*. The fungus attacks mostly crucifers like mustard, radish, cabbage, cauliflower, turnip etc. The most common representative of this genus infecting cruciferous crop is *Albugo candida*.

Structure of mycelium

The fungal body consists of microscopic branched filaments called hyphae. The hyphae constitute the vegetative plant body known as mycelium. Mycelium is coenocytic, branched and intercellular. It sends button shaped haustoria into the host tissue. Haustoria is the hyphal tip that penetrates the host tissue and absorbs nutrients from it. Hyphal cell wall is made up of cellulose. The protoplasm contains a large number of minute nuclei distributed in the cytoplasm. Cytoplasm is granular, vacuolate and multinucleate. Reserve food material is in the form of glycogen and oil-drops. Septa are formed at the base of the reproductive structures. Specialised hyphae that bear spores during asexual reproduction are called conidiophore.

Nutrition

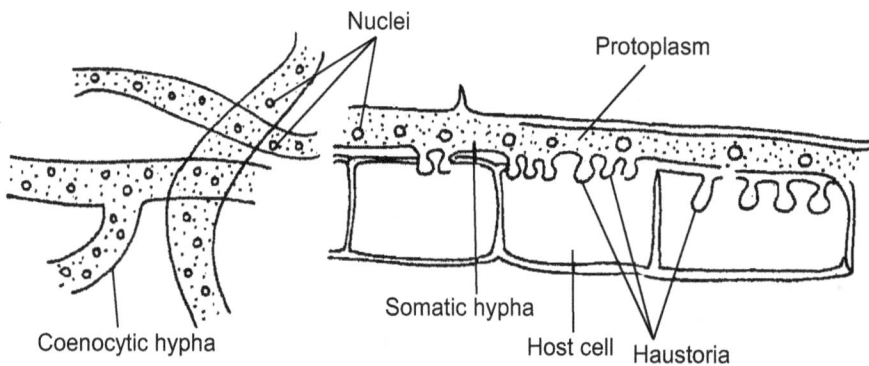

(a) Coenocytic hypha of *Cystopus*   (b) Hypha showing haustoria into the host cells

Fig. 3.1

Albugo shows heterotrophic mode of nutrition and it is an obligate parasite. The absorption of readymade food from host is through button shaped (knob-like) haustoria. Haustorium is a Latin word "haustor" meaning one which draws. Haustoria shows two regions (a) basal penetration tube (b) swollen absorptive region. Fungus spreads rapidly within the host. Hyphae secrete enzymes to simplify the complex organic food which is then absorbed.

Symptoms of "White Rust" Disease

The fungus attacks the entire plant except the roots. The white shining, pustules are seen on the lower side of the leaves, on the stem and inflorescence. It gives rusty appearance hence the name "White rust". Due to the growth of the fungus, cells of the infected organs increase in size and show hypertrophy. Such enormous growth results in swelling of floral parts. In some cases, inflorescence axis is deformed and gets swollen. Leaves become fleshy and irregular. Petals become sepal like and stamens look leafy. The entire plant becomes dwarf.

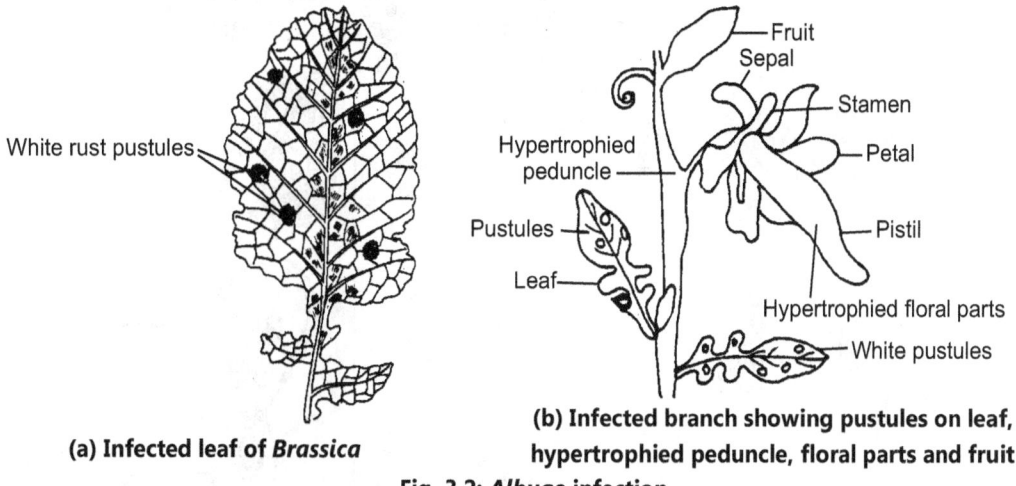

(a) Infected leaf of *Brassica*

(b) Infected branch showing pustules on leaf, hypertrophied peduncle, floral parts and fruit

Fig. 3.2: *Albugo* infection

Reproduction

Reproduction occurs by both asexual and sexual methods.

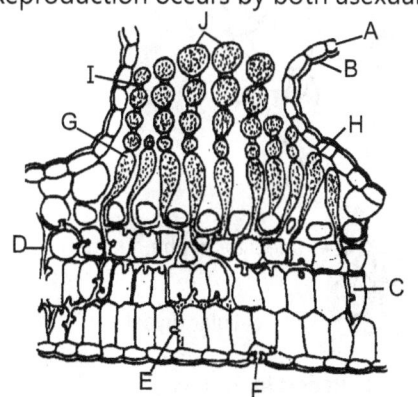

(A) Lower epidermis (B) Cuticle,
(C) Mesophyll cells (D) Inter-cellular coenocytic branched mycelium
(E) Haustorium (F) Stoma (G) Swollen condiophore (H) Youngest condidia
(I) Intercalary disc (J) Oldest conidium

Fig. 3.3: *Albugo*. T.S. of infected host leaf showing

Asexual Reproduction : It takes place during favourable conditions by the formation of conidia. After some growth below the host epidermis, mycelium forms a dense mat. From this mat erect hyphal branches are produced. These are unbranched and club shaped structures called conidiophores (sporangiophores). Condiophores are at right angle to the surface of the epidermis and parallel to each other, forming palisade like layer. The conidiophores cut off conidia in chains at their tips (Fig. 3.4).

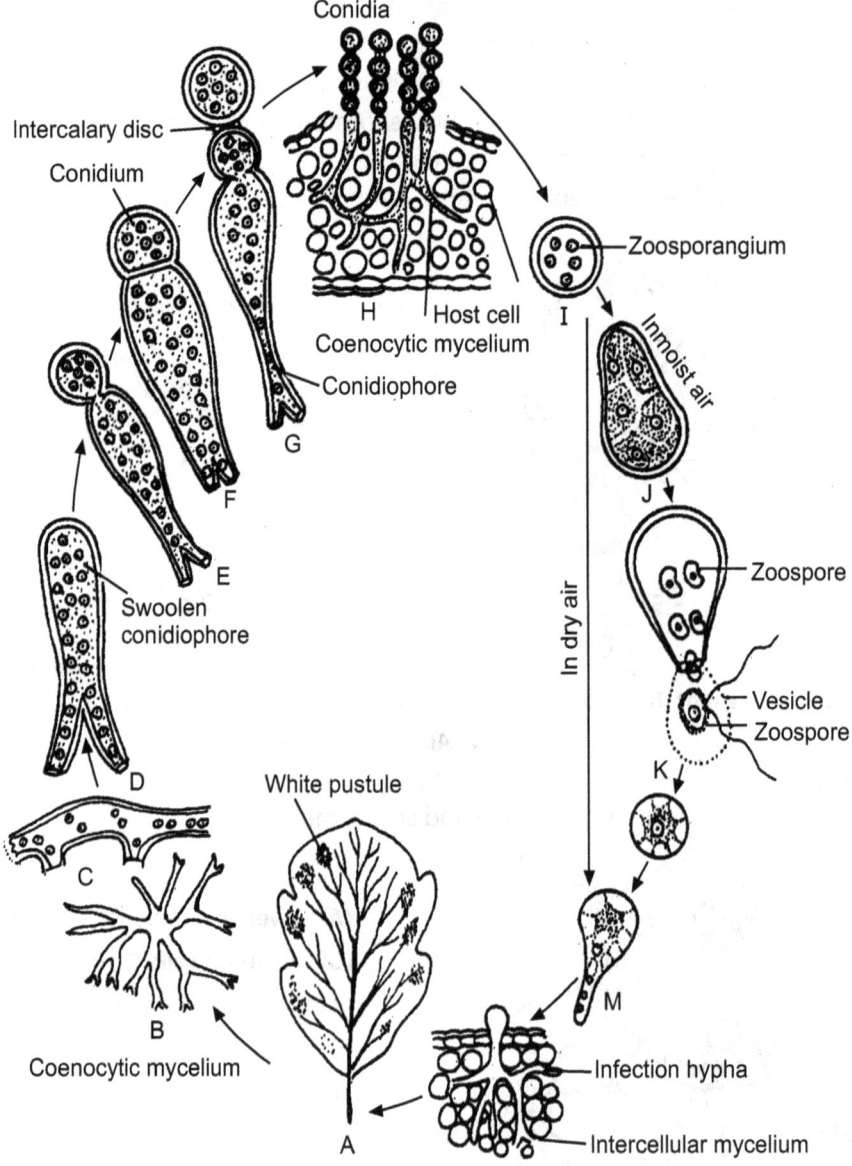

Fig. 3.4 : Showing stages of asexual reproduction in *Albugo*

Formation of Conidia (Fig. 3.5 (a) to (d)) : First of all, the nuclei from the mycelium migrate into the conidiophores along with some protoplasm. The conidiophores become swollen at the tip and develop thick walled structure, enclosing cytoplasm and nuclei in it. Then, a small constriction appears below the swollen end and later on, a septum is formed, resulting into the formation of the first conidium. This process continues giving rise to a chain of conidia. The conidia are produced in basipetal succession i.e. the oldest conidium lying at the top and the youngest at the base.

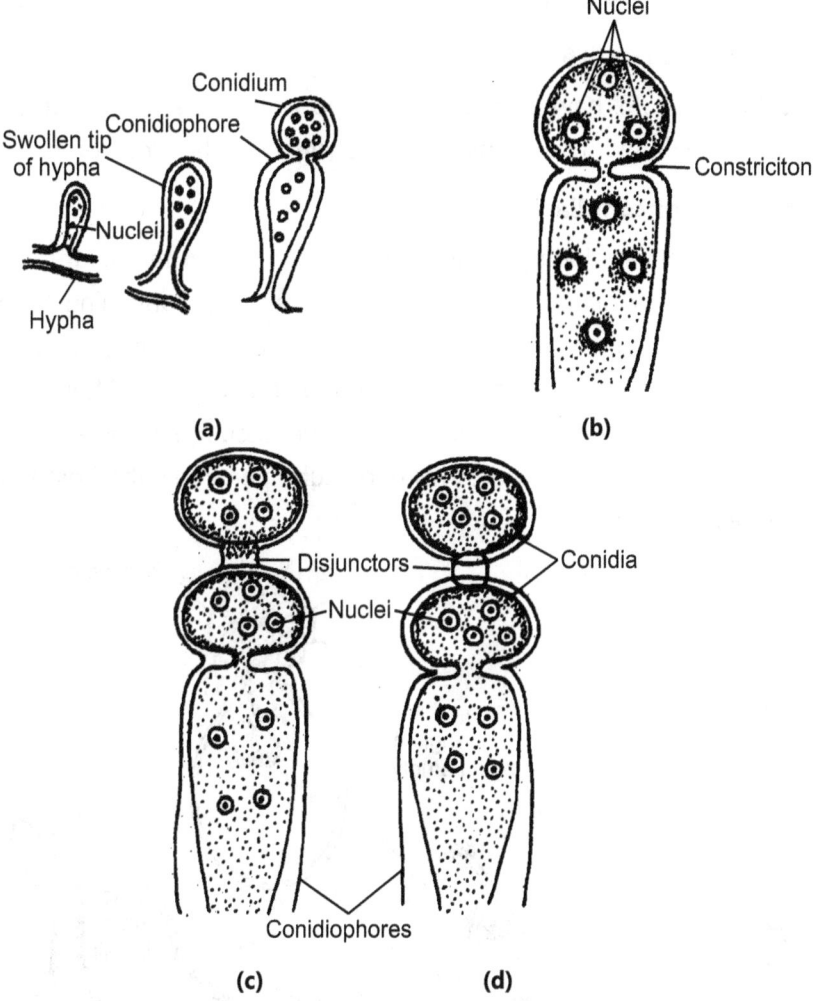

Fig. 3.5 : (a) Hypha developing into conidiophore;
(b – d) Stages in conidial development

Structure of conidium

The conidia are produced in large numbers. Each conidium is unicellular, smooth, spherical, hyaline and multinucleate. The diameter of each conidium (sporangium) is

12 – 18 μ. The outer wall of the conidium is gelatinous and hence the conidia tend to stick to one another. Between successive conidia, a sterile intercalary disc like disjunctor cell is present.

Dispersal or Liberation of conidia (Fig. 3.6 (c))

The conidiophores and conidia are formed just below the epidermis. They exert a pressure on the lower epidermis, due to which it ruptures, finally producing creamy white pustules, hence the name "white rust". The conidia are now dispersed by wind or water.

Germination of conidia (Fig. 3.6 (a to e))

Butler and Jones (1955), have experimentally shown that the conidia do not germinate unless they are partially dried. The germination of conidia may be direct or indirect.

Indirect Germination of conidia (Fig. 3.6 (a to e))

The conidium germinate indirectly under conditions of low temperature and sufficient moisture. The conidium swells up and acts as zoosporangium containing 5 - 8 zoospores. Zoospores are biflagellate, uninucleate and kidney-shaped. By this time, the host plant gets a shower, which facilitates the germination of these motile zoospores. After a brief period of motility, the naked zoospores come to rest on the tissue. Zoospores then germinate immediately by producing a germ tube. This germ tube penerates the host tissues through stomata and cause new infections.

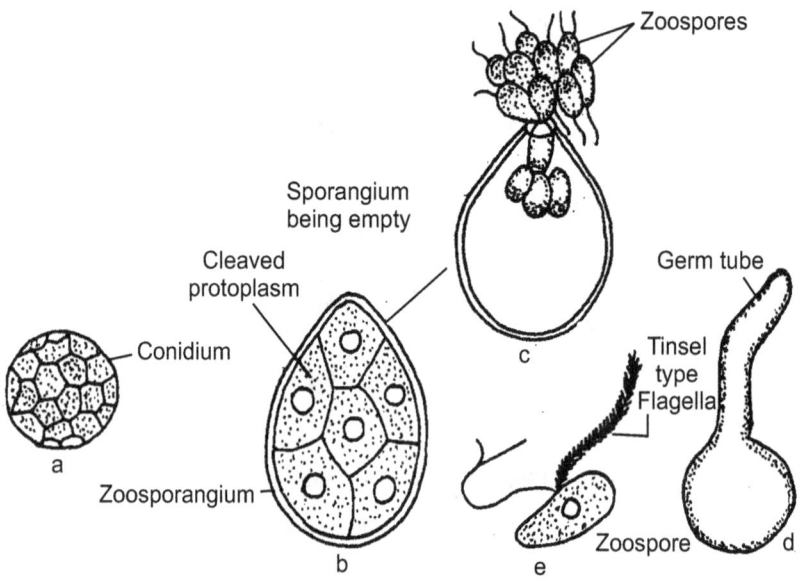

Fig. 3.6: (a to e) Stages in the Indirect germination of conidium

Direct Germination of Conidia (Fig. 3.7)

This is another method of germination of conidia, adapted by the fungus during high temperature and dry climatic conditions. The conidium directly germinates and produces germ tube which enters through stomata or through the injured epidermis and enters into the host body.

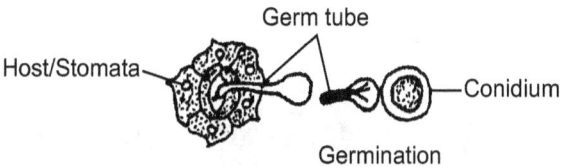

Fig. 3.7 : Stages in the direct germination of conidium

Sexual Reproduction

Sexual reproduction is oogamous. The antheridium is male and oogonium is female sex organ. They are developed on separate hyphae.

Structure of Antheridium (Fig. 3.8)

The antheridium generally develops close to the oogonium therefore is known as paragynous. Tip of the male hypha swells. It is elongated, club shaped and multinucleate. Generally a single antheridium is associated with the oogonium. Out of many nuclei only one is functional and unites with the oogonium.

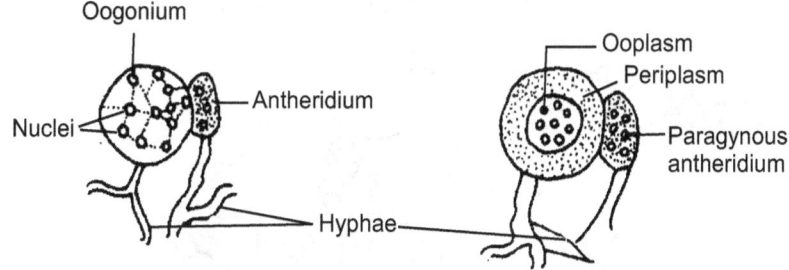

Fig. 3.8 : Antheridium and oogonium of *Cystopus*

Structure of Oogonium

Oogonium develops from side branches of the female hyphae. Oogonia are spherical or globose and terminal in position. They contain about 100 nuclei, at maturity only one remains functional which functions as an egg. Oogonium has outer periplasm and central ooplasm. There are two opinions regarding the uninucleate condition of mature ooplasm. (1) All the nuclei from ooplasm are transferred to the periplasm, except one. (2) All the nuclei of ooplasm except one degenerate.

Fertilisation

The oogonium at the time of fertilisation forms a small papilla which bulges slightly and forms the *receptive papilla*. At the same time, antheridium contacts the oogonium and forms a *fertilisation tube*. This tube penetrates the receptive spot of oogonium and reaches

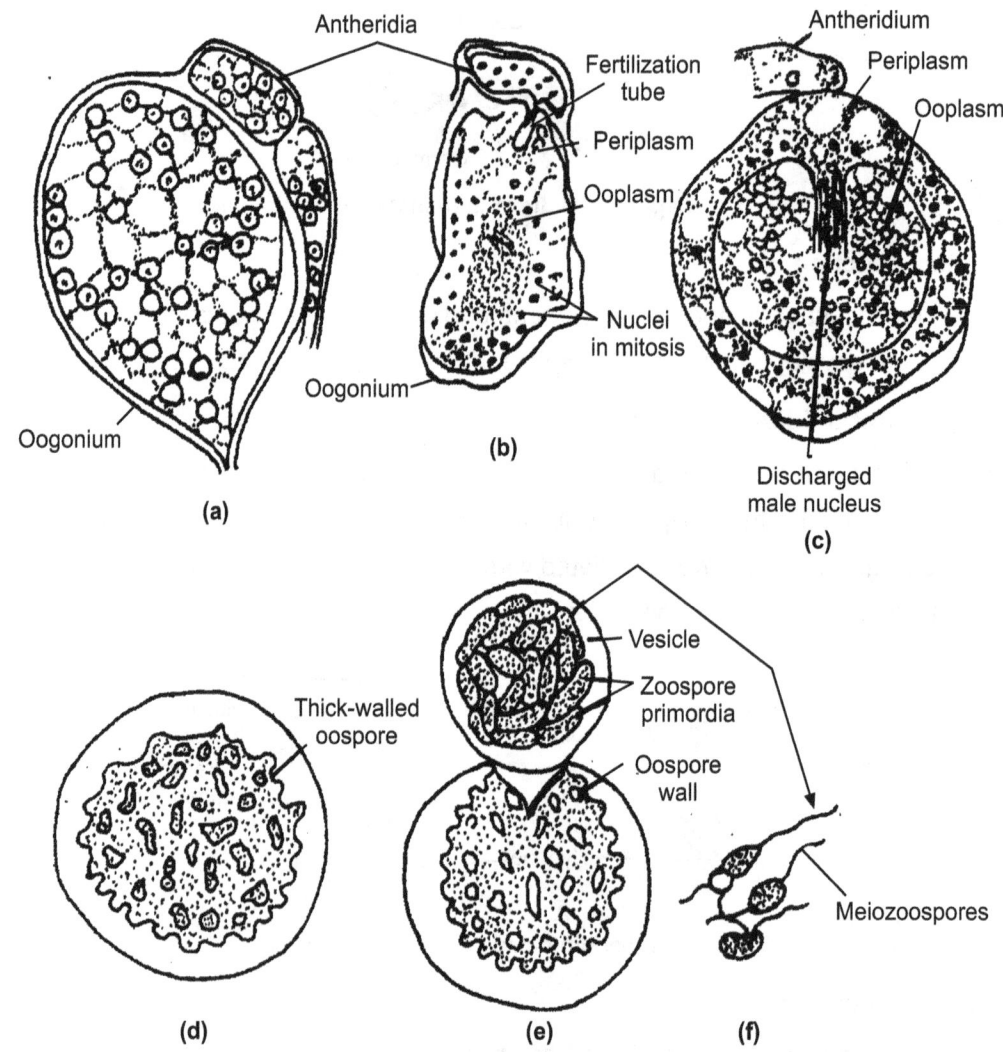

Fig. 3.9 : *Cystopus* sp. (a) Club-shaped multinucleate antheridium applied in the side of globose multinucleate oogonium; (b) Penetration of fertilisation tube through periplasm, presence of deeply granular central region of the oosphere surrounded by multinucleate layer; (c) Fertilisation tube discharging antheridial nucleus; (d) Mature thick-walled oospore; (e) Germinating oospore with vesicle containing zoospore primordia; (f) Meiozoospores

ooplasm through periplasm. Before this, the single functional female nucleus of oogonium gets attached to specialised structure known as *coenocentrum*. It is a spherical, granular cytoplasmic body found in the ooplasm. The fertilisation tube formed by antheridium reaches up to the *coenocentrum*, where it bursts open, liberating the male nucleus. This male nucleus fuses or unites with the female nucleus, forming zygote after fertilisation. Immediately after fertilisation, both, the fertilisation tube and coenocentrum get disintegrated.

The oospore generally does not germinate immediately. If the conditions are unfavourable, it may undergo a period of rest for several months. During this time, the host tissues will be disorganised or disintegrated, liberating the oospore.

Germination of Oospore : (Fig. 3.9 (e))

During favourable conditions the oospore germinates and forms many *meiospores*. The diploid zygotic nucleus first divides meiotically forming 32 nuclei. These, by further divisions form about 100 such nuclei. Each of these nuclei metamorphose into *meiospores*. Each meiospore is a uninucleate, biflagellate and reniform structure. It is now called as *meiozoospore* .

Liberation of meiozoospores (Zoospores)

The meiozoospores are liberated outside from the oospore by two methods (i) The outer wall of oospore will break forming a thin walled vesicle. The zoospores are first set free into the vesicle from the oospore. The vesicle later on perishes liberating the meiozoospores outside (Fig. 3.9 (f)). (ii) In the second method, the oospore forms a small germ tube or may have a small exit and then at the end of germ tube it has a vesicle. The vesicle then disappears, liberating the meiozoospores. They generally swim in water after their liberation from oospore.

Germination of Zoospores (Meiozoospores)

The meiozoospore after coming in contact with a suitable host, gets settled there and enters into a resting state by withdrawing the flagella. It also secretes a wall around itself, becomes rounded and encysted. The encysted meiozoospore germinates under favourable conditions by sending out a germ tube. This germ tube enters through the stomata of host. Then it spreads and establishes its own mycelium in the body of a new host.

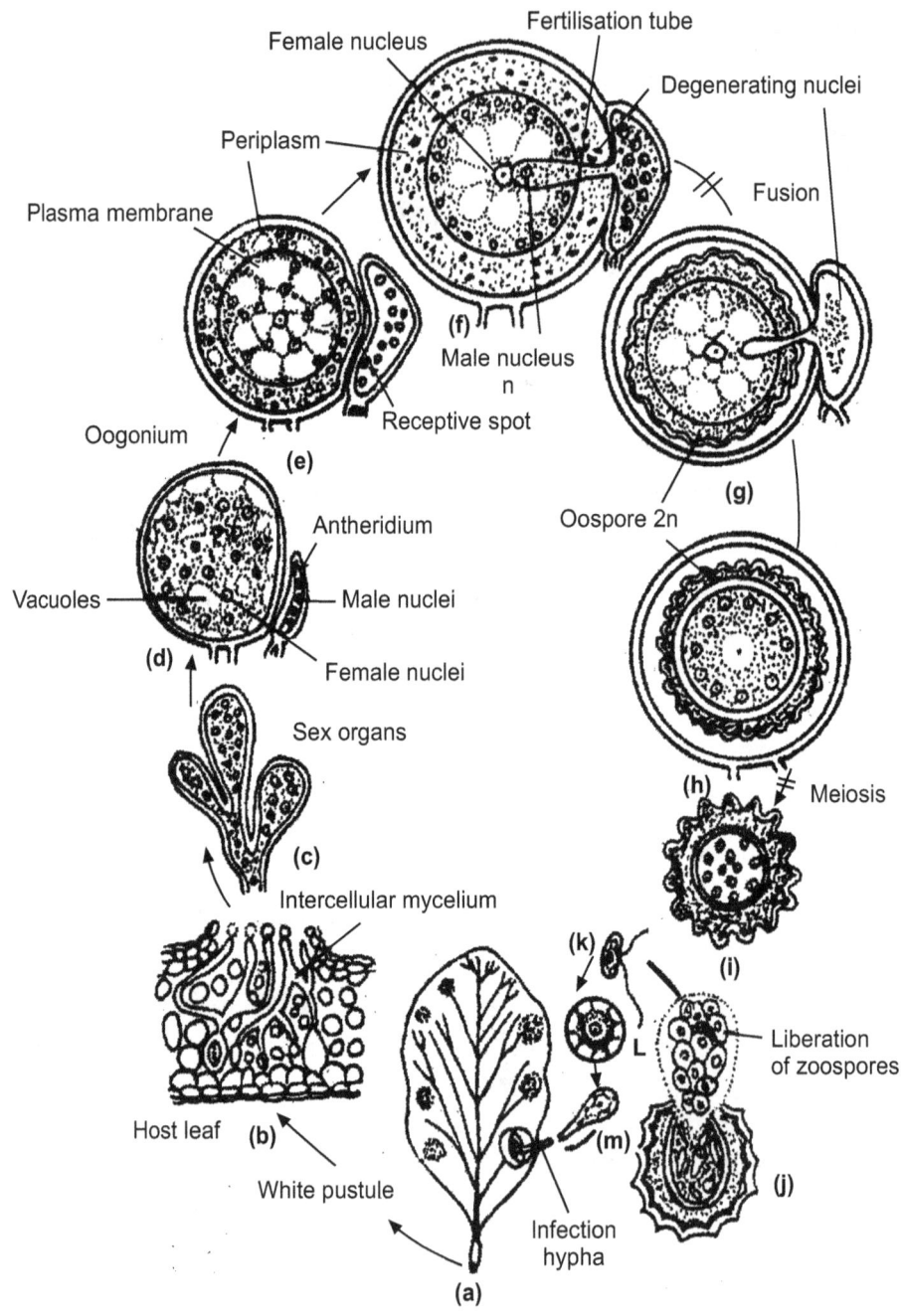

Fig. 3.10 : Diagrammatic representation of the possible sequence of stages in sexual reproduction of *Cystopus* (*Albugo*)

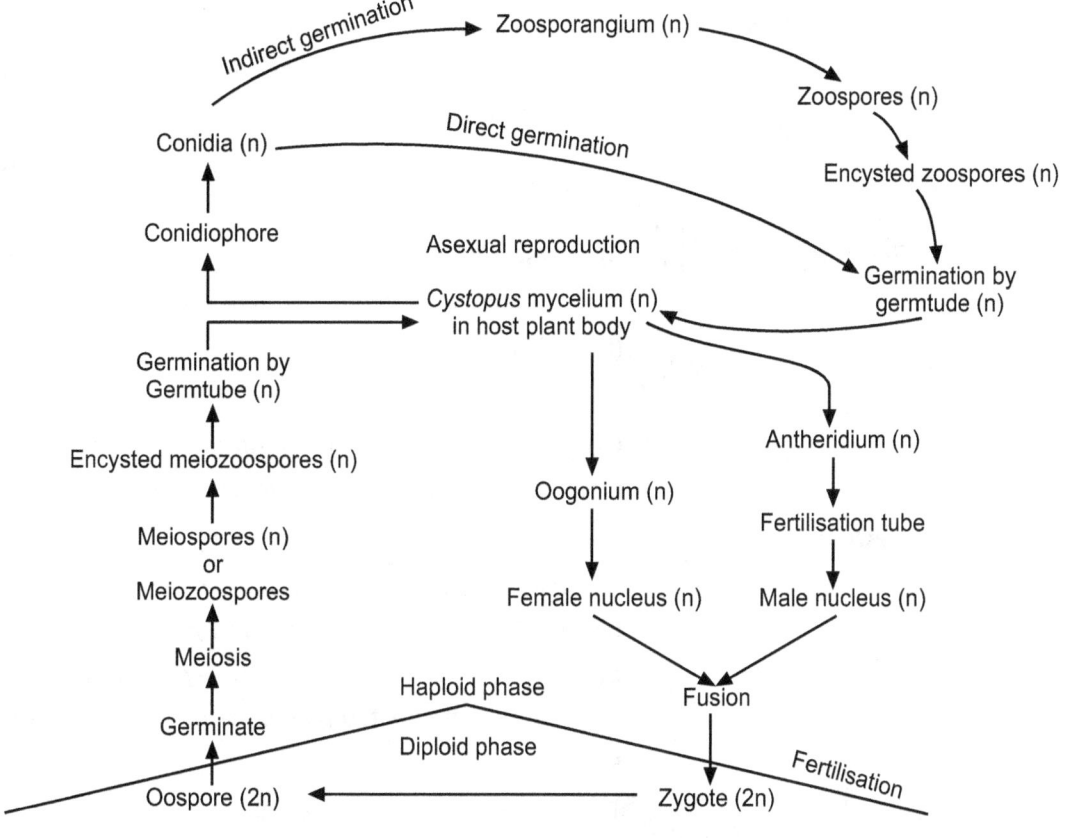

Fig. 3.11 : Graphic life cycle of *Cystopus*

SYSTEMATIC POSITION : (According to G.M. Smith)

Division : Eumycophyta :
(i) Chlorophylls (photosynthetic pigment) absent
(ii) Heterotrophic nutrition (parasites or saprophytes)
(iii) Cell wall made up of fungus cellulose.
(iv) Plant body called as mycelium, uni or multi-cellular

Class : Phycomycetae :
(i) Mycelium aseptate, coenocytic, branched
(ii) Spores many-sporangia or conidia
(iii) Sexual reproduction isogamous or oogamous

Subclass :	**Biflagellatae**	:	(i) Sexual reproduction oogamous
			(ii) Oospores are produced at the end of sexual reproduction
			(iii) Asexual reproduction by means of biflagellate zoospores.
Order :	**Peronosporales**	:	(i) Asexual reproduction by conidia or by sporangia having zoospores in them.
			(ii) Oogamous sexual reproduction.
			(iii) Sporangia detach from mycelium.
Family :	**Albuginaceae**	:	Obligate parasite. Sexual reproduction oogamous. Oospores are formed. Mycelium intercellular.
Genus :	***Cystopus***		
(old name)	***Albugo***	:	Asexual reproduction by chains of conidia which are basipetal in arrangement. Infected plants show white pustules on leaves, hence called as 'white rust'. Hypertrophy of infected plants parts is very commonly seen.
Species :			There are about 25 different species e.g. *A. bliti, A. Candida, A. portulacae* etc.

Points to Remember

Introduction
1. Fungi are nonchlorophyllous thalloid plants.
2. Fungi has attracted the attention of human due to their useful as well as harmful activities.
3. Fungi are mainly classified into two divisions: (a) Myxomycophyta, (b) Eumycophyta.
4. Myxomycetes do not have definite cell structure because of lack of cell wall.
5. Vegetative plant body of myxomycetes is called as plasmodium.
6. Eumycota are true fungi having definite cell structure.

General Characters
1. Fungi are heterotrophic in their mode of nutrition.
2. Vegetative plant body is thalloid and called as mycelium.
3. Reserve food is in the form of glycogen and oil drops.

4. Asexual spores are conidia, aplanospores etc.
5. Sexual reproduction involves plasmogamy, karyogamy and meiosis.

Classification of Fungi by G. M. Smith

1. Fungi divided into Myxomycophyta and Eumycophyta.
2. Myxomycophyta includes three classes

    (1) Myxomycetae,

    (2) Plasmodiophorinae,

    (3) Acrasieae.
3. Eumycophyta includes four classes

    (1) Phycomycetae,

    (2) Ascomycetae,

    (3) Basidiomycetae,

    (4) Deuteromycetae

Life Cycle of *Albugo* (*Cystopus*)

1. Fungus *Albugo* causes white rust disease to cruciferous plants.
2. Mycelium is coenocytic, intercellular and branched. Presence of haustoria.
3. Reproduction is by both sexual and asexual means.
4. Asexual reproduction takes place by means of formation of conidia.
5. Conidia are numerous and in a chain like manner.
6. Conidia germinate directly and indirectly.
7. Sex organs antheridium (male) and oogonium (female).
8. Sexual reproduction is of oogamous type.
9. Oospore is a dormant stage.
10. Oospore germinates and produces meiozoospores.
11. Meizoospores withdraw its flagella and enter into the host tissues.

Exercises

Short Answers Questions

1. Give any five characters of fungi.
2. Write about occurrence of *Albugo* (*Cystopus*).
3. Write in short, the structure of mycelium.

4. Explain mode of nutrition of *Albugo*.
5. Sketch and label asexual reproduction in *Albugo* (*Cystopus*).
6. Write a note on formation of conidia.
7. Write a note on indirect germination of conidia in *Albugo*.
8. Describe female sex organ in *Albugo*.
9. Show diagrammatic representation of sexual reproduction in *Albugo*.
10. Give the symptoms of 'white rust' disease.
11. Give systematic position of *Albugo* with reasons.
12. Write a note on direct germination of conidia in *Albugo*.
13. Describe male sex organ in *Albugo*.

Long Answers Questions
1. Give the general characteristics of fungi.
2. Give the outline classification of fungi proposed by G. M. Smith.
3. Describe asexual reproduction in *Albugo*.
4. Explain germination of conidia in *Albugo*.
5. Describe sexual reproduction in *Albugo*.
6. Describe sex organs in *Albugo*.

Chapter 4...
Lichen Diversity

Contents ...
4.1 Introduction
4.2 Nature of Association
4.3 Types of Lichens on the Basis of Thallus Morphology
4.4 Economic Importance of Lichens
   Points to Remember
   Exercises

4.1 Introduction

A lichen is a composite organism consisting of a fungus living in intimate association with an alga. The fungal partner is called as mycobiont and algal partner called is called as photobiont or phycobiont. Lichens are composite organisms consisting of a fungus (mycobiont) and a photosynthetic partner (photobiont or phycobiont) growing together in a symbiotic relationship. The mycobiont belongs to Ascomycotina, Basidiomycotina or Deuteromycotina and the lichens based on fungal partners are called ascolichens, basidiolichens or deuterolichens. The photobiont is usually either a green alga (chlorophyta) or a blue green alga (cyanophyta). The thallus of most lichens is different from those of either the fungus or alga growing separately. The fungus surrounds the algal cells, often enclosing them within complex fungal tissues unique to lichen associations. In many species, the fungus penetrates the algal cell wall, forming penetration pegs or haustoria similar to those produced by pathogenic fungi. Lichens are capable of surviving at extremely low water levels.

The algal cells are photosynthetic, and as in plants they reduce atmospheric carbon dioxide into organic carbon sugars to feed both symbionts. Both partners gain water and mineral nutrients mainly from the atmosphere, through rain and dust. The fungal partner protects the alga by retaining water, serving as a larger capture area for mineral nutrients and, in some cases, provides minerals obtained from the substrate. If a cyanobacterium is present, as a primary partner or another symbiont in addition to green alga as in certain tripartite lichens, they can fix atmospheric nitrogen, complementing the activities of the green alga.

Lichens have great diversity. There are 13,500 species of lichens distributed all over the world. About 2223 species of lichens are reported from India. Lichens occur in some of the most extreme environments on earth such as arctic tundra, hot deserts, rocky coasts, and toxic slag heaps. However, they are also abundant as epiphytes on leaves and branches in rain forests and temperate woodland, on bare rocks, including walls and gravestones, and on exposed soil surfaces in otherwise mesic habitats. The roofs of many buildings have lichens growing on them. Lichens are widespread and long-lived; however, many are also vulnerable to environmental disturbance, and may be useful to scientists in assessing the effects of air pollution, ozone depletion, and metal contamination.

General Characters

1. Lichens are composite organisms consisting of a fungus living in intimate association with an alga.
2. The mycobiont belongs to Ascomycotina, Basidiomycotina or Deuteromycotina
3. Algal members are unicellular and belong to chlorophyceae or cyanophyceae.
4. Morphologically lichens are classified into three types, crustose, foliose and fruticose.
5. Lichens reproduce by vegetative, asexual and sexual methods.
6. Vegetative reproduction in lichens occurs by fragmentation of thallus and by formation of vegetative propagules like soredia and isidia.
7. Asexual reproduction in lichens takes place by pycnidia.
8. Sexual reproduction in lichens takes place in fungal partner only, since most of the lichens have fungal partner belonging to Ascomycetes.
9. In Ascolichens, the ascospores are produced in asci which are produced in fruiting bodies like apothecia and perithecia. The male and female reproductive organs are called spermogonium and carpogonium respectively.
10. In basiodiolichens, basidiospores are produced on basidia.

4.2 Nature of Association

The association of a fungus and an alga in the lichen is generally believed to be symbiotic. The relationship of two partners was termed as helotism by Schwendener (1867) where the alga was the slave providing food to the fungal master. de Bary (1867) used the term symbiosis for this relationship. Reinke (1896) used the term mutalism, where the both partners are benefited from each other. Bornet, Clements and Shear used the term parasitism for this relationship. However, the simple term symbiosis, first used by de Bary, has been accepted all over the world.

The dominant member of a lichen symbiont is usually the fungus. The lichen thallus is usually found from association of one fungus and one alga, one alga and two fungi or two algae and one fungus or two algae or two fungi.

4.3 Types of Lichens on the Basis of Thallus Morphology

Lichens are classified mainly on the basis of habitat and morphology of thallus. On the basis of habitat they are classified into four groups as follows

1. Saxicolous: Lichens which grow on rocks are called saxicolous lichens.
2. Endolithic: Lichens which form colonies inside the crevices of rocks are called endolithic lichens.
3. Corticolous: Lichens which grow on the leaves and bark of plants are called corticolous lichens.
4. Terricolous: Lichens which grow on soil are called terricolous lichens.

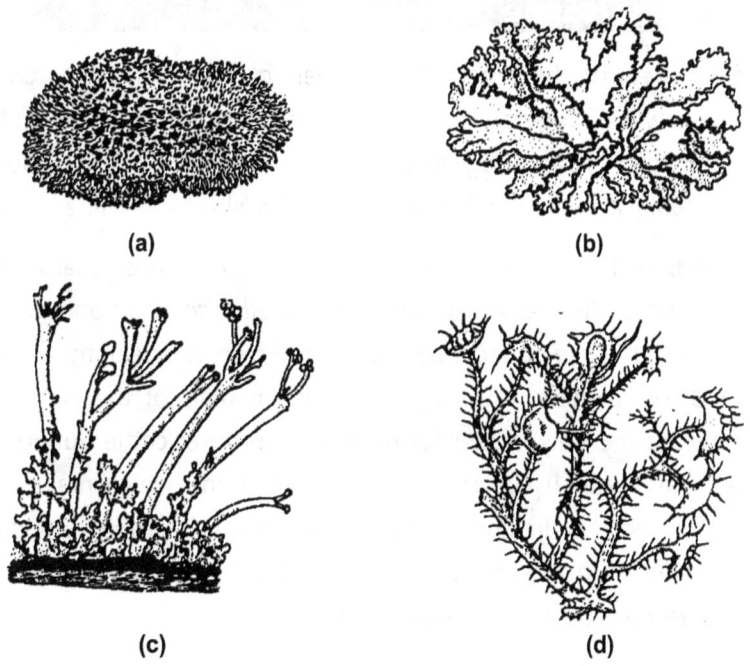

(a) *Graphis*, (b) *Parmelia*, (c) *Cladonia*, (d) *Usnea*

Fig. 4.1: Different types of Lichens

On the basis of morphology of thallus, lichens are divided into three major types crustose, foliose and fruticose lichens.

1. **Crustose lichens:** Crustose lichens are firmly attached to the substrate so that they cannot be separated easily from it. They are thin, flat and crust-like without lobes. They are found growing on the surface of rocks, barks of trees or on surface of soil. These lichens produce apothecia or perithecia on the thallus. The common examples are *Graphis, Lecanora, Lecidia, Verrucaria* and *Haematomma*. (Fig. 4.1)

2. **Foliose lichens:** Foliose lichens have thin, flat and leaf like thallus with lobes. The thallus is dorsiventral, which is partially attached to substrate by hair like rhizinae. The rhizinae are absorptive in nature and provide support to thallus. These lichens produce apothecia on dorsal surface at maturity. e.g. *Physcia, Parmelia, Peltigera, Cetraria, Xanthoria, Stricta* and *Collema*. (Fig. 4.1)

3. **Fruticose lichens:** The thallus is erect, shrubby or pendent, branched structure. The branches may be cylindrical or flat -ribbon like. The thallus is attached by means of a flat disc. They grow on rocks and branches of trees. They produce apothecia at maturity. e.g. *Usnea, Cladonia, Ramalina* and *Evernia*. (Fig. 4.1)

4.4 Economic Importance of Lichens

1. **Pioneers of vegetation:** The lichens are pioneering organisms which contribute in soil formation and growth of vegetation. Through weathering of the rocks and accumulation of organic debris, they make a region suitable for growth of other plants. The series of succession eventually allows growth of mosses, herbs, shrubs and finally trees.

2. **Lichens as food:** Numerous small creatures like mites, slugs, snails, caterpillars and termites are known to feed upon lichens like *Aspicilia calcarea* and *Lecanora saxicola*. Some lichens like *Cladonia rangiferina* the well known reindeer moss is an important source for food for reindeer, musk ox and other animals of the arctic and sub arctic regions. Lichens are the only fodder for reindeer and other cattle during winter. Lichens contain lichenin as a starch like carbohydrate compound which makes some of them useful for human food. In Ireland, Sweden and Norway, *Cetraria islandica* is taken as food. In South India, *Parmelia perlata* is used for making delicious curry. A desert lichen, *Endocarpon miniatum* is used as vegetable in Japan.

3. **Application to Pharmacology Medicines:** Several species of lichens are used to treat different diseases but today they have been replaced by more effective drugs.
   a. *Peltigera caniana* is used in hydrophobia.
   b. *Xanthoria parientina* is used in cases of jaundice

c. Species of *Cladonia* and *Cetraria* for intermittent fever and as laxatives.
d. *Lobaria pulmonaria* and *Cetraria islandica* were used in for treating lung diseases.
e. The antibiotic effect of many lichen metabolites have been found significant for Gram positive bacteria.
f. The usnic acid derived from lichens has antibiotic properties against a number of fungi and bacteria.
g. Lichens are used in commercially available antiseptic creams.

4. **Dyes:** Lichens are commonly used for making dyes and perfumes from the time of the ancient Greeks.
   a) Erythrolitmin, the dye used in litmus paper to indicate pH is extracted from variety of lichens. *Rocella, Evernia, Parmelia* are some dye yielding lichens.
   b) *Rocella* gives 'orchil' which is used in dyeing woolen and fabrics.

5. **Perfumes:** Several species of lichens are used in preparation of dhup, hawan samagris and perfumes. *Evernia prunastri* and *Pseudovernia furfuracea* are the sources of an oily substance used in perfume.

6. **As pollution indicators:** Lichens grow in pollution free areas. They are killed even at low levels of sulphur dioxide, which accumulates in lichen thallus.

7. **Nest building:** The bird, golden plover uses *Thamnolia vermicularis* in its nests. More than 50 species of birds in North America are known to use lichens in nest building.

8. **Tanning Industry:** Some lichens such as *Lobaria pulmonaria* and *Cetraria islandica* are used as agents in tanning industry.

9. **Packing material:** One of the more strange uses of lichens from the past is as packing material for ancient Egyptian mummies.

10. Recently the species of lichen is named in honor of U.S. President - Barack Obama. e.g. *Caloplaca obamae*.

Points to Remember

- Lichens are composite organisms consisting of a fungus living in intimate association with an alga.
- The mycobiont belongs to Ascomycotina, Basidiomycotina or Deuteromycotina. Algal members are unicellular and belong to chlorophyceae or cyanophyceae.
- Morphologically, lichens are classified into three types, crustose, foliose and fruticose. There are 13500 species of lichens distributed all over the world. About 2223 species of lichens are reported from India.

- Lichens occur in some of the most extreme environments on earth such as arctic tundra, hot deserts, rocky coasts, and toxic slag heaps. However, they are also abundant as epiphytes on leaves and branches in rain forests and temperate woodland, on bare rocks, including walls and gravestones, and on exposed soil surfaces in otherwise mesic habitats.
- The association of a fungus and an alga in the lichen is generally believed to be symbiotic. The dominant member of a lichen symbiont is usually the fungus.
- On the basis of morphology of thallus lichens are divided into three major types crustose, foliose and fruticose lichens.
- Lichens have many applications. They are pioneers of vegetation, used as food, packing material and pollution indicators, in pharmacology and medicines, for making dyes and perfumes, in nest building and tanning industry.

Exercises

Short Answer Questions
1. What are lichens?
2. What is mycobiont?
3. What is phycopbiont?
4. Enlist the general characters of lichens.
5. Give economic importance of lichens
6. Enlist examples of crustose lichens.
7. Enlist examples of foliose lichens.
8. Enlist examples of fruticose lichens.

Long Answer Questions
1. Explain thallus diversity in lichens.
2. Describe thallus diversity in lichens based on morphology.
3. Comment on nature of association in lichens.
4. Write short notes on
   (i) Crustose lichens
   (ii) Foliose lichens
   (iii) Fruticose lichens

Chapter 5...

Bryophytes

Contents ...

5.1 Introduction
5.2 General Characters
5.3 Outline of Classification
5.4 Life Cycle of *Riccia*
    Points to Remember
    Exercises

5.1 Introduction

Bryophytes are among the oldest primitive, thalloid, nonvascular, cryptogamic land plants that flourished during the middle Devonian period which include liverworts, hornworts and mosses. These are the "amphibians" of the plant kingdom. The term Bryophyte is of Greek origin. Bryon-mosse means 'phyton' plant. Bryophytes occupy an intermediate position between algae and vascular cryptogams i.e. pteridophytes. Bryophytes are essentially small plants ranging from a few millimeters to a few centimeters in size; because of their dependence on water for fertilisation. The gametophyte (haploid) is the most conspicuous and dominant phase in life cycle which is nutritionally independent i.e. autotrophic. However sporophyte (diploid) is dependent on gametophyte for its nutrition. Bryophytes have a sharply defined heteromorphic alteration of generation. **Late Prof. S.R. Kashyap** due to his memorable contribution to Indian bryophytes is known as **"Father of Indian Bryology"**.

As on today, about 1025 genera and 24,000 species of bryophytes are reported. Amongst these, liverworts are represent 320 genera and more than 10,000 species. While mosses are at the top having 700 genera and 14,300 species, hornworts is the smallest group with only 5 genera and 100 species.

Liverworts grow horizontally and are flattened or "leafy", whereas mosses have an upright stalk with spirally arranged leaf like structures. The bryophytes are now being used in pollution monitoring, as the new sources of pharmaceutical products, medicines, food, horticulture, industry, construction and for various household uses. They are even used as fuel. Moss peat produces methane, ethylene, natural gas etc.

5.2 General Characters

1) It is a small group of primitive, nonvascular and cryptogamic land plants
2) The plant body is a gametophyte. They grow in areas which are in between the aquatic and terrestrial habitats i.e. amphibious zone and hence known as amphibious plants.
3) They have thalloid or leafy multi cellular green plant body.
4) The smallest form is microscopic (e.g. *zoopsis*). The largest form belong to Australian Dawsonia which is about 70 cms in length.
5) The dominant plant body is a gametophyte (n) which is independent.
6) The plant body lacks true roots, stem or leaves.
7) Rhizoids – (root like structure) serve the function of roots.
8) The plants are green and possess chloroplasts.
9) They show autotropic mode of nutrition.
10) Vascular tissues are completely absent.
11) Sexual reproduction is oogamous.
12) Sex organs are multicellular and jacketed.
13) Male reproductive organ is known as antheridium. It is a club shaped structure bearing a narrow stalk. It produces biflagellate and motile male gametes or antherozoids. Both the flagella are of whiplash type.
14) The female sex organ is known as archegonium. It is a flask shaped structure having a swollen base and a narrow neck.
15) Water is essential for fertilisation.
16) The fertilised egg is retained within the venter of the archegonium. The venter wall enlarges with the developing embryo forming a protective multicellular calyptra.
17) The diploid zygote undergoes repeated divisions to form a multicellular sporophyte.
18) Sporophyte is dependent on the gametophyte for nutrition, partially or wholly.
19) Sporophyte generally consists of foot, seta and capsule. But in some species, seta is absent, while in others, both foot and seta are absent.
20) Spores on germination give rise to gametophytic plant.
21) Gametophyte and sporophyte differ in form which alternate with each other, thus heterologous alternation of generation is seen in bryophytes.

5.3 Outline of Classification

Gilbert M. Smith (1955) had classified Division Bryophyta in to three distinct classes

  i) Hepaticae (Liverworts)
  ii) Anthocerotae (Hornworts)
  iii) Musci (Mosses)

i) Distinguishing features of Class Hepaticae

Hepatica is a latin word for liver. The thallus structure of the members of the class resemble the lobes of human liver. The plants belonging to this class are supposed to have remedial values for liver problems. Therefore they are called as liverworts. They show the following features

1) The plant body is a thalloid, dorsiventrally flattened or with a leafy axis.
2) If the leaves are present, they are arranged in two or three rows on the axis.
3) Rhizoids and scales are present on the ventral surface.
4) Rhizoids are usually unicellular and unbranched. They are of two types i.e. smooth and tuberculate.
5) Sex organs develop from the superficial single initial cell situated on the dorsal side of the thallus, but in some cases they develop at the terminal position.
6) The sporophyte is totally dependent on the gametophyte as it is without chlorolphyll.
7) The sporophyte may be simple or may be differentiated into foot, seta and capsule or foot and capsule. It has no meristematic tissues.
8) Sporogenous cells develop from the endothecium of the embryo.
9) Capsule wall may be one layer thick or multilayered. Stomata are absent on the capsule wall.
10) The dehiscence of the capsule is due to irregular rupture of its wall.
11) The gametophyte has photosynthetic tissues. The cells constituting the gametophyte have simple or compound oil bodies and numerous, small chloroplast. The chloroplast lack pyrenoids.
12) The sterile cells elongate to form elaters with spirally thickened walls.
13) The columella is absent.

Examples : *Riccia, Marchantia, Pellia, Porella.*

ii) Distinguishing features of Class Anthocerotae

These are also called as 'Hornworts'. They show the following features

1) The plants are thalloid, dorsiventrally flattened and lobed.

2) Rhizoids are smooth walled.
3) Ventral scales are absent.
4) Internally, the thallus shows no differentitation of tissues, i.e. the thallus is homogenous.
5) There are no air chambers or air pores but intercellular mucilage cavities are present.
6) Each cell of the thallus has a single large choroplast with a conspicuous compound central pyrenoid. The cells lack oil bodies.
7) The sex organs are embeded in the gametophytic tissue.
8) Antheridia develop in groups from hypodermal cells of the dorsal side of the thallus in the antheridial chambers.
9) Archegonia develop from dorsal superficial cells.
10) The sporophyte consists of a bulbous foot, a meristematic region and a long cylindrical capsule. The sporophyte has the peculiar property of being able to continue growth throughout the growing season by means of a characteristic intercalary meristem.
11) The wall of the capsule is 4 to 6 layers thick, rich in chlorophyll and is provided with stomata.
12) Dehiscence of the capsule takes place in two halves.
13) The sporogenous tissue develops from the amphithecium and arches over the columella.
14) Sporophyte is partially dependent on the gametophyte.
15) Pseudo elaters are present as they do not have thickened bands.

Examples : *Anthoceros, Megaceros, Dendroceros and Notothylas.*

iii) Distinguishing features of Class Musci

They are commonly called as 'Mosses'. The show the following features

1) The gametophytic plant body is differentiated into rhizoids, stem (axis) and leaves, which are radially symmetrical.
2) The rhizoids are multicellular with oblique septa.
3) The leaves are arranged in 3 – 8 rows on the axis.
4) At maturity, the plants bear sex organs which develop from the superficial cells of the gametophyte.
5) The sporophyte is differentiated into foot, seta and capsule.
6) The capsule wall is multilayered with stomata.
7) The sporogenous tissue or archesporium develops from the outer layer of the endothecium. The endothecium develops central columella also.

8) In many cases, peristome teeth are present in one or two rows. They surround the terminal opening of the capsule.
9) Capsule dehisces by means of operculum.
10) Internally, the stem shows differentiation into cortex and conducting strand, but there is no true vascular tissue.
11) The gametophyte consists of two growth stages - the protonema and the leafy gametophyte.
12) With the exception of *Sphagnum*, the leaf of mosses usually has a midrib.
13) The sex organs are stalked.
14) The venter of archegonium is massive.
15) The sporophyte is more elaborate and complex and shows high degree of specialisation and sterilisation.
16) There are no elaters.

Examples : *Sphagnum, Funaria, Polytrichum* etc.

5.4 Life Cycle of *Riccia*

Systematic position

    Division - Bryophyta
    Class - Hepataceae (liverworts)
    Order - Marchantiales
    Family - Ricciaceae
    Genus - *Riccia*

Occurrence

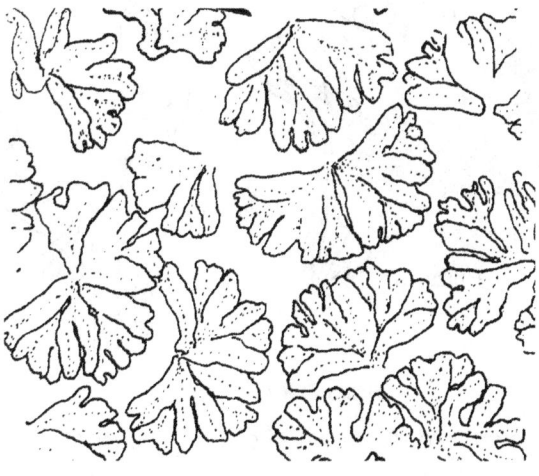

Fig. 5.1: *Riccia* thalli forming rosette

This name of the genus is given to honour the Italian Botanist F.F. Ricci. This cosmpolitan genus with more than 200 species is mostly found in southern hemisphere. The species are terrestrial, except *Riccia fluitans*, and *R. natans* which are free floating or submerged, reported from Dal lake, Kashmir, Garhwal, Madras and Kupurthala (Punjab).

The terrestrial species grow for a very short span of time on damp soil forming rosettes. (Fig. 5.1) In India, approximately more than 30 species of *Riccia* are reported mainly from Eastern Himalayas and hills of South India.

Gametophyte: (External structure) Morphology

The plant body is thalloid, small, green, flat and fleshy; with an indistinct to distinct midrib and dichotomous branching. It grows prostate on the ground and takes up rosette. The dichotomously branched thallus becomes lobed. Each lobe is thickened at the middle and gradually becomes thin towards the margin.

The lobes of thallus may be linear to wedgeshaped or obcordate. The upper surface of lobe shows a median groove or furrow which is known as dorsal groove, which ends in a depression at the apical region, forming an apical notch. The growing point of thallus is situated in this notch. The dorsal groove is meant for retaining water, required for fertilisation. (Fig. 5.2)

On the ventral surface, rhizoids and scales are present. The thallus is attached to the substratum by slender, simple, unicellular rhizoids, which arise from the lower surface of the thallus. The rhizoids are of two kinds (i) smooth-walled and (ii) tuberculated. The smooth walled rhizoids are simple, colourless and smooth. (Fig. 5.3)

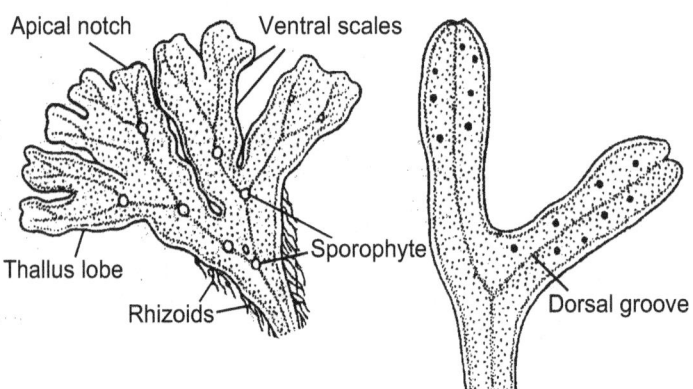

Fig. 5.2: *Riccia* **thallus**

These rhizoids are brown to dark brown in colour. The rhizoids function as the organs of attachment of thallus to the substratum and absorb water and solutes from soil.

In addition to rhizoids, on the ventral surface of thallus, they are many scales which are membranous, one cell in thickenss multicellular and violet in colour. The scales are arranged in one transverse median row near the apex. They are situated closely and project forward to protect the growing point and provide moist environment by capillary conduction of water (Fig. 5.3). Posterior to the growing point, an increase in width of thallus splits the scales in two parts. Therefore, the older parts of thallus have two rows of scales along the two lateral margins.

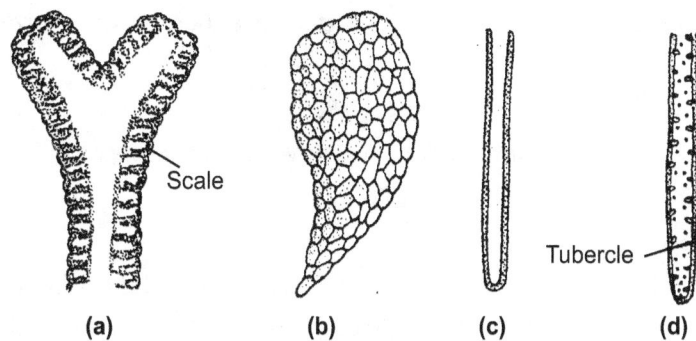

Fig. 5.3: (a) Scales on thallus (ventral side), (b) Scale enlarged, (c) Smooth walled rhizoid, (d) Tuberculated rhizoid.

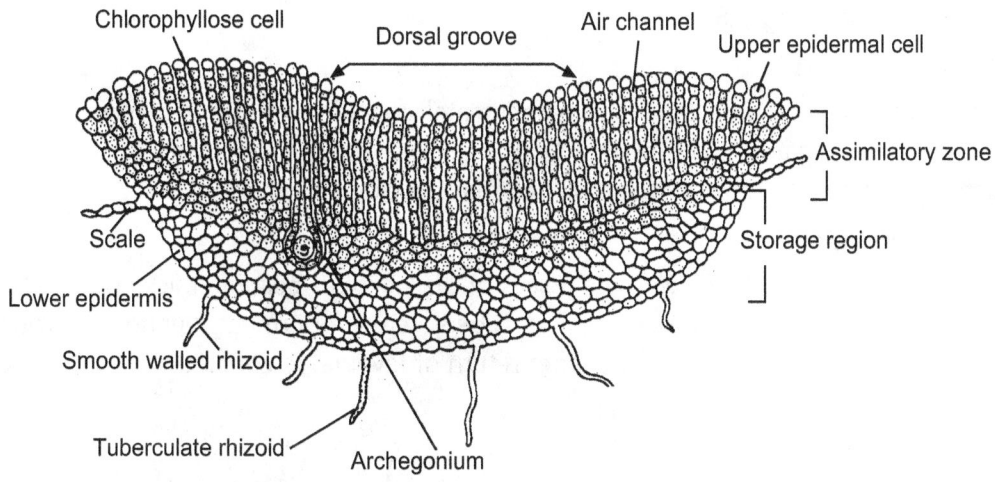

Fig. 5.4: Internal structure of *Riccia* thallus

Internal Structure of Thallus

In the cross section, the thallus shows two distinct zones (Fig. 5.4) (i) Upper assimilatory region and (ii) Lower storage region.

(i) The upper assimilatory or photosynthetic region consists of assimilatory cells stacked over one another which are rich in chloroplast, and forms filaments or coloumn of an air chamber. But the upper most cells of the filament are without chloroplasts, which combine to form loose epidermis. It shows presence of many air chambers.

(ii) Storage region : It is made up of parenchymatous, nonchlorophyllous, compactly arranged cells, which are full of starch, water and reserve food. The lowermost cell layer of this zone forms lower epidermis. Its central cells elongate and from rhizoids (Fig. 5.4) while marginal cells form scales.

Reproduction

At maturity, the gametophyte starts reproducing either by vegetative methods, or by sexual methods.

Vegetative reproduction

It takes places by (a) Fragmentation, (b) Adventitious branches, (c) Persistant apices (d) Tuber formation.

(a) Fragmentation

Due to ageing of vegetative cells, the thallus cells decay and die; as a result of this, young lobes separate and they grow into new thallus by means of apical growth. (Fig. 5.5 (a) to (d))

(b) Adventitious branches

In some species like *Riccia fluitans*, special adventitious branches developed from the ventral surface of thallus in the midrib regions. These branches separate from parental thallus and form new thalli. (Fig. 5.6 (g))

(c) Persistent apices

Sometimes due to unfavourable environmental conditions e.g. dry season, the whole thalli except growing apices completely die. But the surviving persistant apices again resume growth with the onset of the rainy season and they develop new thalli.

(d) Tuber formation

In some species like *R. discolor*, the apices of thallus lobes become thick, forming tubers at the end of the growing season. The tubers remain dormant during unfavourable conditions, but give rise to new plants after return of favourable conditions. (Fig. 5.6 (e) and (f)).

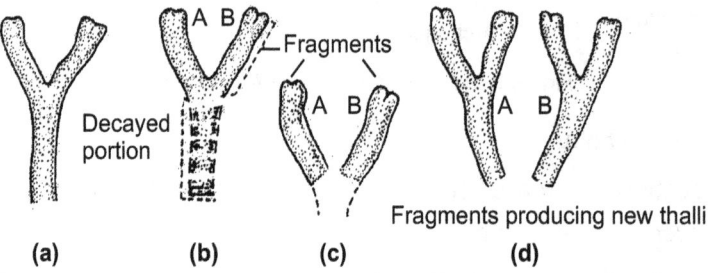

Fig. 5.5 : Different modes of vegetative reproduction in *Riccia*

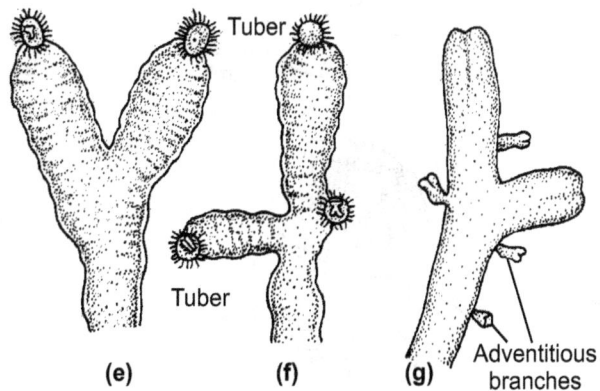

Fig. 5.6 : Different modes of vegetative reproduction

Sexual Reproduction

Almost all the species of *Riccia* are monoecious i.e. antheridia (male sex organ) and archegonia (female sex organ) occur on the same thallus. The sex organs are formed on thallus in acropetal succession (younger at the apex and older at the base). The monoecious thallus shows intermittent and mixed development of antheridia and archegonia.

Structure of Antheridium

The antheridium is formed in an antheridial chamber, which opens at the upper surface of thallus by a narrow pore known as ostiole. The antheridium is attached to the bottom of antheridial chamber by means of its multicellular stalk. Its body is a void or pear shaped, having antheridial wall, made up of a jacket of sterile cells, which is protective in function. The antheridum mainly consists of a mass of androcyte mother cells, which are small, cubical, fertile cells. Each androcyte mother cell has a denser cytoplasm and a relatively larger nucleus. It divides to form two sperm cells known as spermatids or androcytes, each of which turn into spermatozoid or antherozoid with two whiplash flagella at the anterior end. (Fig. 5.7, Fig. 5.8 and Fig. 5.9)

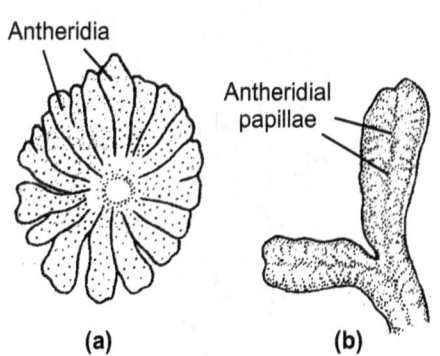

Fig. 5.7: Antheridia

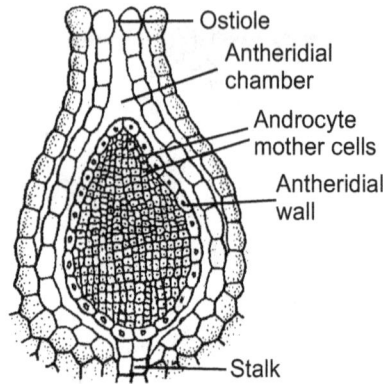

Fig. 5.8: Structure of antheridia

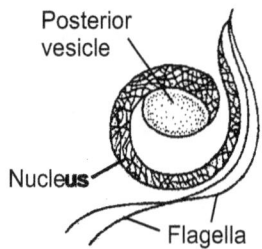

Fig. 5.9: Antherozoid

Structure of Archegonium

The archegonium is a flask shaped body, consisting of venter – the basal swollen part and neck – long, slender part. Venter is attached to the tissue of the thallus. The venter has six longitudinal rows of sterile cells forming a protective jacket around the lower and larger

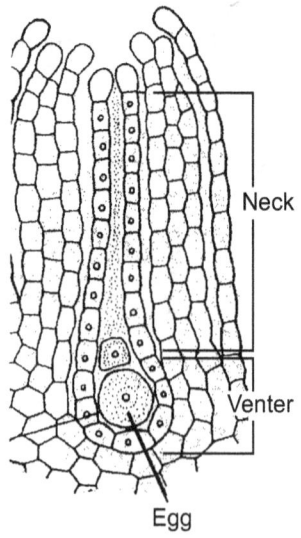

Fig. 5.10: Structure of Archegonium

egg cell and the upper and smaller ventral canal cell. The neck consists of 6 – 9 layers of elongated cells arranged in 6 vertical rows and encloses a narrow canal consisting of 4 – 6 neck canal cells in a single row. Cover or lid cells are present at the top of the neck. Each archegonium lies in a cavity but the neck projects above the surface of the thallus into the dorsal furrow.

Fertilisation

At maturity, the antheridium in presence of moisture or water bursts open, liberating thousands of sperms or antherozoids outside, at the upper surface of thallus. The antherozoids swim freely in a thin film of water in the dorsal furrow.

The archegonium also matures at the same time, its neck canal cells degenerate forming a mass of mucilage, which absorb water and swell, forcing the neck-canal apart and making a clear passage for the entry of the antherozoids.

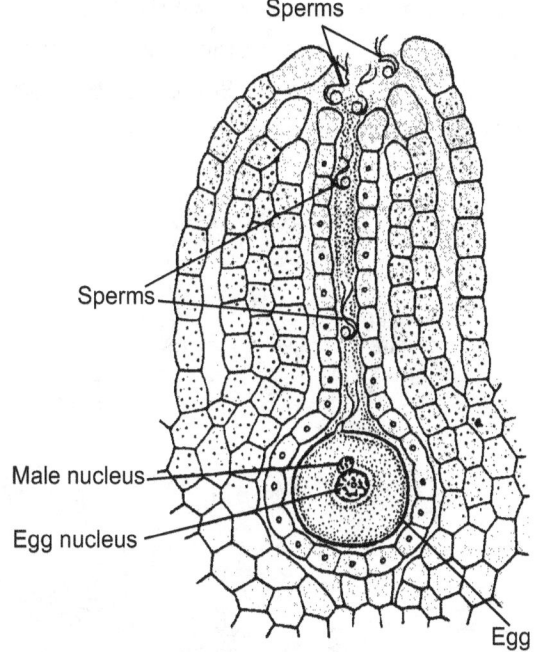

Fig. 5.11: Fertilisation

These enter into the venter of the archegonium and finally one of them successfully unites with the egg completing the act of fertilization and forming zygote. It is the end of gametophytic phase of life cycle and beginning of the sporophytic phase.

Structure of Sporophyte

It is the most simple sporophyte, among all liverworts having only a capsule while foot and seta are absent and hence described as sporogonium.

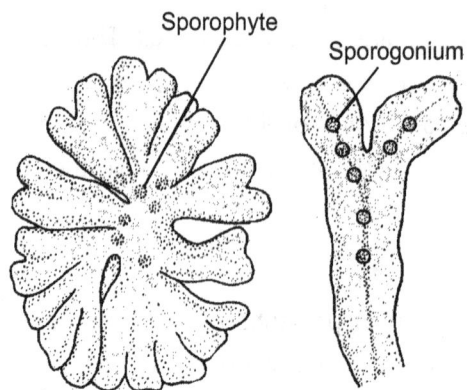

Fig. 5.12: *Riccia* sporophyte/sporogonium position on thallus

The zygote divides and gives rise to embryo. The embryo after many divisions forms the spherical, young sporogonium; having amphitecium (outerwall) and endothecium (inner wall). The cells of endothecium form archesporium which after several divisions form a mass of sporogenous cells. These function as spore mother cells or sporocytes. At last all the spore mother cells divide meiotically to form spores. But a few of them become nurse cells to provide nutrition. The sporophyte is completely dependent on the gametophyte.

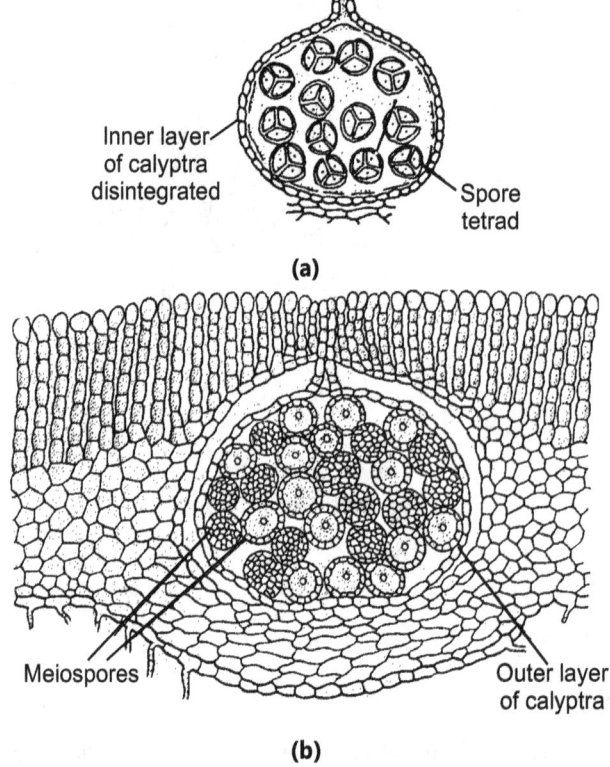

Fig. 5.13: Internal structure of sporophyte of *Riccia* (a and b)

Dehiscence of Sporogonium

The spores are liberated by the decay of surrounding outer layer of calyptra and thallus tissue. The thallus perishes in the dry season. The wall of the capsule disintegrates and the spores are liberated outside and finally dispersed by air currents or more commonly by splashing of rain drops.

Structure of Spores

All the spores are of similar size, hence *Riccia* is homosporus.

The spores are formed in tetrad and each spore is pyramidal in shape consisting of cytoplasm and haploid nucleus. The outer wall of spore is thick, black and sculptured. The ornamentation of the spore wall is a distinguishing feature of each species of *Riccia*.

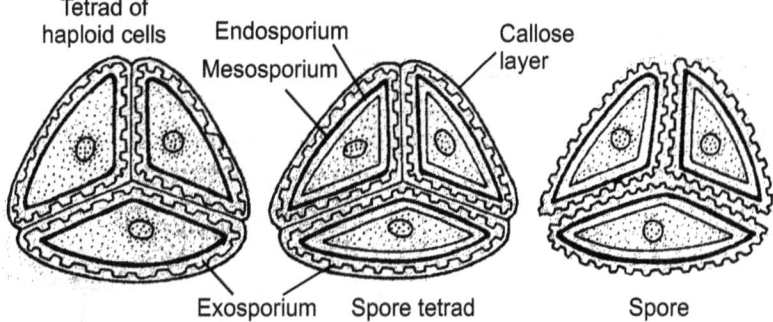

Fig. 5.14: *Riccia*: Structure of spore

Germination of Spores

The spores germinate during favourable conditions, especially in presence of moisture by producing a germ tube, which form the new gametophyte after various types of cellular divisions. The first rhizoid emerges from the base of the germ tube.

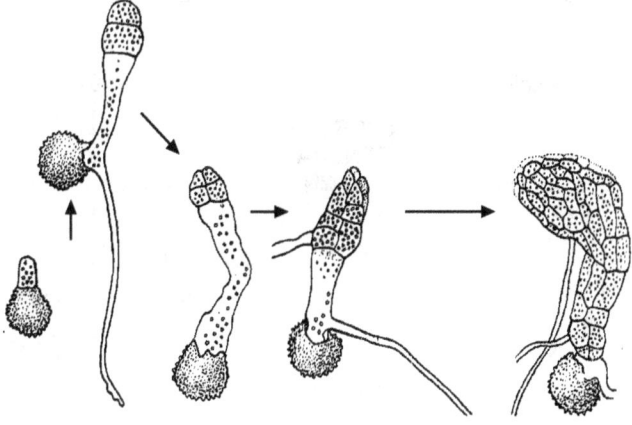

Fig. 5.15: *Riccia*: Germination of spore

Alternation of Generation

A regular alternation between the two generations i.e. gametophyte (gametes – producing) and sporophyte (spore producing) complete the life cycle of *Riccia*. The gametophyte is haploid and represents sexual generation. It is independent and autotrophic in nutrition. It bears sex organs i.e. antheridia and archegonia, which produce antherozoids and egg respectively. The antherozoid or sperm unites with the egg and complete the act of fertilisation resulting into the formation of diploid zygote.

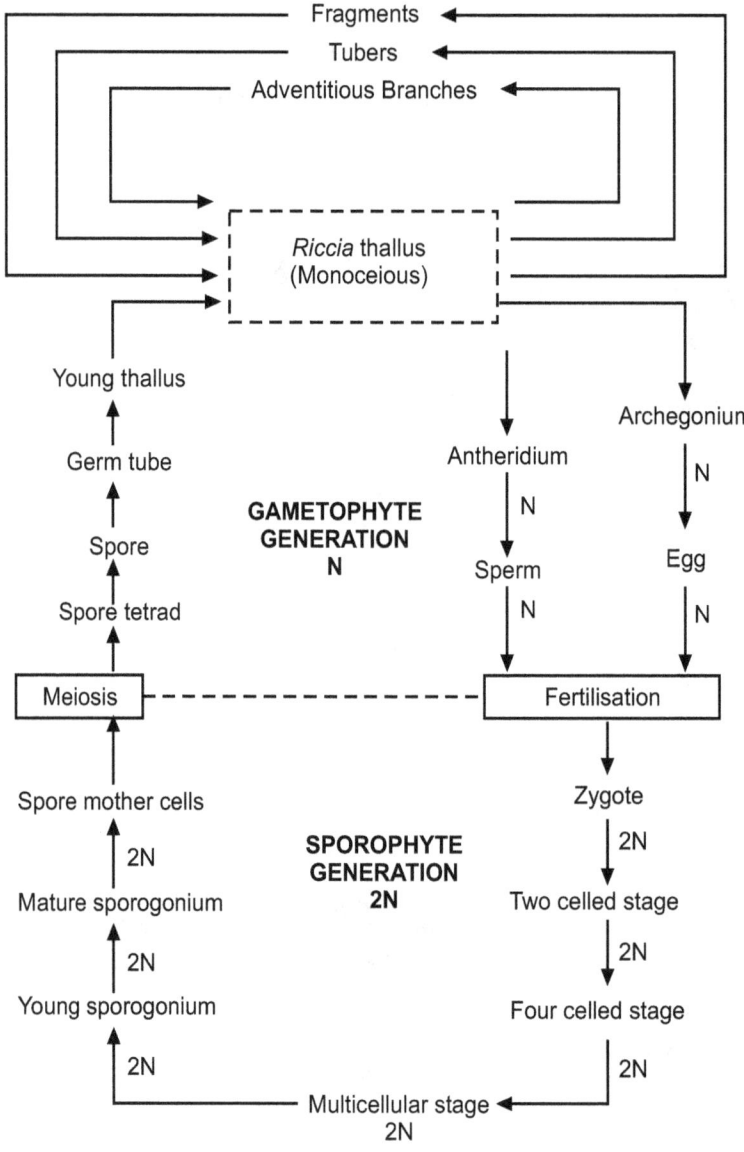

Fig. 5.16: Graphic life cycle of *Riccia*

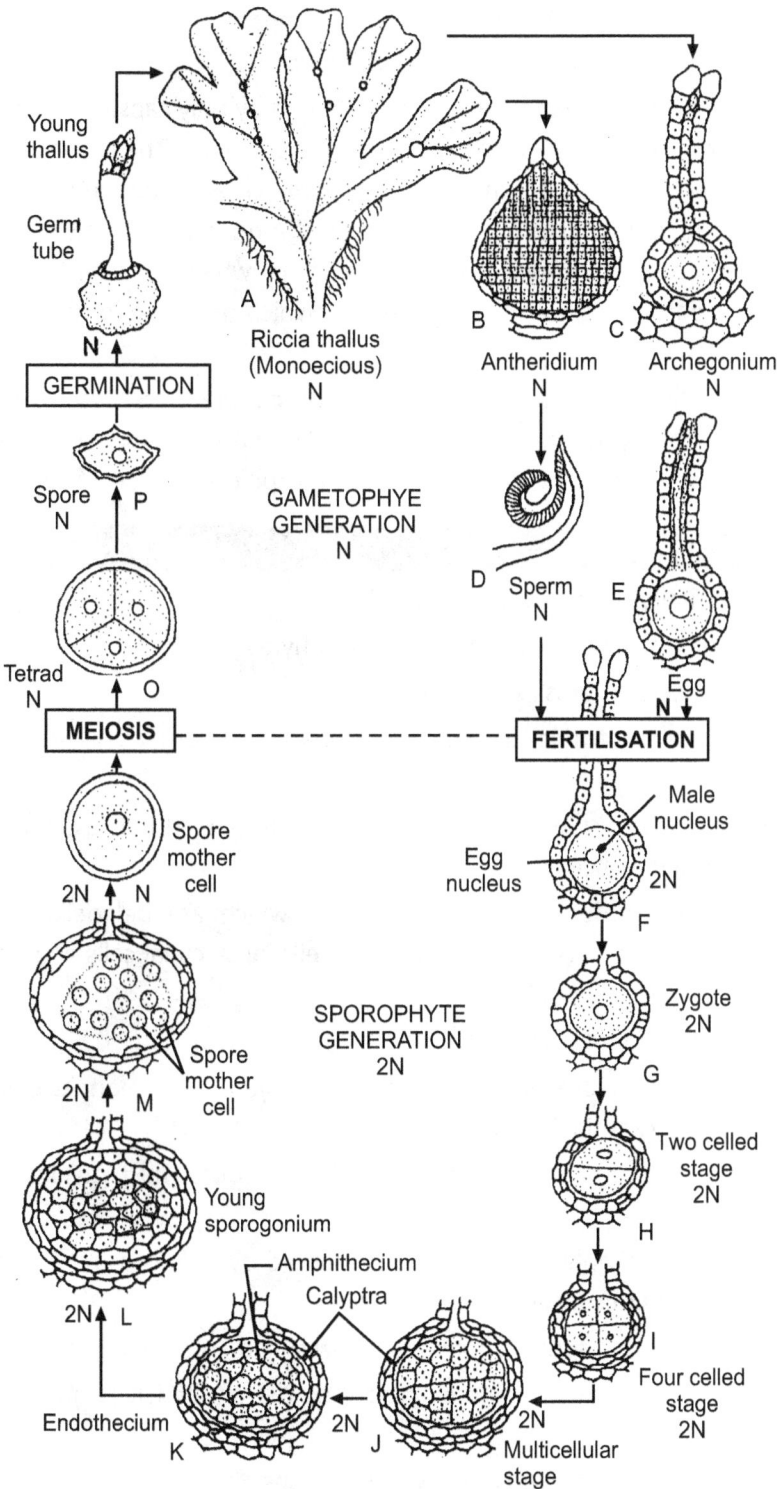

Fig. 5.17: Diagrammatic life cycle of *Riccia*

It is the end of gametophytic / sexual / haploid phase and beginning of sporophytic (spore producing) or diploid phase of life cycle of *Riccia*.

The sporophyte in *Riccia* is highly simple, represented by only capsule while foot and seta both are absent, because of this it is also known as sporogonium. The sporophyte of *Riccia* is completely dependent on gametophyte for nutrition. The sporogenous tissues (Spore mother cells), undergo meiosis (reduction division) and form many spores. All the spores are similar in size and hence it is homosporus. The spore when released from the capsule germinates in moist conditions, forming a germ tube which gives rise to thalloid, green plant body of the gametophyte.

Thus, in *Riccia*, there is distinct alternation of generations. Both the generations (gametophytic and sporophytic) are morphologically different and hence this type of alternation of generation observed in *Riccia* is heteromorphic alteration of generation.

Points to Remember

1. Amphibious thalloid plants except mosses.
2. Transitory group between algae and pteridophytes.
3. Non vascular cryptogams.
4. Gametophyte autotropic in nutrition, bears sex organs like antheridia and archegonia.
5. Sex organs are hidden, not exposed; hence described as cryptogams (Gr. Kruptos=hidden, concealed, Gamos=wedded)
6. The antheridia produce many antherozoids which are biflagellated and motile. Archegonia consist of venter, ventral canal cells, neck canal cells and enclose egg in venter.
7. Water is essential for fertilisation.
8. Both the sex organs are either present on a single thallus (monoecious) or they are present on different thalli (dioecious).
9. Antheroids and egg unite together giving rise to zygote which divides and forms the sporophyte.
10. It may be highly simple as in *Riccia*, represented by only capsule but in others foot and seta along with capsule is present.
11. Spores are formed in spore tetrad, they show ornamentations.
12. Released outside and germinate by producing germ tube which gives rise to haploid gametophyte.
13. Distinct heteromorphic alternation of generations.

14. G. M. Smith classified Bryophytes in three distinct classes : (i) Hepataceae (liver worts) (ii) Anthocerotae (Hornworts) (iii) Musci.
15. *Riccia* is the member of *Hepataceae*.
16. Simple thalloid gametophyte has rhizoids and scales; Rhizoids are of two types smooth and tuberculated.
17. Vegetative reproduction by fragmentation of apical growing point and by tuber formation.
18. Most of the species are monoecious bearing both antheridia and archegonia, producing antherozoids and egg respectively.
19. Antherozoids unite with egg to produce a zygote which then forms a single sporophyte having only the capsule.
20. Sporophyte is dependent on gametophyte for nutrition and support.
21. Spores are formed by meiosis; hence they are haploid. They germinate and give rise to gametophyte.
22. *Riccia* shows distinct heteromorphic alternation of generations.

Exercises

Short Answer Questions

1. Explain the general characters of Bryophytes.
2. Describe the gametophyte of Hepataceae.
3. Give a brief account of sporophyte of Hepataceae.
4. What is alternation of generation?
5. Explain heteromorphic alternation of generation.
6. Explain why bryophytes are known as "amphibians" of plant kingdom?
7. Give distinguishing features of Hepataceae.
8. Give distinguishing features of Anthocerotae.
9. Give distinguishing features of Mosses.
10. Describe rhizoids in Bryophytes and give their function.
11. Give systematic position of *Riccia*.

Long Answer Questions

1. Describe the special features of bryophytes.
2. Explain the modes of vegetative reproduction in *Riccia*.
3. Give an account of sexual reproduction in *Riccia*.

4. Describe the sex organs in *Riccia*.
5. Explain the morphological structure of gametophyte of *Riccia*.
6. Describe the structure of antheridium of *Riccia*.
7. Describe the structure of sporophyte of *Riccia*.
8. Explain the internal organisation of thallus of *Riccia*.
9. Explain the life cycle of *Riccia*.
10. Explain graphically the life cycle of *Riccia*.
11. Sketch and label the parts of
    i) Thallus of *Riccia*
    ii) Sporophyte of *Riccia*
    iii) Sex organs of *Riccia*
    iv) T. S. of thallus of *Riccia*

Chapter 6...
Pteridophytes

Contents ...
6.1 Introduction
6.2 General Characters
6.3 Classification According to G. M. Smith (1955)
6.4 Life Cycle of *Nephrolepis*
   Points to Remember
   Exercises

6.1 Introduction

Pteridophytes are the first group of vascular cryptogams having a long fossil history. They are known to exist from as far back as the Silurian age of Paleozoic era and flourished well during the Devonian age. The tree ferns and giant horsetails are the dominating fossil forms of the pteridophytes. This group is generally represented by both fossils as well as living genera. Pteridophytes are represented by about 15,000 species. Most of them are native to moist tropical forest. The ferns are the main representatives of the group, cosmopolitan in distribution. Plant body in pteridophytes is well organised and sporophytic in nature.

6.2 General Characters

1. These are vascular cryptogamic plants with well developed plant body possessing roots, stem and leaves.
2. Plant body is sporophytic but without flowers.
3. Sporophyte produces asexual reproductive bodies known as spores. Spores are produced in sporangium. Sporangia develop on sporophylls. In many members sporangia bearing structures are grouped in a cone (strobilus).
4. Plants may be homosporous or heterosporous (with megaspores and microspores).
5. Spores after germination produce gametophytes (prothalli). Megaspore develops into female gametophyte and microspore develops into male gametophyte.
6. Gametophytic thallus is with rhizoids and chlorophyllous tissue, thus it is independent.
7. Gametophytes develop antheridia and archegonia.
8. Antherozoids are multiflagellate.

9. Water is necessary for fertilisation.
10. Zygote remains in gametophyte, which further develops into simple embryo. Embryo develops into the sporophytic plant. Thus, at early stage sporophyte is dependent on gametophyte.
11. Sporophytes possess vascular tissues. Xylem is without vessels and phloem is without companion cells.
12. Plants show distinct alternation of generations. Sporophytic phase is dominant phase while gametophytic phase is independent, short living phase. The sporophytic plant and gametophytic plant have different morphological characters thus their life cycle is known as diplontic and heteromorphic. e.g. *Psilotum, Selaginella, Equisetum, Adiantum, Marsilea.*

6.3 Classification of Pteridophytes According to G. M. Smith (1955)

G. M. Smith (1955) classified the group pteridophytes into four divisions by considering the following points.
1. Nature of sporophytic plant body
2. Nature of vascular strand of sporophytic plant body
3. Nature of spore producing organs and type of spores produced (homospores or heterospores)
4. Structure and origin of sporangium
5. Nature of gametophyte
6. Structure of sexual organs (antheridium and archegonium)

Outline Classification

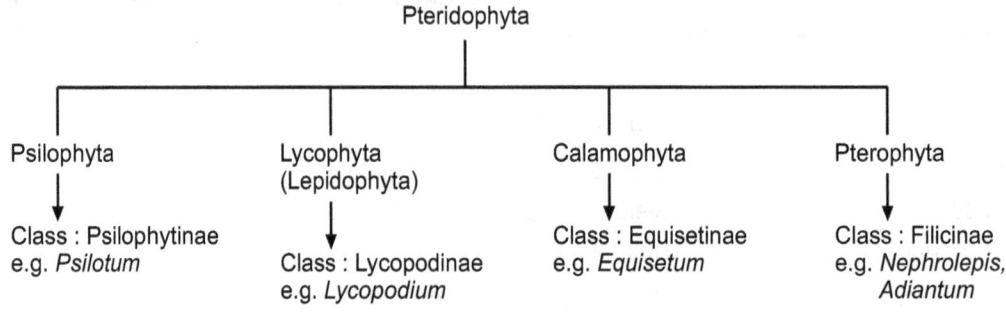

Division Psilophyta – Class Psilophytinae

It is the most primitive division of pteridophytes represented by a few fossil genera and only a single living genus *Psilotum*.

1. Sporophyte with simple plant body consist of subterranean rhizome with dichotomously branched aerial shoots.
2. True roots are absent but rhizoids are present.

3. True leaves are absent, scaly leaves are present.
4. Vascular strand is protostelic.
5. Cambium is absent so secondary growth is absent.
6. Sporangia are borne singly at the tip or in a group in the axil of scaly leaves.
7. Sporangia are homosporous.
8. Gametophyte is poorly developed with endophytic fungi.
9. Anthrozoids are multiflagellate.

e.g. Fossil genera – *Rhynia* and *Asteroxylon*; e.g. Living genus *Psilotum*.

Division – Lycophyta / Class lycopodinae

1. It is also represented by fossils and a few living genera.
2. Sporophytic body is differentiated into root, stem and leaves.
3. Leaves simple, microphyllous and may be dimorphic.
4. Vascular cylinder is protostelic or siphonostelic.
5. Sporophyll arranged in strobilus (cone) and dimorphic.
6. Sporophyte may be homosporous or heterosporous.
7. Gametophyte is thalloid and autotrophic endosporic or exosporic. e.g. *Lycopodium, Selaginella, Isoetes*.

Division – Calamophyta / Class Equisitinae

The members of this group are commonly called as horse tails and represented by fossil members and only a single living genus *Equisetum*.

1. Sporophyte is with jointed hollow stem and scaly leaves in whorls at the nodes.
2. True roots develop on underground rhizomatic stem.
3. Reproductive shoot bears cone at the tip.
4. The sporangia develop on sporangiophore.
5. The living form is homosporous.
6. Gametophyte is autotrophic and exosporic.

e.g. *Equisetum* and *Calamostachys*.

Division – Pterophyta / Class – Filicinae

The members of this group are commonly known as 'ferns'. They are represented by fossil as well as living genera.

1. Plant body is sporophytic, perennial and differentiated into root, stem and leaves.
2. Stem is usually subterranean rhizome with true roots.
3. Leaves are usually pinnately compound with circinate venation.

4. The plants are homosporus or heterosporous.
5. The sporangia develop in sori on lower surface of sporophyll.
6. Gametophytes are usually heart shaped; autotrophic.

e.g. *Nephrolepis, Adiantum, Marsilea* etc.

6.4 Life Cycle of *Nephrolepis*

The genus **Nephrolepis** consists of 30 species which are distributed in the tropics of the world. They show diversity in habits and habitat. They are mostly terrestrial in habit. They are usually moisture and shade loving plants found in tropical rain forest. In India, about five species are found in Northern and Southern part of the country. The common Indian species is **Nephrolepis exaltata**.

The life cycle of **Nephrolepis exaltata** shows alternation of generations in which sporophytic generation is dominant and diploid (2n) in nature and gametophytic generation is haploid (n) in nature.

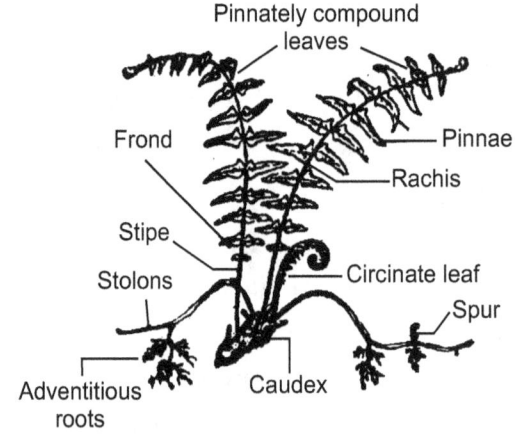

Fig. 6.1 : *Nephrolepis* : Sporophyte

External morphology of sporophyte

Fern plant is a sporophyte. It is perennial, dominant and differentiated into roots, stem and leaves.

Roots are adventitious which develop on rhizome and stolon. They are small, fibrous, branched and possess persistent root hairs. The primary root of the young sporophyte is short lived and dies very early.

Stem is erect, short, thick, condensed cylindrical and obliquely placed in the soil. Such a stem is commonly known as root stock or rhizome or caudex. It is very rough due to persistent leaf bases. Rhizome gives out large number of extra axillary branches which are called as stolons. Stolons are green when young and turn brown at maturity. The caudex is fully covered with scales with peltate base and thin pale edges often bearing fine hair. At intervals, stolons produce adventitious roots below and bud or spur above the ground which develop into a new plant under favourable conditions. Thus, they perform the function of vegetative propagation. Leaves are large, pinnately compound and spirally arranged towards the apex of the caudex. Each leaf is differentiated into the basal part without leaflets, known as stipe and upper part produces leaflets which are known as frond. The stipe is brown in colour, smooth and polished. The frond consists of a central axis called as rachis which bears leaflets or pinnae. They are arranged on either side. The pinnae are slightly falcate and are articulated to the rachis. The young frond is silvery white and coiled inward from apex to base like the spring of the watch. Such type of folding of a young leaf is called circinate ptyxis.

Leaflet or pinna is sessile, auriculate, lanceolate with acute apex and slightly crenate margin. Each pinna or leaflet is about 6 to 8 cm in length and 2 to 3 cm in width. They show a distinct midrib with forked lateral veins ending into white dots which are called as hydathode.

Each hydathode is present at the vein endings. These are white dots arranged in two longitudinal rows on the dorsal surface along the margins of each pinna or leaflet. The central part of the hydathode consists of a group of small, thin walled, parenchymatous cells sunk into a minute oval depression which is covered by two to three layers of rectangular epithelial cells. These cells of the hydathode are hygroscopic in nature. They are also called as water stomata. They exude water in the form of liquid, this process is known as guttation.

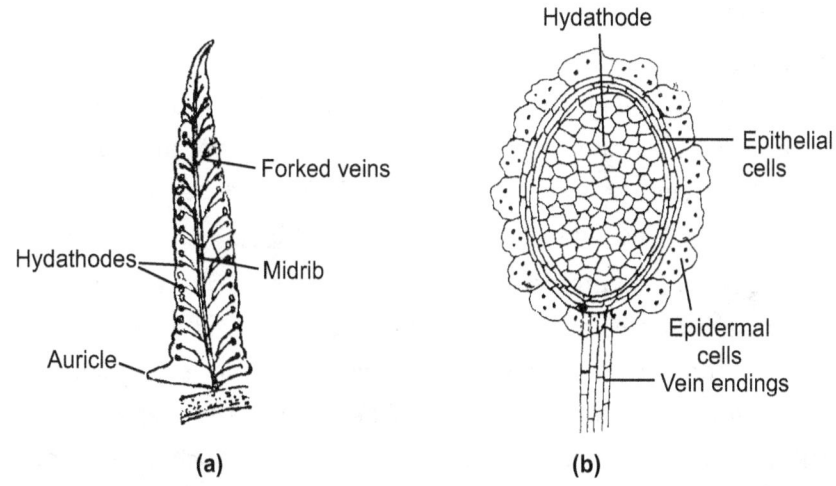

Fig. 6.2 : (a) Position of Hydathode in pinna and (b) Structure (enlarged) of Hydathode

The stem and leaves usually when young, are covered by many brown scale-like structures known as ramenta, which protect the young parts of the plant against adverse climatic conditions. Each ramentum is membranous, multicellular, triangular in shape and made up of a single layer of cells. These cells are dry with thick brown walls with the marginal cells giving out hair-like structures. They are protective in function; i.e. they protect the plant from heavy rain water and high temperature.

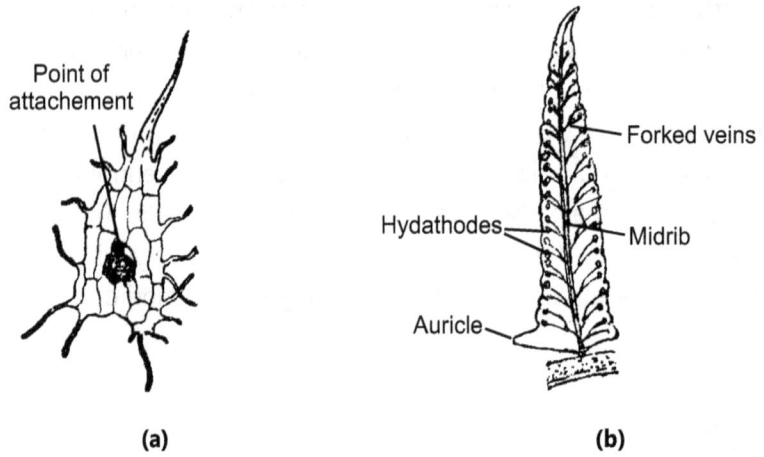

Fig. 6.3 : (a) Structure of ramentum (b) Single pinna

Internal structure of sporophyte

1) T. S. of stolon

Internally, it is differentiated into epidermis, cortex, endodermis, pericycle and stele.

i) **Epidermis:** It is the outermost, single layer of rectangular parenchymatous cells. The cells of the outer wall are cutinised.

ii) **Cortex:** The outer region consists of thick walled cells, which are compactly arranged layers of lignfied cells forming hypodermis. The inner region is formed by thin walled parenchymatous cells, which are loosely arranged with sufficient intercellular space. These cells store food. The innermost layer of the cortex is called endodermis. Endodermis is made up of rectangular, thick walled parenchymatous cells.

iii) **Stele :** It is single and protostelic in nature. It consists of a solid column of vascular tissue without pith. It is externally surrounded by pericycle made up of two to three layers of thin walled cells. If consists of a single vascular bundle which is conjoint, concentric and amphicribral as xylem is surrounded by phloem. The xylem is star shaped with metaxylem in the centre and protoxylem radiating towards the periphery. Such type of protostele with stellate or star-shaped xylem is also called *actinostele*. The xylem consists of tracheids and xylem parenchyma. The phloem consists of phloem parenchyma and sieve cells which completely surround the xylem but more prominent in between the radiating protoxylem group.

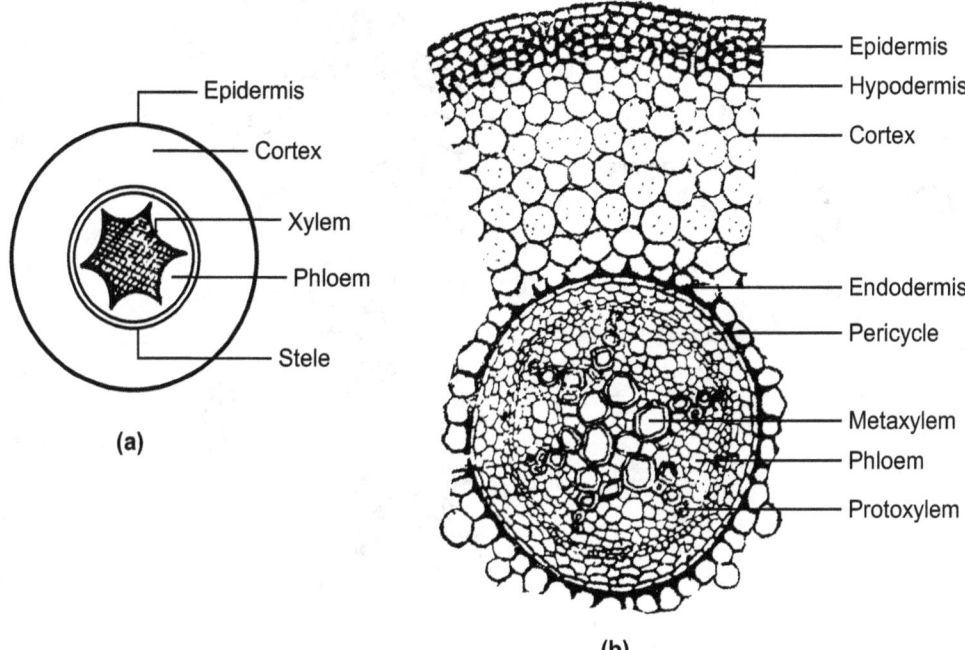

Fig. 6.4 (a) : T.S. of stolon (Diagrammatic) (b) T.S. of stolon

2) T.S. of Rachis

Internally, the rachis is differentiated into epidermis, hypodermis, endodermis, percicyle and vascular bundles.

i) **Epidermis:** It is the outermost single layer of rectangular cells with cutinised outer walls.

ii) **Hypodermis:** Ground tissue is differentiated into the outer zone of thick walled, compactly arranged, without intercellular space and lignified cells forming hypodermis. It gives mechanical support and strength. The inner ground tissue are parenchymatous, thin walled, loosely arranged with intercellular space and they contain starch grains and chloroplasts when young. A layer of the ground tissue surrounds each vascular strand.

Vascular system consists of 2 to 5 vascular strands embedded in the ground tissue. They are arranged in a horse shoe-shaped manner open towards the groove. Each vascular strand contains a single vascular bundle surrounded by its own endodermis and pericycle. Each vascular strand consists of single layer of parenchyma. Therefore, they are known as meristele.

The vascular bundle is conjoint, concentric and amphicribral or hadrocentric as xylem is surrounded by phloem. Xylem is exarch, C-shaped or comma-shaped and consists of tracheids and xylem parenchyma. Vessels are absent; phloem is made up of sieve cells and phloem parenchyma. Sieve tubes and companion cells are absent.

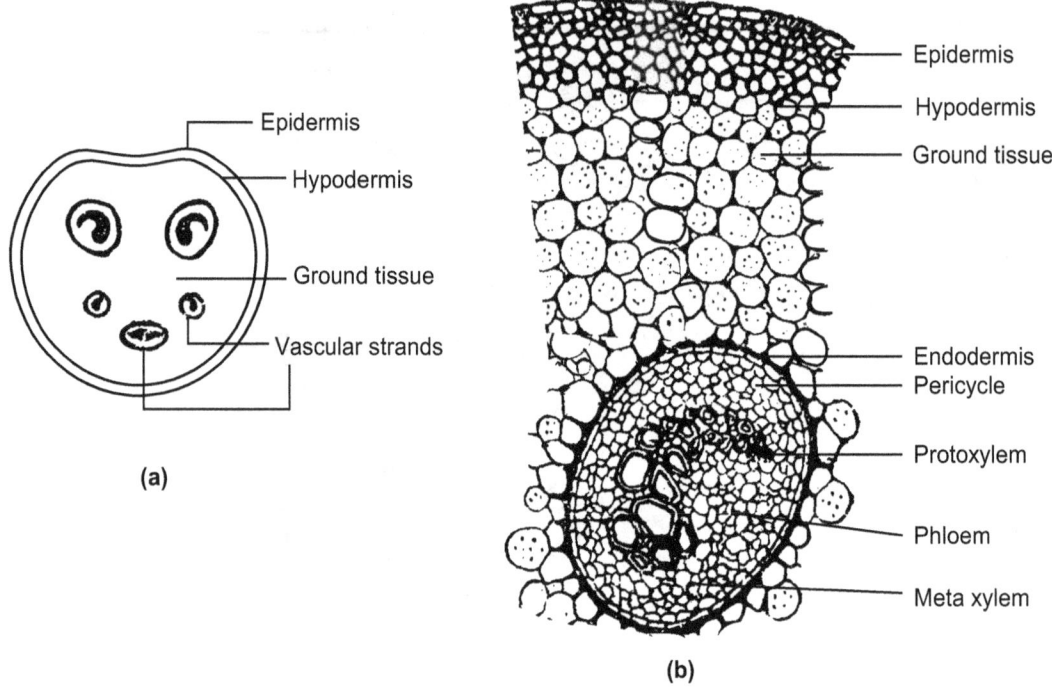

Fig.6.5 (a) : T. S. of rachis (Diagrammatic)
(b) T. S. of rachis (Enlarged section)

3) T.S. of pinna or leaflet

T.S. of pinna or leaflet shows upper epidermis, mesophyll, lower epidermis and sorus.

i) **Upper epidermis:** It consists of a single layer of compactly arranged brick shaped cells with chloroplast and outer wall is cutinised. It is distinguished by the presence of hydathode as shallow depressions above vein endings and absence of stomata.

ii) **Mesophyll :** It consists of spongy tissue containing one type of cells. Therefore pinna is said to be isobilateral. However the upper spongy tissues are more compact than the lower one. It also shows vein ending in the lower one. It also shows vein ending in the form of group of tracheids below the hydathode.

iii) **Sorus:** Sorus remains attached to lower epidermis at the vein ending and consists of placenta, sporangia and indusium. Placenta is a cushion-like structure which is made up of thin walled parenchyma. It provides nourishment to the developing sporangia. Sporangia are present on either side of the placenta, each sporangium consists of a stalk and capsule containing spores. Indusium is protective covering which is single layered. It is attached to the placenta by massive short stalk of parenchyma cells.

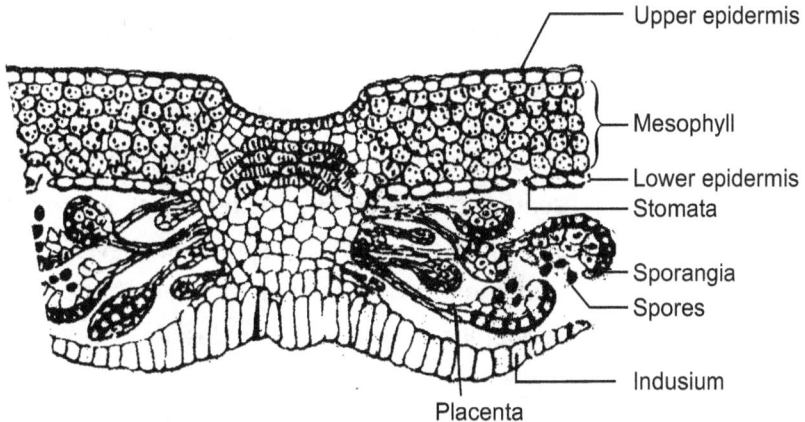

Fig 6.6: T.S. of pinna passing through sorus

Reproduction

It reproduces by vegetative, asexual and sexual methods.

(i) Vegetative reproduction

It takes place by death and decay process of rhizome. When the progressive death and decay of the older part of a rhizome reaches upto the place of branching, it separates into two branches and continues to grow as a separate individual.

(ii) Asexual reproduction

The fern plant is a sporophyte. It reproduces asexually by the formation of spores. At maturity, some of the leaflets or pinna produce reproductive bodies in the form of sori on ventral (abaxial) surface of the leaflets. Such a leaf producing leaflets with sori or fertile pinnae is known as sporophyll.

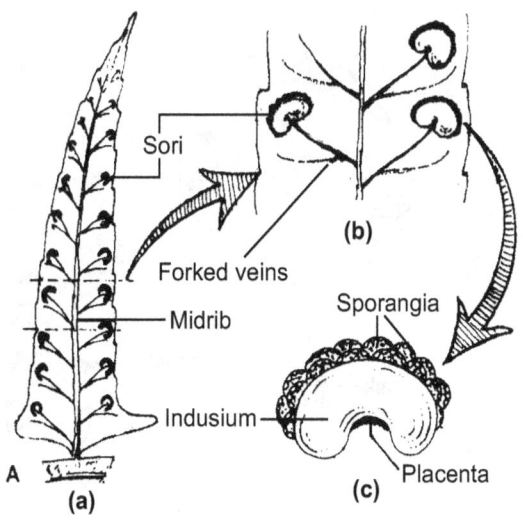

Fig 6.7: (a) Position of sori in pinna (b) Single sorus

The sori are a group of asexual reproductive bodies which develop in two rows on the ventral surface of the pinna along the margins. They develop on one of the vein endings of the forked vein, which is towards the apex. They are light green to brown in colour. Each sorus consists of a group of sporangia which develop on cushion like outgrowth of parenchymatous cells, called placenta and covered by a membrane structure called indusium. The indusium is kidney-shaped in surface view. The sporangia develop all around the placenta except at the notch. Sporangia produce large number of spores. The placenta provides food material to the developing sporangia and indusium covers and protects the sporangia.

Structures of sporangium

The sporangia are asexual reproductive structures. Each sporangium consists of basal stalk and distal capsule. The stalk is multicellular, long, slender and made up of two to three vertical thick-walled rows of cells. The capsule is oval, biconvex and disc-like structure. The wall of the capsule is made up of a single layer of flat thin walled cells. Along the periphery it shows a distinct incomplete ring of cells, which is vertically placed, known as annulus. The cells of the annulus are thick and brown along the inner tangential and radial walls while the outer wall is slightly thin. On one side of the capsule, the annulus is replaced by large size, thin walled transversely arranged elongated cells. At maturity, sporangium opens through these cells forming the stomium. When young, the sporangium contains sixteen diploid spore mother cells. At maturity, each spore mother cell undergoes reduction division (meiosis) forming tetrad or four haploid (n) spores. Therefore, each sporangium contains sixty four spores.

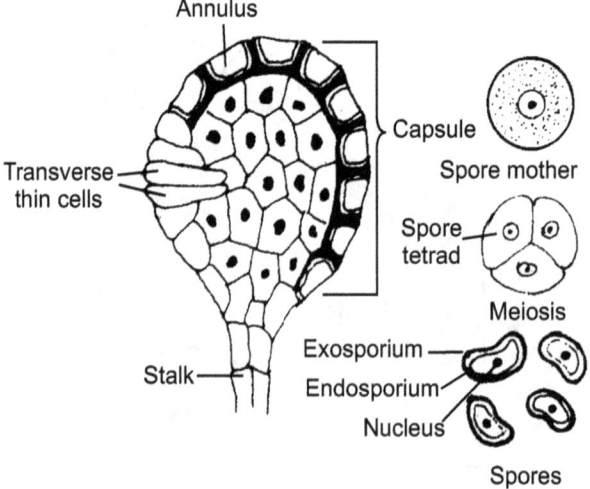

Fig. 6.8 : Sporangium, spore mother cells and spores

Mechanism of dehiscence of sporangium

When the sporangium is mature and the weather is dry, the dissemination of spores takes place. The annulus and the stomium play a very important role in the dehiscence of the sporangium. At maturity, the wall of the sporangium start to lose moisture and dries up; at the same time, cells of the annulus lose water. As a result, the drying of the annulus creates an equal tension on the cell wall. This tension makes the annulus cells straigthten up and this results into breaking of the sporangium by rupturing the thin walled cells of stomium. Thus, the spores are dispersed. Each spore is more or less kidney-shaped, slightly flattened, dark brown in colour. Spore is haploid (n), uninucleate with protoplast. It is made up two layers, in which the outer layer is thick brown known as exosporangium and the inner layer is thin called as endosporium. All spores are of the same type, therefore *Nephrolepis* is homosporous type.

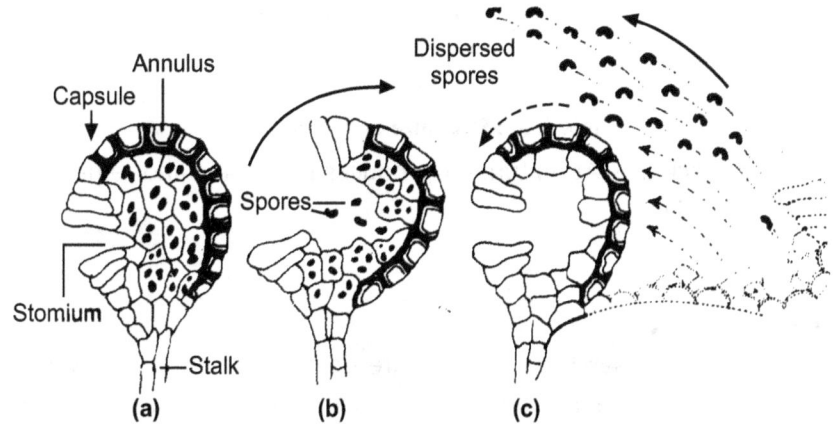

Fig. 6. 9: Dehiscence of sporangium

Germination of spores

During favourable conditions, the spore germinates. The exosporium breaks and the endosporium grows into a short germ tube. After some time, they divide into two unequal cells, viz. rhizoidal cell and prothalial cell. The rhizoidal cell is small and colourless which gives rise to unicellular rhizoid. The latter by repeated transverse cell divisions, give rise to green filamentous structure. Soon the division takes place in other planes to form green plate like body. Due to more rapid division and growth of the marginal cells, the plate like structure gets converted into more or less heart-shaped structure called as prothallus.

Gametophyte

Prothallus is the gametophyte of fern. It is haploid (n), dorsiventrally flattened, green, delicate and heart-shaped structure, measuring about 5 mm across. At the broader end it shows a notch, while ventrally at the narrow posterior end it produces unicellular hair-like structures called rhizoids. Their main function is absorption of water and minerals from the soil and fixation of gametophyte. The prothallus is one-cell thick except towards the notch where it is many layered forming a cushion like structure. The cells of the prothallus are closely arranged, thin-walled and full of chloroplasts. They are autotrophic in nature.

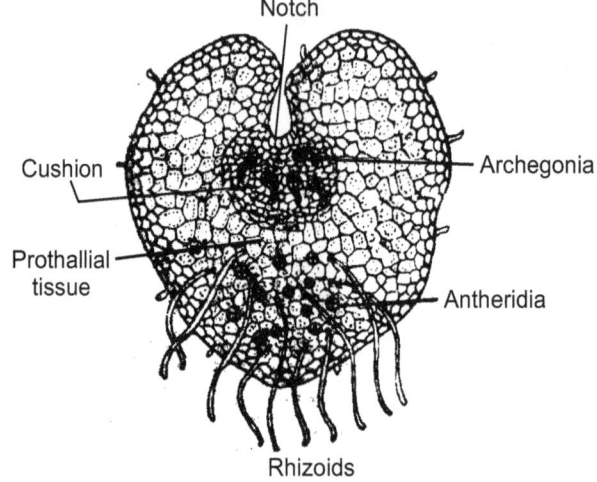

Fig. 6.10 : Structure of prothallus

Prothallus is monoecious - At maturity it produces both male and female sex organs i.e. antheridia and archegonia.

Structure of sex organs

(i) Antheridia

The antheridia are male sex organs which are developed ventrally towards the narrow posterior end in between the rhizoids. Each antheridium is sessile and has a globose structure. The wall of the antheridum is made up of three cells viz., the proximal shallow first ring cell, the middle second ring cell and the apical third cap cell. The body of antheridium is filled with antherozoid mother cells or androcytes each of which metamorphoses into a single male gamete called as antherozoid or spermatozoid. Each antherozoid is haploid (n).

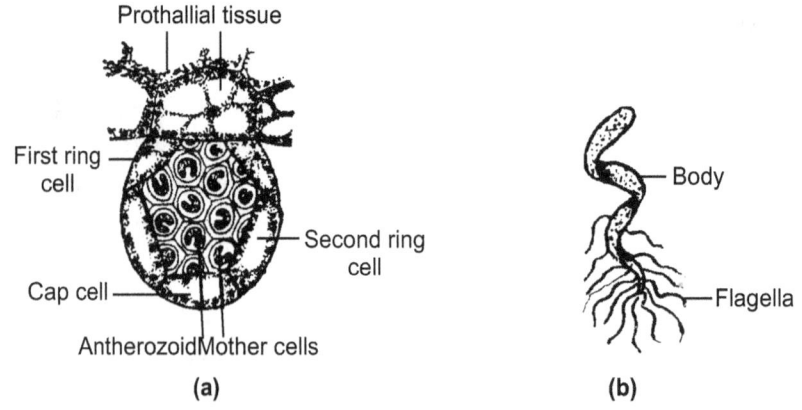

Fig. 6.11 : (a) V.S. of antheridium (B) Antherozoid

It is a multiflagellate, coiled structure. Under humid conditions, the antheridium absorbs water, the mucilaginous contents swell up and as a result, the lid cell comes off and the antherozoids coated with mucilage are liberated. Mucilage dissolves in water and the antherozoids are free to swim in the film of water.

(ii) Archegonia

The archegonia are the female sex organs which develop ventrally on the anterior cushion like area towards the notch of the prothallus. Each archegonium is a sessile, inverted flask-shaped structure that consists of a globular venter and tubular neck. The venter is completely embedded in the prothallial cells. It contains a single large egg or oospore towards the base and venter canal cell towards the neck. The neck is short and curved towards posterior end. The wall of the neck is single layered in thickness with cells arranged in four longitudinal rows and closed at the tip by lid cells. It consists of a single elongated binucleate neck canal cell.

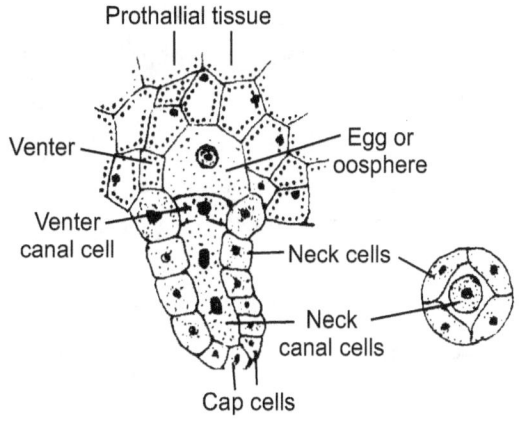

Fig. 6.12 : Structure of archegonium

Fertilisation

It takes place only in the presence of water. Water is essential for antherozoids to swim towards archegonia and to break open the neck of archegonium. Prothallus is monoecious, as a rule there is cross fertilisation as antheridia mature much before the archegonia. When the archegonium matures, the venter canal cell and neck canal cell disintegrate to form mucilaginous substance. The latter absorbs water and swells, as a result, lid cells break open and the mucilage oozes out. The mucilage contains some chemical substance which attracts swarms of antherozoids. Therefore the fertilisation takes place by the process of *chemotaxis*.

The antherozoids enter the venter through the neck and one of them penetrates the egg and fuses with the egg nucleus to form diploid nucleus or zygote (2n). The zygote produces a cell wall around itself and forms a oospore. It is initiation of sporophyte.

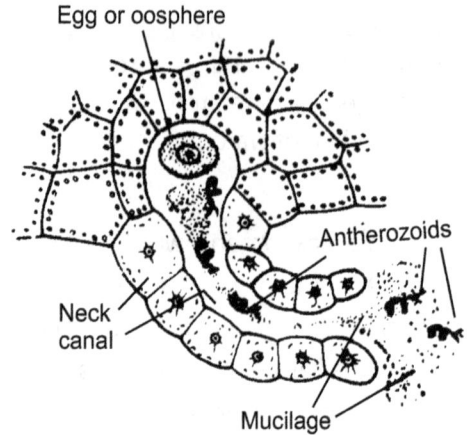

Fig. 6.13 : Fertilisation

Young sporophyte

Many archegonia of the prothallus are fertilised but only one oospore divides and redivides mitotically within the venter to develop embryo. The early embryo consists of foot, root, stem apex and cotyledon.

The foot is embedded into the prothallus and absorbs nourishment for the developing sporophyte till it becomes independent. Therefore, initially the sporophyte is dependent on the gametophyte. Later on, root enters into the soil while the cotyledon and stem apex bend, come up through the notch of the prothallus and develop into a young sporophyte. The prothallus degenerates and young sporophyte develops into a new fern plant.

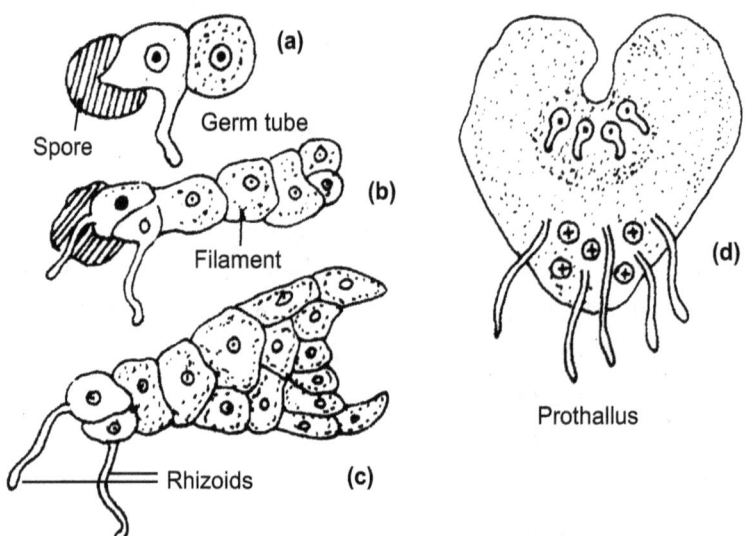

Fig. 6.14 : Prothallus with young sporophyte

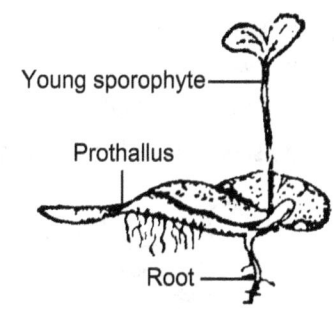

Fig: 6.15: Prothallus with embryo

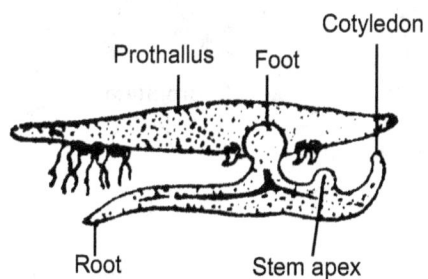

Fig. 6.16: Germination of spore and development of prothallus

Alternation of generations

The life cycle of *Nephrolepis* shows two distinct alternation of generations in which sporophytic generation is the dominant phase and gametophytic generation is reduced,- they alternate one after another in the life cycle of *Nephrolepis* plant. The sporophyte is the asexual generation. It is diploid (2n) and dominant stage. It is differentiated into roots, stem and leaves. Therefore, it is physiologically independent. At maturity, some of the leaflets or pinna develop into sporophylls. Sporophylls produce a group of sporangia called as sori on the lower surface of the pinnae. Each sporangium consists of sixteen diploid (2n) spore mother cells, which undergo reduction division (meiosis) and develop sixty four haploid (n) spores. The formation of spores is the indication of the beginning of gametophyte. Spores are dispersed in dry climatic condition. When a spore falls on a suitable surface, it germinates and gives rise tothe gametophyte.

The gametophyte of fern is called prothallus. It is an independent stage in the life cycle. The gametophyte is the sexual generation which is haploid (n) as it is produced from spore.

Prothallus is green and monoecious. At maturity, it produces both antheridia and archegonia which develop male gametes called as antherozoids and female gametes called as egg cells. The fertilisation takes place in presence of water by the process of chemotaxis. The gametes fuse to form diploid (2n) zygote which produces a wall around the developing oospore. Oospore is the beginning of sporophyte. After the period of rest it germinates within the venter to develop into an embryo which further develops into a young sporophyte. The prothallus gradually degenerates and the young sporophyte develops into an independent fern plant. In this way, sporophytic generation alternates with the gametophytic generation and this is called as alternation of generations.

The life cycle of *Nephrolepis* can be schematically represented as follows

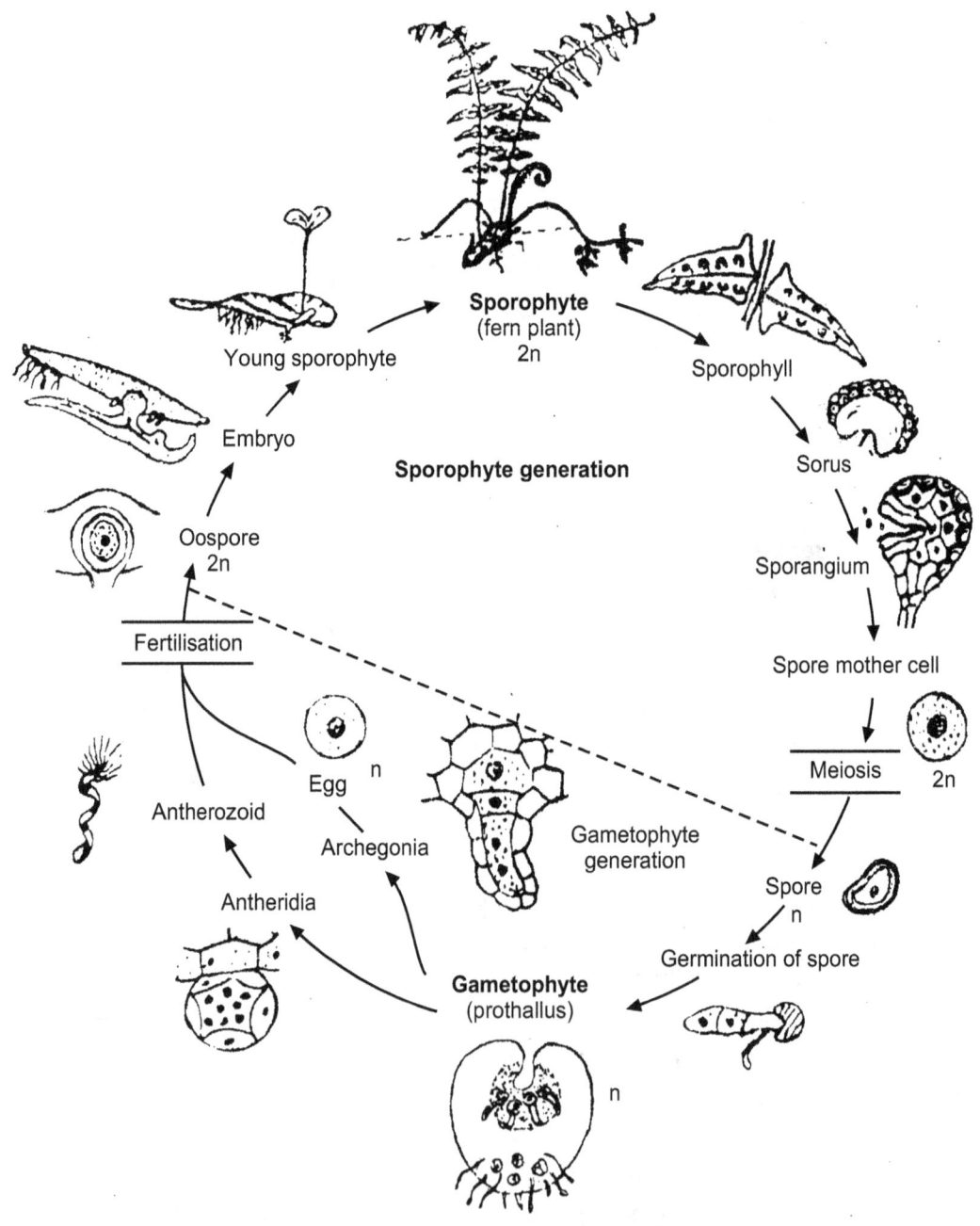

Fig. 6.17: Life Cycle of *Nephrolepis*

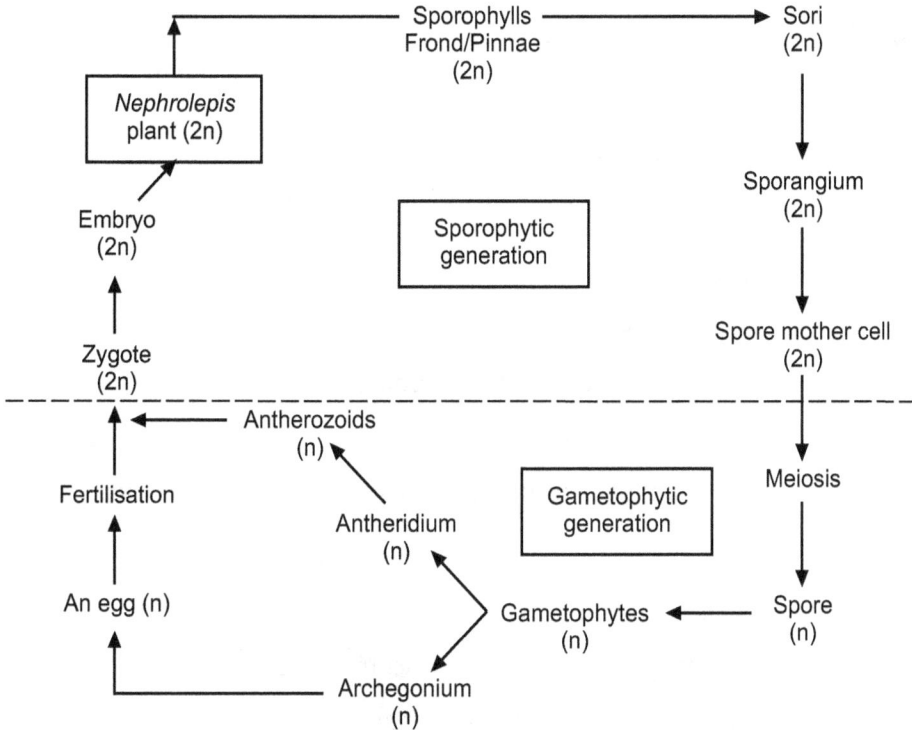

Fig. 6.18: Graphic life cycle of *Nephrolepis*

Systematic position with reasons.

As per G.M. Smith (1955)

Group – Pteridophyta

1. Plant is sporophytic with well developed roots, stem and leaves.
2. Vascular tissue present.
3. Antherozoids are multiflagellate.

Division – Pterophyta

1. Sporophyte is differentiated into roots, stem and leaves.
2. The stem is a subterranean rhizome and sometimes stems are upright.
3. The leaves are large with petiole and central rachis.
4. The plants are homosporous. The spores are produced in sporangia.
5. Gametophyte is usually heart shaped.

Class – Filicinae

1. Plants are perennial.
2. Sporophyte grows subterranean.
3. The sporangia are grouped in sori.

Order – Filicales

1. The plants are homosporous.
2. The prothallus or gametophyte is monoecious.
3. The sporangia develop on the surface of the sporophyll.
4. The sporangia are grouped in sori.
5. The wall of the sporangium consists of a single layer of cells with annulus.

Family – Polypodiaceae

1. The sporangia are usually aggregated together into sori.
2. The sporangium has a long stalk with vertical incomplete annulus.
3. About 32 to 64 spores are produced in a sporangium.
4. The gametophyte is green, flat and heart-shaped.
5. The body of antheridium consists of a jacket layer with 3-cells, 2-ring shaped cells and one cap cell at the apex.

Genus – *Nephrolepis*

1. Plants are usually terrestrial.
2. The stem is erect and condensed called as rootstock.
3. The pinnae are slightly falcate and articulated to the rachis.
4. The entire plant body is covered with scales.
5. The sori are rounded or elongated and produced at terminal position on veins.
6. The rootstock shows typical dictyostele vascular arrangement.

Species – *exaltata*

i. Frond erect
ii. Pinnae auriculated, upper auricle larger.

Points to Remember

- The group pteridophyta is divided into division psilophyta, lycophyta, calamophyta and pterophyta.
- The division of pteridophyta is divided into class psilophytinae, lycopodinae, equisetinae and filicinae.
- The life cycle of *Nephrolepis* shows alternation of generations.
- The plant itself is a sporophyte which is a dominant, diploid (2n) stage and differentiated into roots, stem and leaves.
- The sporophyte develops fixed number of haploid (n) spores i.e. 64 in each sporangium.
- The prothallus or gametophyte is the haploid (n) stage, independent and heart-shaped.
- Prothallus is monoecious as it produces both archegonia and antheridia.
- Fertilisation takes place in the presence of water by the process of chemotaxis.
- Zygote or oospore develops into young sporophyte.

Exercises

Short Answer Questions

1. Describe mechanism of dehiscence of sporangium and dispersal of spores.
2. Describe the structure of gametophyte or prothallus of fern.
3. Describe briefly of the following
   (a) Antheridium
   (b) Archegonium
   (c) Process of fertilisation
4. What is alternation of generations? Explain the phenomenon with reference to life cycle of fern.
5. Describe the structure and dehiscence of sporangium of fern.
6. Describe the structure of sex organs of fern.
7. Describe the structure and dehiscence of sporangium of *Nephrolepis*.

8. What is alternation of generations? Give the cyclic representation of life of *Nephrolepis*.
9. Explain the position, structure and functions of hydathode and ramentum of fern.

Long Answer Questions

1. Give systematic position of *Nephrolepis*. Explain the structure of fern pinna passing through the sorus.
2. Give an account of the structure of prothallus of *Nephrolepis*.
3. Describe T. S. of pinna of fern passing through sorus.
4. Describe the gametophyte of fern.
5. Describe a T. S. of fern rachis.
6. Describe the structure and dehiscence of sporangium of fern.
7. Give an account of the position and structure of the sex organs in *Nephrolepis*.

❖❖❖

Chapter 7...
Gymnosperms

Contents ...
7.1 Introduction
7.2 Classification of Gymnosperms
7.3 Life Cycle of Cycas
   Points to Remember
   Exercises

7.1 Introduction

Flowering plants or phanerogams consist of two major groups of land plants (i) Gymnosperms (ii) Angiosperms. The gymnospermic plants are characterised by presence of naked seeds. The great Taxonomist – Theophrastus, who is known as "Father of Botany" had coined the term gymnosperms for the first time. This group of plants originated in the Devonian period i.e. about 350 million years ago. These plants dominated the vegetation during Palaeozoic and Mesozoic era. This group includes fossilised as well as living plants. The plants belonging to the orders like pentoxylales, cycadeoidales, cordaitales etc. have completely fossilised or become extinct, while plants belonging to the orders like cycadales, ginkgoales, coniferales, taxales, and gnetales survive today.

Presently, gymnosperms are represented by about 69 - 70 genera and 750 to 760 species. These plants form an evolutionary link or bridge between pteridophytes and angiosperms. The gymnospermic plants have originated from pteridophytic ancestor stock, and in the course of time they have given rise to angiosperms. Because of this, they share the characters of both the groups i.e. pteridophytes and angiosperms. Many botanists have described the gymnosperms as "*proangiosperms*".

General Characters

Gymnospermic plants have their own characteristic features of morphology, anatomy and reproduction.

The salient features or general characters of gymnosperms are given below
1. Growth of the gymnospermic plants is very slow, they are generally, perennial.

2. They are mostly evergreen, dwarf or tall trees and shrubs. The tallest plant in the world, *Sequoia sempervirens* (red wood tree) is approximately 112 meters in height, is from the order coniferales of this group. Some species like *Ephedra* is a scrambling shrub, while *Gnetum* is a woody climber or lina.
3. The cycadales look like palms, while coniferales have pyramidal appearance.
4. The stem is aerial, stout, columnar, branched or unbranched, woody, showing normal or abnormal secondary growth as in *Gnetum*. The stem in *Zamia* and *Welwitschia* is underground. Shoot dimorphism (long shoot and dwarf shoot) is present in *Ginkgo*, and members of coniferales. Long shoot is vegetative, while dwarf shoot is reproductive.
5. The root system is tap root type, very deep going. In addition, there are some special type of roots present in some plant species like *Cycas*, which are known as *"Coralloid roots"* as they appear like corals. These roots are adventitous, apogeotropic with lenticels and infected by blue-green algae. They perform the function of nitrogen fixation. In *Pinus*, the roots show association with mycorrhiza and hence they are known as *"mycorrhizal roots"*.
6. The leaves are of diverse nature and dimorphic
    (a) Foliage leaves
    (b) Scale leaves
7. Foliage leaves in *Cycas* and other genera of cycadales are very large, 1 - 2 metres in length, pinnately compound, formed in crowns every year at the top of the columnar stem. They are ever green and photosynthetic in nature. The leaflets are thick, leathery, and mostly sessile, with or without midrib, showing circinate venation. The leaf bases are persistent on stem. '
8. In *Ginkgo,* the leaves are fan shaped, lobed, ever green and very beautiful.
9. In *Pinus* and other coniferales, the leaves are highly reduced, needle like, remaining ever green for years together.
10. In *Gnetum,* the leaves are similar to that of dicot plants. They are ovate, thick, alternate showing reticulate venation. But in *Ephedra*, the leaves are almost reduced to scales.
11. The leaves of *Welwitschia* are very peculiar. It has only a pair of leaves throughout the life, which are about three meters in length, persistent and continuously growing.
12. Scale leaves – These are reduced, dry, deciduous, brown coloured or colourless. Mostly protective in nature. Present on stem, male and female cones etc.

13. The anatomical characters of stem, root and leaf of gymnosperms are also very specific. The wood anatomy of gymnosperm is quite interesting. The stem shows presence of conjoint, collateral, open vascular bundles. The cortex, pith and even secondary xylem, shows presence of mucilage or resin canals. Growth rings are distinct in stem.

14. The xylem is endarch or mesarch, secondary growth is normal due to intra and interfasicular cambium ring. But abnormal secondary growth is seen in stem of *Gnetum*. The cambium behaves abnormally or its origin may be abnormal (cortical cambium).

15. The xylem shows only tracheids, but vessels are absent (except in Gnetales). Similarly, the phloem is without companion cells.

16. In gymnosperms the wood is of two types
    (a) Manoxylic, (b) Pycnoxylic.
    (a) Manoxylic wood is soft, porous, mainly formed by pith. Secondary xylem is scanty or very less. It has no economical or commercial value e.g. *Cycas*.
    (b) Pycnoxylic wood is hard, compact, with less amount of pith and maximum amount of secondary xylem tissues. It is economically and commercially important wood. e.g. *Pinus, Taxus* etc.

17. The root is exarch and diarch, triarch, tetra or pentarch.

18. The leaves show thick cuticle, multilayered hypodermis – acting as heat screen, compactly arranged or even folded palisade tissues with sunken stomata. The leaf shows many xeromorphic characters. Transfusion tissues are present in species like *Cycas* for lateral conduction of food material as the side veins are absent.

19. The vegetative methods of reproduction are limited, occurs only through bulbils as in *Cycas*.

20. The plants are generally dioecious – male and female cone bearing plants are separate, but some are monoecious also.

21. The male and female cones are very distinct and formed in all the genera. (Except in *Cycas*, in which loose megasporophylls are formed on female plants).

22. The male cones, present on male plants are formed by many compactly arranged, microsporophylls. The microsporophylls bear microsporangia. These are grouped in 3 to 4 or many, forming sori as in *Cycas*. The microsporangia contain inside them many microspores or pollen grains.

23. The pollen grains are formed in huge amounts, sometimes yellowish clouds of pollen grains are formed in coniferales. The pollen grains are liberated outside in three or four celled condition.
24. The pollination is anemophilous, the pollen grains are colourless, light in weight, smooth walled, with or without wings.
25. The female cones formed on female plants are composed of many, compactly arranged megasporophylls. The megasporophylls bear ovules on them. The size, shape and number of ovules differ in different genera. The ovules are naked and freely exposed. The ovules in gymnosperms are the largest in the plant kingdom. In coniferales, ovuliferous scale bears the ovule. The ovule of *Ginkgo* has distinct collar, while in *Taxus* it has an aril like structure. In Gnetale, the male and female cones look like the angiospermic inflorescence, enclosing male and female flower like structures.
26. The male gametophytes are formed by the germination of microspores. Prothalial cells are formed during the germination of microspores.
27. Male gametes are top shaped and motile, due to presence of bands of flagella in cycadales and ginkgoales. In other genera, the male gametes are non-motile. They are carried through pollen tubes towards the egg. Thus zooidogamy (motile gametes) and siphonogamy (siphon-pollen tube carrying the male gametes) are observed in gymnosperms.
28. The female gametophytes bear 2 to 5 or more archegonia (Cycadales), containing egg, with neck-canal cells and venter canal cells. The archegonia are not formed in the most advanced order like gnetales.
29. There is no double fertilisation. The endosperm develops before fertilisation and hence it is haploid.
30. Polyembryony is the most significant feature of all gymnosperms. The embryos develop from many zygotes (simple polyembryony) or they are formed by the divisions in a single zygote (cleavage polyembryony). In addition to this, in coniferale, rosette and suspensor polyembryony are also observed.
31. Inspite of polyembryony, finally only single embryo matures and all the remaining are aborted.
32. The embryo is usually dicotyledonous, with radicle, plumule and suspensor.
33. The naked ovules form the seeds; these have hard, stony seed coat.
34. Seed germination is epigeal type.
35. The gymnospermic plants show distinct heteromorphic alternation of generations.

e.g. *Cycas, Pinus, Thuja, Taxus, Gnetum, Ephedra, Welwitschia.*

7.2 Classification of Gymnosperms

There are different systems of classification of gymnosperms proposed from time to time by different taxonomists. While proposing a particular system of classification, main importance was given to both vegetative and reproductive characters alongwith anatomy, embryology, palynology, cytology and even phytochemistry. Many of them have also considered fossil records.

Chamberlain's system of classification of gymnosperms

Prof. C.J. Chamberlain (1935) proposed his system of classification of gymnosperms on the basis of habit of plants, stem anatomy and leaf morphology. Chamberlain's system of classification of gymnosperms was also supported by Arnold (1948) by giving palaeo-botanical evidences.

Chamberlain divided the gymnosperms into two main classes. The classes were further divided into different orders

Class – Cycadophyta : Comparatively smaller plants, unbranched stems, pinnately compound leaves, thick cortex, scanty wood, large pith, simple cones, including the orders like (i) Cycadofilicales (fossilised), (ii) Cycadeoidales (extinct genera), (iii) Cycadales (living).

Class – Coniferophyta : Tall plants, extensively branched stem, simple leaves, scanty cortex, thick wood, small pith, simple male cones but compound female cones, including the orders like (i) Cordaitales (fossilised), (ii) Ginkgoales (living), (iii) Coniferales (living), (iv) Gnetales (living).

Brief Outline of Chamberlain's System of Classification of Gymnosperms (1935)

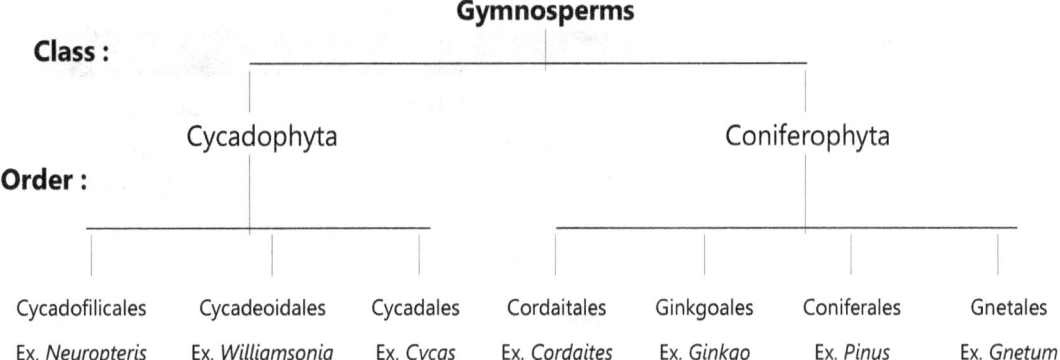

Distinguishing features of various orders of Cycadophyta

(i) **Cycadofilicales :** Seeds formed on leaves. All genera are fossilised. Most of the characters are similar to pteridophytic plants (Pteridospermales)

(ii) **Cycadeoidales :** Leaves very big, pinnately compound, leaving persistent leaf bases on stem. Megasporophylls grouped into cones but microsporophylls loose, not forming the cones. It includes both living and extinct genera.

(iii) **Cycadales :** Palm like habit, unbranched, columnar stem, crown of leaves with persistent leaf bases. Manoxylic wood. Male and female cones are large (except *Cycas*).

Distinguishing features of various orders of Coniferophyta

(i) **Cordaitales :** Tall plants with crown of branches. Leaves strap shaped, spirally arranged, showing parallel venation. Male and female cones are compact. It includes all fossilised genera.

(ii) **Ginkgoales :** Leaves are fan shaped, lobed with dichotomously branched venation. Male cones pendent, female cones with two ovules showing collar. Shoot dimorphism - two types of shoots – long shoot and dwarf shoot. Only one living genus *Ginkgo*, all others are fossilised.

(iii) **Coniferales :** Tall trees with ever green leaves. Resin canals throughout the plant body, male and female cones distinct. Ovuliferous scale and bract scale present in female cones. Pollen grains winged, wood pycnoxylic.

(iv) **Gnetales :** Woody climbers or shrubs, leaves with reticulate venation. Most of the characters are similar to angiosperms. Male and female cones look like inflorescence.

Most of the systems of classification of gymnosperms are based on criteria proposed by Chamberlain (1935) and Arnold (1948).

7.3 Life Cycle of *Cycas*

A total of six species of *Cycas* have been reported from India, of which four species occur as wild plants and the two species are cultivated in gardens, parks etc. The most common Indian species of *Cycas* are *C. circinalis, C. pectinata, C. beddomei, C. rumphii, C. revoluta* and *C. siamensis*.

Sporophyte

The *Cycas* plant looks like a palm tree with a columnar aerial trunk and a crown of pinnately compound leaves. Generally, the stem is unbranched, but older trees sometimes exhibit branching. The branch is developed from the adventitious bud called bulbil which arises from the leaf base. Thus the bulbil helps in vegetative propagation of the plant. The stem is covered by armour of alternating bands of large and small rhomboidal leaf bases. These leaf bases are persistent, of which the large bases belong to foliage leaves, while the small ones belong either to scale leaves (in male plants) or to sporophyll (in female plants). *Cycas* exhibits leaf dimorphism in possessing large green foliage leaves and small scale leaves or cataphylls. The primary tap root system is replaced by a number of strong, branched, adventitious roots arising from the stem.

Fig. 7.1 : *Cycas*

Root

External morphology

At the beginning, there is a primary root system in *Cycas*. This normal tap root system is short-lived and is replaced by large, fleshy, persistent, branched adventitious roots arising from the stem. Some of the lateral branches grow horizontally in the soil and become apogeotropic. They have numerous lenticels on their surface. These roots frequently get infected with bacteria (*Pseudomonas, Azotobacter*), fungi and blue green algae or Cyanobacteria (*Anabaena, Nostoc, Oscillatoria* and *Calothrix*). The infection causes a distortion of their shape. The infected roots repeatedly dichotomise to become a mass of tubercles which apparently look like corals. These are called coralloid roots which grow horizontally in soil and get swollen at the

Fig. 7.2 : *Cycas* : Coralloid root

tip. The exact role of these endophytic Cyanobacteria is not known. However, it has been reported that these Cyanobacteria can fix nitrogen and promote the growth of *Cycas* plant.

Internal structure

Anatomically, a normal primary root is differentiated into epidermis, cortex and a central vascular system. Epidermis is comprised of single layered parenchymatous cells with occasional hairs. The cortex is multilayered, made up of parenchymatous cells filled with starch. Some cells of the cortex contain tannins and sphaeraphides. The single-layered endodermal cells have characteristic casparian bands and the multilayered pericycle is made up of parenchymatous cells. The stele is diarch with exarch xylem. A mature tap root shows secondary growth in thickness both instrastelar and extrastelar. Anatomically, the coralloid roots are more or less identical with the primary tap root except for a well-defined algal zone in the cortex having abundant intercellular spaces occupied by blue-green algae or Cyanobacteria. Besides, some fungi and bacteria are also reported from this zone. The stele is diarch to tetrarch. There is a little or no secondary growth in the coralloid roots.

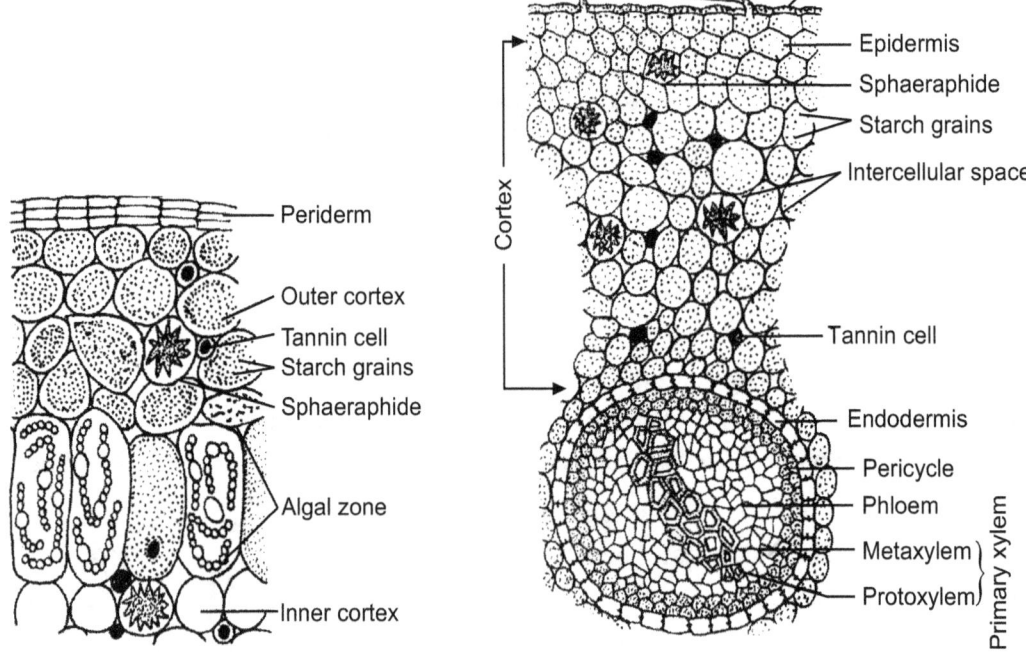

Fig. 7.3 : T.S. of coralloid root of *Cycas*   Fig. 7.4 : T.S. of primary root of *Cycas*

Stem

External morphology: The *Cycas* stem is columnar with thick armour of persistent leaf bases. However, *C. siamensis* has underground short tuberous stem. The stem is usually unbranched, but sometimes it shows branches which are produced from the bulbil. The stem is irregular in outline because of a number of persistent leaf bases.

Internal structure

Internally, the stem shows similarity to a dicot stem which is differentiated into epidermis, cortex and vascular cylinder. The single-layered epidermis in discontinuous due to the presence of leaf-bases. The epidermis is covered with a thick cuticle. The cortex is massive, made up of parenchymatous cells rich in starch grains. The cortex is traversed by several mucilaginous canals and leaf bases.

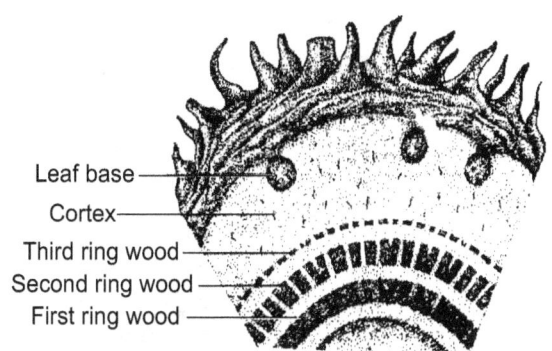

Fig. 7.5 : T. S. of *Cycas* stem

The endodermal and pericycle layers are not distinct. In the young stem, the vascular cylinder is very small comprising of several vascular bundles arranged in a ring. Thus, the *Cycas* stem shows ectophloic siphonostelic configuration. Each vascular bundle is conjoint, collateral and open which is separated by parenchymatous medullary rays. The xylem is endarch,

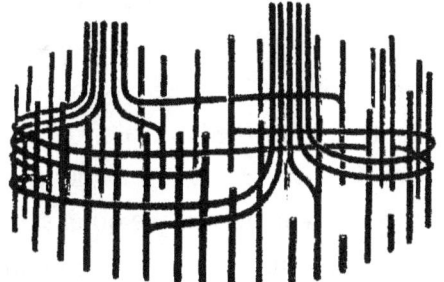

Fig. 7.6 : Girdling of leaf traces

comprising of tracheids and xylem parenchyma only. Several leaf-traces are observed in a T.S. of stem. Each leaf receives four traces. Out of the four traces, two traces enter directly into the leaf after arising from the stelar cylinder on the same side and is called direct traces.

The other two traces arise from the stelar cylinder on the opposite side of the leaf and enter the leaf after turning round a semicircle or girdle around the stelar cylinder. These traces are called girdle traces. The girdle of leaf traces is a characteristic of *Cycas* and allied members of Cycadaceae. The two girdle traces join with the direct traces and branches of other girdle traces finally enter the leaf as two traces. The central part of the stem is occupied by a large parenchymatous pith rich in starch grains. Pith cells also contain tannins and mucilaginous substances.

Secondary growth

The normal instrastelar secondary growth is observed in early stages due to the bifacial activity of cambium ring. This primary cambium ring is short-lived, and so remains functional for a short time. The secondary xylem produced centripetally shows tracheids with 4-5 rows of bordered pits and scalariform thickenings and one row of thin-walled cells in between. Three types of vascular rays are produced: (i) uniseriate rays, (ii) multiseriate rays, and

(iii) foliar multiseriate rays. The phloem is well developed which may exceed the volume of xylem. The sieve elements contain numerous sieve areas on their radial wall. The companion cells are absent, instead some phloem parenchyma termed albuminous cells are formed, closely associated with sieve cells. The stem does not produce any annual ring.

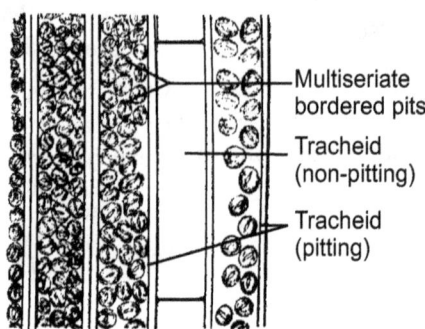

Fig. 7.7: *Cycas*: L. S. of mature wood

A peculiarity of *Cycas* stem is that the young stem which is monoxylic becomes polyxylic at maturity due to the formation of accessory cambium rings in the cortex. The second cambium similarly forms ring around the secondary xylem towards the inner side and secondary phloem towards the outer side. The second cambium ring remains functional for a short time, after that its activity ceases. In a similar fashion, successive cambium rings initiate in the cortical region. The first two vascular rings are thicker than the other vascular rings, of which the second vascular ring is wider than the first. The subsequent rings are narrower than these two rings, gradually diminishing towards the periphery. Usually 3-4 rings of wood are produced in *Cycas*, but in *C. pectinata* as many as 20 rings of wood may be formed. The extrastelar secondary growth has also been observed in the stem of *Cycas* which forms the periderm.

Leaf

External morphology: *Cycas* exhibits leaf dimorphism in possessing green foliage leaves and scale leaves. The scale leaves are small, dry, non-green and triangular in shape, covered with rementa. They have small persistent leaf bases. Their only function is to provide protection to apical meristem and other aerial parts. The foliage leaves are large, unipinnately compound. A single leaf bears 75- 100 pairs of leaflets which are arranged on either side of the rachis in opposite or alternate manner. The leaflets are sessile and elongated. Each leaflet is provided with a single unbranched mid vein without having any lateral veins. The leaves possess a very long and strong rachis with a short petiole. The base of the petiole is provided with two rows of small stiff spines. The young rachises as well as leaflets are circinately coiled like those of ferns.

Fig. 7.8: *Cycas* : A single leaf   Fig. 7.9: *Cycas*: A young leaf

Internal structure

The T.S. of rachis shows circular outline. The outermost layer is the epidermis which consists of cuticularised thick walled cells interrupted by sunken stomata. The epidermis is followed by hypodermis, which is composed of a variable mixture of chlorenchyma and sclerenchyma followed by a parenchymatous ground tissue with many mucilage canals. Initially, two endarch bundles enter the leaf base and then they split up into several bundles. These bundles are then dispersed in the ground tissue and are arranged in an inverted Greek letter 'omega' like arc. The vascular bundles are conjoint, collateral and open, bearing both the centrifugal and centripetal xylem. Thus, they are diploxylic or pseudomesarch in nature. As the bundles move up into pinnae, they become exarch without having any centrifugal xylem. The phloem lies on the side of the protoxylem. The bundles are covered with a bundle sheath. The *Cycas* leaflet is dorsiventral showing strongly xerophytic characteristics. The T.S. of a leaflet shows a thick-walled, highly cuticularised epidermis. The upper epidermis is continuous, while the lower epidermis is interrupted by stomata. The stomata are haplocheilic, situated in pits with overarching rims. The two guard cells are bordered by 8-10 subsidiary cells arranged in a ring. The hypodermis is 1-2 layer thick except for the midrib or at the margins where it becomes 3-4 layered. The hypodermal cells are thick-walled, highly lignified. The mesophylls are differentiated into palisade cells which are arranged vertically below the hypodermis. These cells have long fibrous thickenings that make them resistant against the external radial and longitudinal pressures. The lower part of the mesophyll consists of spongy parenchymatous cells with intercellular spaces. The vascular bundle is diploxylic in nature, made up of a broad, triangular, centripetal, exarch metaxylem and two small patches of centrifugal endarch primary xylem.

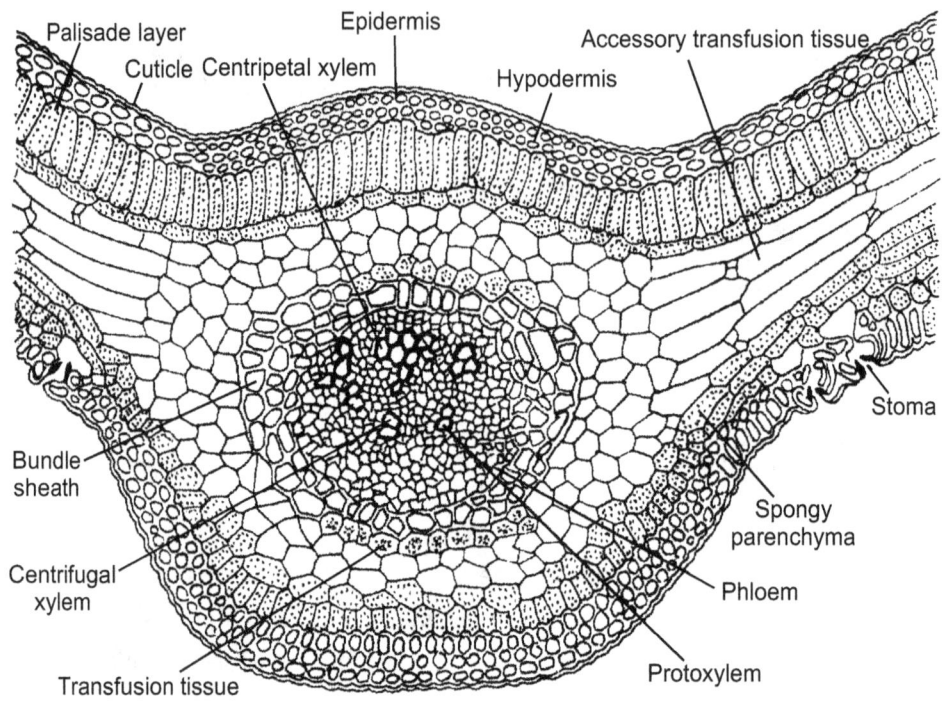

Fig. 7.10: T.S. of leaflet of *Cycas*

The centripetal xylem is separated from centrifugal xylem by a few parenchymatous cells. Some tracheidal cells situated on either side of the centripetal metaxylem are termed transfusion tissue. Additionally, there are 3-4 layers of transversely elongated thin-walled colourless tracheidal cells in between the upper palisade layer and the lower spongy layer. These cells constitute the accessory transfusion tissue which serves for lateral conduction in the portion of leaflet that lacks veins. The phloem is situated on the abaxial side below the xylem which is made up of sieve cells and parenchyma only. A small arc of cambium is present in between the centripetal xylem and phloem. Many calcium oxalate crystals are found in the parenchymatous tissue below the vascular bundle. The vascular bundle is surrounded by a fibrous bundle sheath.

Reproduction

Cycas reproduces both by vegetative and sexual methods.

Vegetative reproduction

Cycas reproduces vegetatively by means of bulbils or adventitious buds. These bulbils develop from the parenchymatous cells of the cortex in the base of the stem at the crevices between persistent leaf bases. Initially, bulbils are covered only with scale leaves, but a few foliage leaves develop with further growth. Bulbil arising on male plant gives rise to male plant; if it forms on female plant it produces a female plant. This is a very common method of vegetative propagation. In *C. revolute*, the vegetative propagation in *C. circinalis* takes place by suckers that develop on roots. With further growth they start producing new plants.

Sexual reproduction

Cycas is strictly a dioecious plant, but the male and female plants are indistinguishable at the vegetative stage. The compact male cone develops at the apex of the stem in the male plant. However, *Cycas* is the only genus of Cycadaceae which does not produce any female cone. Instead, several megasporophylls arise spirally in acropetal succession around the stem apex of the female plant.

Male cone

The surface of male cone is covered with brown scales at young stage. At maturity, the male cone becomes very large (40-80 cm in length), oval or conical in shape which emits odour that can be smelt from a moderate distance. The male cone of *Cycas* is the largest among the plant kingdom.

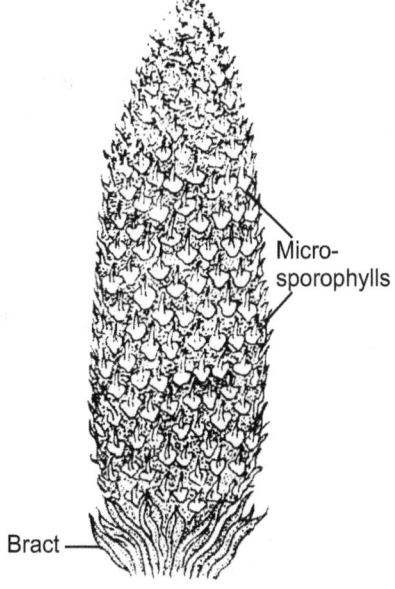

Fig. 7.11: *Cycas* : **Male cone**

The male cone has a central cone axis and numerous microsporophylls are arranged spirally and acropetally around the axis. A single microsporophyll is a triangular flattened woody structure. It is differentiated into a proximal wedge-shaped fertile part and a distal sterile part, tapering into an up curved apex called apophysis.

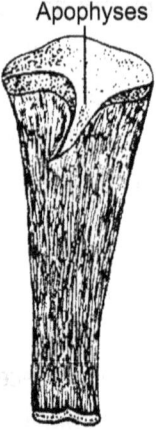

Fig. 7.12: *Cycas* **: Microsporophyll**

Numerous microsporangia *are* borne on the abaxial (lower) surface of the microsporophyll except at the apex and the base. Microsporangia are borne in groups of 3-5 forming sori that are surrounded by many single celled delicate hair.

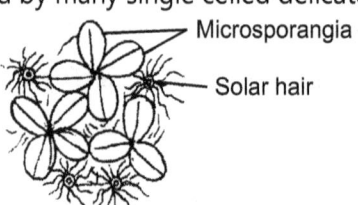

Fig. 7.13: Microsporangia

Each sporangium is oval or circular in shape having a very short massive stalk. The dehiscence of sporangia takes place by a longitudinal slit. The development of sporangia is of eusporangiate type. The sporangial wall is multilayered with a thickened epidermis and an ill defined tapetum enclosing numerous microspore (pollen) mother cells. Further, microspore mother cells through meiotic division produce numerous microspores or pollen grains. The pollen grain is oval-shaped having a large rounded monosulcate aperture. The pollen is bounded by two concentric wall layers; the outer thick exine and the inner thin intine.

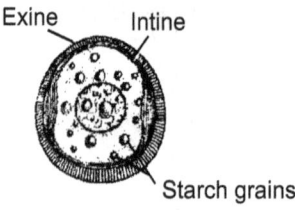

Fig. 7.14: *Cycas* **: Pollen grain**

Megasporophyll

The megasporophylls of *Cycas* are not organised into a definite cone. Instead, they arise at the stem apex spirally and acropetally forming a loose crown. The megasporophylls are pinnate in nature and are covered with brown hair called rementa. Hence, the megasporophylls of *Cycas* are considered to be the modified foliage leaves. Megasporophylls are produced every year like the foliage leaves, though they are produced more in numbers than the foliage leaves. A single megasporophyll is a flat dorsiventral structure, measuring upto 30 cm in length. It is differentiated into an upper pinnate lamina and a basal stalk that bears two rows of opposite or sub-opposite, one to six pairs of ovules.

There is a great variation in structure of megasporophylls and in number of ovules per megasporophyll in *Cycas* and these criteria can be applied to identify the species of *Cycas*. There is a great reduction in the structure of megasporophylls and in number of ovules among the various species of *Cycas*. *C. revoluta* is the most primitive species where the megasporophyll lamina is much dissected and tapers into a point, bearing 3-4 pairs of ovules. In *C. pectinata*, only the lowermost megaspore becomes functional. The upper free opening of the integument forms the micropyle and a concavity in the top of the nucellar tissue forms the pollen chamber. After pollination, the pollen grains are collected in the pollen chamber and the development of pollen grains takes place in the nucellar tissue.

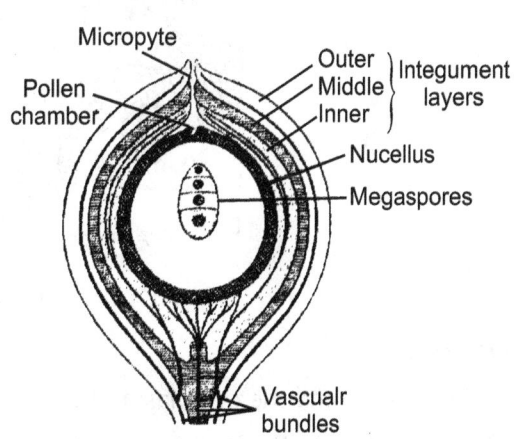

Fig. 7.15: *Cycas*: A megasporophyll   **Fig. 7.16:** *Cycas*: Ovule

Gametophyte

The spore is the first phase of gametophytic generation. The microspore or pollen grain is the male gametophyte, while the megaspore represents the first stage of female gametophyte which develops to form a female gametophyte.

Pollination

Cycas is anemophilous i.e., wind pollinated. The airborne pollen grains remain suspended in the air and at the same time, some cells of the nucellar beak in the ovule are disorganised to form a viscous fluid. This fluid comes out through the microphyle in the form of a 'pollination drop'. Thus, some of the airborne pollen grains come in contact with the fluid and are sucked into the pollen chamber through the micropylar canal. The pollen grains are then deposited and concentrated within the pollen chamber as a result of drying off the fluid. At this stage, the ovule increases in size.

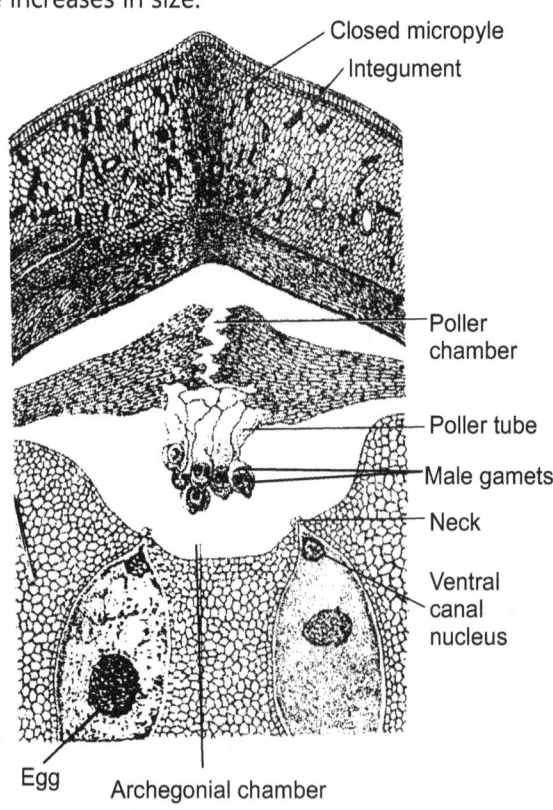

Fig. 7.17: Closed top of ovule after pollination

Fertilisation

The sperms and the cytoplasm of pollen tube are released in the archegonial chamber by the rupture of the basal end of pollen tube. The osmotically rich pollen tube cytoplasm causes the rupture of neck cells. The motile sperms enter into the archegonium with a forward and circular motion, with the ciliary band forming the anterior end. The archegonial chamber is flooded with the fertilisation fluid produced by nucellar cells. The ciliary band of the sperm is left behind on the top of the egg cell. The sperm nucleus fuses with the egg nucleus and thus a zygote in formed.

Embryogeny

The zygote enlarges considerably and undergoes numerous free nuclear divisions. As much as 256 (*C. revoluta*) to 512 (*C. circinalis*) free nuclei have been reported. A large central vacuole is formed and the nuclei are arranged around the central vacuole. Most of the free nuclei move to the base of the proembryo. The cell formation in the proembryo begins from the basal part and extends up the periphery. The entire embryo never becomes cellular. The basal cells are smaller with dense cytoplasm forming an embryo. A dicotyledonous embryo is developed at the tip. The upper cells elongate greatly to form the suspensor which may be coiled and twisted. Several egg cells may be fertilised to form many zygotes, but ultimately only one embryo in an ovule attains maturity. The layer of cells covering the outer curved face of the embryonal mass is called the cap.

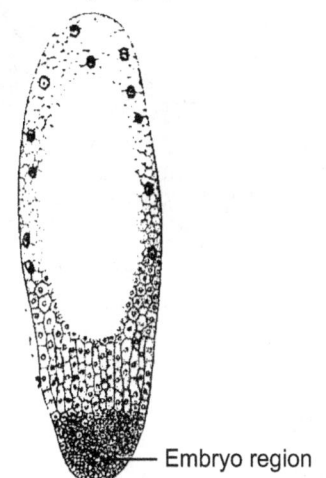
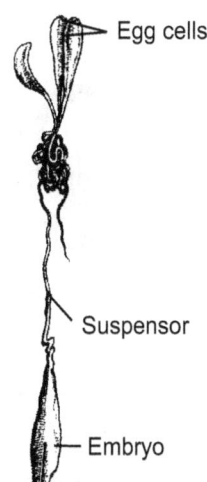

Fig. 7.18: *Cycas*: Embryo   Fig. 7.19: *Cycas*: Embryo with suspensor

Seeds

Cycas seeds are fleshy and remain covered with an orange red-coloured thick seed coat. The embryo in the seed enlarges much. The nucellus is used up and the seed is covered with a three-layered seed coat. The coleorrhiza is the first region to differentiate in the embryo proper which is quite hard. The plumule develops later inside the base of the cotyledons.

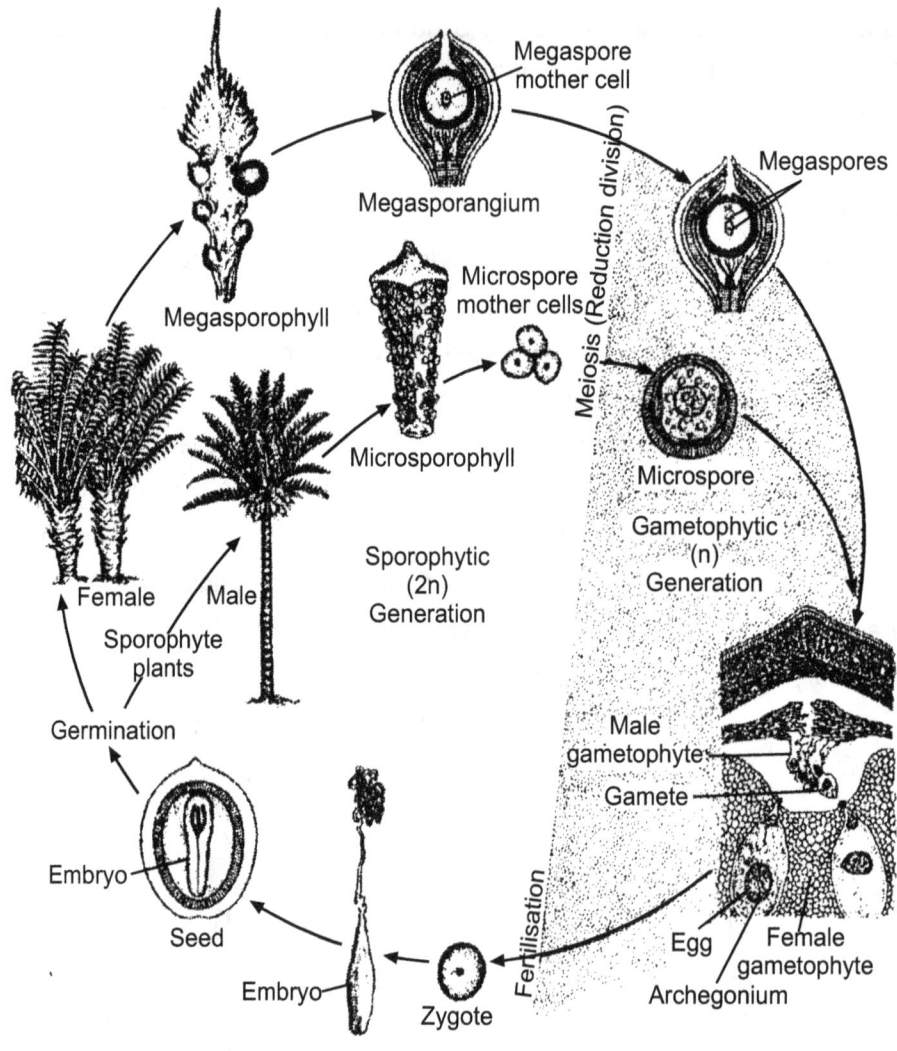

Fig. 7.20 : Life cycle of *Cycas*

Subsequently, the suspensor dries up. The growth of the embryo in seeds is very slow, taking over a year to mature. *Cycas* shows a three years reproductive cycle where pollination occurs in the winter of the first year, fertilisation in the summer of the second year and seed shedding in the summer of the third year. The development of embryo continues even after the seeds are shed. The seeds are dispersed by birds due to their attractive fleshy outer pulp. The germination of the seed is epigeal. The first leaves come out at right angles to the cotyledons in a decussated fashion, although the remaining leaves develop spirally.

Points to Remember

- Most gymnosperms are evergreen trees or shrubs with xerophytic adaptations.
- The plant body is sporophytic and differentiated into root, stem and leaves.
- The roots are diarch or polyarch.
- The young stem has a ring of conjoint collateral open vascular bundles.
- The leaves have thick cuticle and sunken stomata.
- Most of the gymnosperms lack lateral veins in leaves.
- The ovules are characterised by the presence of archegonia.
- Pollination takes place by wind i.e. anemophily.
- Endosperm is haploid and formed before fertilisation.
- Double fertilisation and triple fusion are absent.
- *Cycas* is a dioecious plant i.e. male and female plants are different.
- The *Cycas* plant looks like a palm tree with a columnar aerial trunk and a crown of pinnately compound leaves.
- *Cycas* exhibits leaf dimorphism in possessing large green foliage leaves and small scale leaves or cataphylls.
- The stem of *Cycas* shows a similarity with a dicot stem which is differentiated into epidermis, cortex and vascular cylinder.
- *Cycas* reproduces both by vegetative and sexual methods.
- The male cone of *Cycas* is the largest among the plant kingdom.
- The megasporophylls of *Cycas* are not organised into a definite cone, instead, they arise at the stem apex spirally and acropetally forming a loose crown.
- *Cycas* shows reproductive cycle of three years where pollination occurs in the first year's winter, fertilisation in second year's summer and seed shedding in third year's summer. The development of embryo continues even after the seeds are shed.

Exercises

Short Answer Questions

1. Enlist the general characters of Gymnosperms.
2. Describe the classification system of Chamberlain.
3. Describe the internal structure of *Cycas* root.
4. Describe the internal structure of *Cycas* stem.

5. Describe the internal structure of *Cycas* leaf.
6. Write a note on fertilisation in *Cycas*.
7. Describe the ovule of *Cycas*.

Long Answer Questions

1. Describe habit, habitat and external morphology of *Cycas*.
2. Give an account of the structure of male cone and megasporophyll of *Cycas*.
3. Describe the pollination, fertilisation and seed structure of *Cycas* in detail.
4. Describe the life cycle of *Cycas*.

Chapter 8...

Angiosperms

Contents ...

8.1 Introduction

8.2 Salient Features of Angiosperms

8.3 Causes of Evolutionary Success of Angiosperms

8.4 Comparative Account of Dicotyledons and Monocotyledons

Points to Remember

Exercises

8.1 Introduction

The angiospermic plants show great variation in size, some are very minute and almost microscopic in nature e.g. *Lemma, Wolfia*, while others are giant trees e.g. *Eucalyptus*, Banyan etc. The angiospermic plants are cosmopolitan in distribution. They occur in every ecological niche. They are found at every altitude, from the sea level to the highest mountain peaks. The span of life is variable from a few weeks (e.g. ephemerals) to several hundred years (perenials). These are mostly autotrophic, but a few plants like *Cuscutta, Loranthus* etc. are complete or partial parasites respectively. They are even saprophytic (*Monotropa*) and carnivores (*Drosera, Nepenthes,* etc.)

This highly evolved and very successful group of plants, with about 12,500 genera and more than 3,00,000 species dominate the vegetation on earth. These flowering plants have seeds enclosed in the carpel or carpels or in the fruit and hence they are known as angiosperms (Greek word, Angeion-means vessel and sperma - means seed). Literally, angiosperm means plant bearing seeds in a vessel or ovary. These are considered as geologically young plants, and hence called as 'modern' seed plants'. Angiospermic plants have undergone intensive evolution in many directions, under different environmental conditions, and due to this, they have attained an extraordinary level of morphological and ecological diversity. The greatest diversity seen in them is mostly due to adaptive specialisation in response to great climatic changes. Some of them show highly elaborated characters, while others have evolved by reduction of characters.

8.2 Salient Features of Angiosperms

Angiosperms are characterised and distinguished from other plant groups by the following important features

1. These flowering plants have seeds enclosed in ovary.
2. They show greatest diversity in size, shape, occurrence, habit, habitat, and in life-span.
3. The sporophytic plant body shows distinction of root, stem and leaves.
4. The plant body is characterised by the presence of vessels in xylem.
5. These plants have very efficient and highly evolved conducting tissues. The phloem has phloem parenchyma and companion cells.
6. They have complex and advanced reproductive structures (the flower).
7. The carpel is differentiated into style, stigma and ovary.
8. These are heterosporous plants, with microspore in microsporangium and megaspore in megasporangium.
9. Both the male and female gametophytes are highly evolved. Male gametophyte lacks prothalial cell, while the female gametophyte is without archegonium.
10. Siphonogamy and act of double fertilisation are the significant features of angiosperms.
11. Endosperm is generally triploid and formed after fertilisation.
12. They show polyembryony, parthenocarpy and even apomixis.
13. They reproduce very effectively even by vegetative methods of propagation.
14. In the life cycle of angiospermic plants, the gametophytic phase is highly reduced, while the sporophytic phase is well pronounced and dominant.
15. Angiosperms, on the basis of some morphological, anatomical, flower and seed characters are grouped into monocotyledonous (seed with single cotyledon) and dicotyledonous (seeds with two cotyledons) plants. These have some common characters of the group angiosperms and at the same time their own special features.
16. Thus angiosperm is a highly evolved, very vast and varied assemblage of group of plants dominating the earth's vegetation.

8.3 Causes of Evolutionary Success of Angiosperms

Today Angiosperm is the most evolved, successful, largest and dominating group of higher plants, existing on earth. These are represented by about 330 families, with 12,500 genera and more than 30,00,00 species of monocots and dicots. Their numbers itself indicate their great success for survival and continuation of species for years together.

Palaeobotanical research convincingly shows that during the geological period different taxa (group of plants, like algae, fungi, bryophytes, pteridophytes etc.) originated, flourished and eventually became extinct. But angiosperms have, highly succeeded during the course of evolution. The evolutionary success of angiosperms is mainly because of the following reasons

Angiosperms most probably evolved during the lower cretaceous and spread enormously by the middle cretaceous. During upper cretaceous, they become the dominant and luxuriant component of the earth's vegetation. This happened within a short evolutionary period of about 25 million years. The secret behind this may be due to their great evolutionary plasticity and unusually high adaptability. These characters enabled angiosperms to occupy the whole world.

The late Cretaceous period was marked by a very high diversity of physico-geographical conditions. The plants like Bennettitales, Ginkgoales, Cycadales and Ferns did not possess sufficient evolutionary plasticity to enable them to produce new forms, adaptations to new conditions of more diverse and rapidly changing environments and hence they became extinct. On the other hand, angiosperms adapted very quickly, adjusted themselves with changing environment and spread rapidly throughout the world. The diversity and dynamic nature are the key points of evolutionary success of angiosperms.

The main reasons of their evolutionary success are given below

1. Most diversified and varied nature of habitat.
2. Tremendous adaptation and adjustment with each and every type of habitat available for growth and multiplication.
3. Highest degree of perfection in the vascular system. This highly developed vascular system contributed in their evolutionary success.
4. Great adaptations and timely evolution of flowers for entomophilous pollination. The most important factor in the rapid development of angiosperms was their complex inter-relationship with insects. The role of insects in the evolution and

development of angiosperms has been emphasised by many scientists like Arber and Parkin (1907), Ehlrich and Raven (1964).

5. Bisexual nature of flower, beneficial for cross or self pollination, providing guarantee of fertilisation and seed formation.

6. Formation of ovules within the ovary.

7. Highly efficient modes and devices for most successful dispersal of fruits and seeds. Agents like insects, birds, animals, wind and water are used very efficiently for dispersal of fruits and seeds.

8. Additional modes of efficient, rapid and varied types of vegetative propagations along with normal sexual or seed propagation. Hence, if one method fails for multiplication, it was immediately replaced by other alternative methods. Thus, anyhow, the multiplication of species never stopped.

9. Seed propagation is a very effective mode of multiplication.

10. Highly important for food, fodder, fiber, fuel, medicines, shelter, clothing etc. hence human beings have always conserved, protected and grown them.

11. The pollen economy, profitable use of nectar and exploitation of insect visitors for pollination mechanism.

12. The protection of ovules against chewing insects was successfully offered by closure of the carpel. Thus, the development of ovules within the ovary ensured protection to the developing ovules and seeds.

13. The advancement in flower morphology helped a lot to this group to form seeds. Bisexuality ensured self pollination but, if it fails then cross pollination takes place, thus seeds are formed in any case.

Stebbins (1974) proposed that the survival of the seedlings and adult plants under a variety of environmental conditions, cross pollination, development and dispersal of seeds and establishment of seedlings provided evolutionary success and the potentiality for further diversification of angiosperms.

14. The genetic variations, gene mutations, recombinations, apomixis, amphimixis etc. have added to the evolutionary success of angiosperms.

15. Some special features like parthenocarpy and polyembryony have helped these plants to flourish and grow luxuriently.

8.4 Comparative Account of Dicotyledons and Monocotyledons

	Dicotyledons	**Monocotyledons**
Roots :	Tap root system	Adventitious root system.
Stem :	Mostly without distinct nodes and internodes.	Always with distinct nodes and internodes.
Leaves :	Leaves with reticulate venation.	Leaves with parallel venation.
Flowers :	Flowers tetra or pentamerous	Flowers always trimerous.
Seeds :	i) Embryo with two cotyledons	i) Embryo with a single cotyledon
	ii) Seed germination is epigeal or hypogeal.	ii) Germination of seed is always hypogeal
Anatomical features :	i) In roots diarch, triarch or tetrarch vascular strands are present with radial vascular bundles.	i) Roots with polyarch vascular strands with radial vascular bundles.
	ii) Stem shows conjoint, collateral and open vascular bundles arranged in a ring.	ii) Stem shows conjoint, collateral and closed vascular bundles scattered in ground tissues.
	iii) In leaves, mesophylls are differentiated into spongy and palisade tissues. Hence, leaves are dorsiventral.	iii) In leaves mesophylls are the only spongy tissues. Hence, leaves are isobilateral.

Points to Remember

- Angiosperms is the most evolved, highly successful and dominant geological young group of plants.
- Angiosperms are cosmopolitan and diversified group of plant kingdom.
- About 12,500 genera and 3,00,000 species of angiosperms are dominating the vegetation.
- Angiosperms are modern seed plants.
- Angiosperms have attained an extra ordinary level of morphological and ecological diversity.

Exercises

Long Answer Questions

1. Describe the salient features of Angiosperms.
2. Explain the causes of evolutionary success of Angiosperms.
3. Explain why angiosperms are dominating the whole world?
4. Give comparative account of dicotyledons and monocotyledons.

Paper - II Term - I

Chapter 1...
Introduction to Industrial Botany

Contents ...
1.1 Concept of Industrial Botany
1.2 Plant Resources and Industries
    1.2.1 Food Industry
    1.2.2 Fodder Industry
    1.2.3 Fibre Industry
    1.2.4 Medicine Industry
    1.2.5 Timber Industry
    1.2.6 Dyes Industry
    1.2.7 Gums Industry
    1.2.8 Tannins Industry
    Points to Remember
    Exercises

1.1 Concept of Industrial Botany

The basic science which deals with the study of plants like bryophytes, pteridophytes, gymnosperms, the highly evolved angiosperms, lichens, bacteria, blue green algae and fungi is known as botany. The science of botany has contributed in the well-being and welfare of mankind. The basic needs of human beings such as food, clothing and shelter are fulfilled by the plant world.

As stated by Lord Kelvin "The life and soul of any basic science including botany is its practical application". Every application always emerges from basic science or fundamental science.

The various branches of applied botany are industrial botany, agriculture, silviculture, forestry, horticulture, plant breeding, pharmacognosy, etc have gained popularity all over the world and have immense importance in our life. The large scale commercial applications of botany at the industrial level is known as industrial botany. Industrial botany has tremendous scope and importance as it is the most practical, commercial and need based branch of botany. Industrial botany is becoming more popular and gaining ground as it has tremendous job potential for the youth.

The industrial application of food, fibre, fodder and medicinal plants has become highly commercial and popular, which is the main stay of the Indian Economy. The British "East India Company" for the first-time explored and then exploited the plant resources in India, such as spices, cotton and timber at an industrial level; this was the beginning of Industrial Botany. At present, the seed industry, horticulture, floriculture, fruit and vegetable processing, micropropagation (tissue culture), herbal pesticides, herbal drugs are the most important examples of industrial botany. Most recently, industries using enzyme technology, biofuel technology, breweries, biotechnology industries and those that use plant dyes (natural colours) have come into lime light.

1.2 Plant Resources and Industries

India is gifted with rich biodiversity and therefore has a variety of plant resources. These plant resources such as fibre plants - cotton, jute, *Agave*, natural dye yielding plants like *Bixa sp*, gum yielding plants like *Acacia* sp, and tannin yielding plants like Hirda, Amla, Beheda have been used by mankind since the beginning of human civilization at household or small scale industry level.

Even today, the small scale industries based on local plant resources are the backbone of sustainable development of rural population,. Some of major plant resources and industries depending on them are briefly summarised below

1.2.1 Food Industry

India is the world's second largest producer of fruits and vegetables. The optimum utilisation of the crops produced in such huge amounts is possible only if supported by a strong food processing industry. It is one of the biggest industries that plays a major role in the Indian economy and provides great job opportunities.

Food grains like wheat, rice, maize are now processed and several by-products derived from them are available in the market. Many ready to eat or instant food products like noodles, pasta, soups, etc. are now popular in the market. Millets which are rich in minerals are also the sources of food industries involved in the preparations of highly nutritional

"Satvas". The barley and sorghum grains are used as starch source for fermentation in the alcohol industry.

Along with food grains, many fruit and vegetable resources also contribute to the food industry. The most common, widely accepted and popular products of the fruit and vegetable processing industry are pulps, ready to serve fruit juices, canned seasonal fruits, jam, jellies, pickles, squashes, etc.

Multinational companies like "Mapro" is famous for its strawberry products; and "Kissan" for its jams, ketchup, pickles, etc.

Frozen fruits, dehydrated and freeze dried vegetables, canned mushrooms etc. are also becoming popular among Indian consumers.

India is the largest producer of pulses in the world. Pulses form an integral part of the Indian diet due to the high protein content. The pulse industry has become a vital and growing segment of agricultural economy, providing employment in the farm input, grain processing, and transportation sectors.

Organically produced products command a good value in the market depending upon the distribution channels and market conditions. Some of the organically produced agricultural crops in India are spices, pulses, fruits, vegetables and oil seeds, etc. which are important commodities in food industry.

1.2.2 Fodder Industry

These industries have flourished because of "Operation Flood" in the milk industry. The dairy industry is growing by leaps and bounds at the state, national as well as international levels. The fodder industry plays a key role in dairy and as well as the poultry farms as it is used to feed the domesticated livestock.

Domesticated animals like buffaloes, horses, goats, sheep, etc. prefer good palatable fodder. On an average, the dairy animals require 6-8 kg dry and 20 – 25 kg green fodder per day. The quality of fodder is important to maintain the health of the animals, increase production of eggs, the body weight of animals and to milk production. Lusarn grass or alfalfa (*Medicago sativa*), berseem (*Trifolium alexandrinum*), maize (*Zea mays*), elephant grass, sorghum, millet, oat, barley, sugarcane tops are used as food sources in the fodder industry. The green leaves of *Sesbania, Alysicarpus rugosus, Leucaena leucocephala, Acacia nilotica* are also very important fodder resources. In deserts, the grass and leaves of xerophytic trees like *Acacia chundra* are the major resources of fodder industry.

Dry fodder is prepared by sun drying the freshly harvested fodder crops like sorghum, bajra, maize. Dried leaves of pulse crops like pigeon pea, cowpea, horse gram, mung bean and groundnut are very popularly used in fodder industry. These leaves are mixed with some minerals and salts and used for dairy animals.

"Sugrass" a mixture of different types of food grains and minerals is a very popular fodder. The cake left behind after the extraction of oil from seeds of groundnut (*Arachis hypogaea*) Safflower (*Carthamus* sp), cotton (*Gossypium hirsutum*) are popular sources of fodder for milch animals. Some hybrids grass varieties have also been developed mainly for the fodder purpose e.g. Elephant grass, etc.

Thus, there is a wide scope and a very high potential for fodder industry.

1.2.3 Fibre Industry

At present, all over the world, the trend in clothing has changed from synthetic fibres to natural fibres like cotton. There are more than 2000 species of yielding plants. The is obtained from leaves, stem, fruits, seeds, roots, etc.

Like food, the industry is also fast growing and is the second most employment generating industry in India. The major textile fibre yielding plant is cotton (*Gossypium* sp), which has captured the world market. The hybrid cotton varieties and Bt-cotton (genetically modified) have revolutionised the textile industry. The regions like Marathwada, Vidarbha, Khandesh are the major cotton producing areas in Maharashtra where textile industries have established very well.

*Cannabis (*Hemp*), Linum usitatissimum, Hibiscus, Cannabis sativa, Musa paradisiaca, Agave sisalana and Cocos nucifera* are the most important fibre resources for this industry.

Jute industry is the leading industry in West Bengal, while coir industry is the leading industry in South India. In Maharashtra, sisal fibre and agave fibre have gained very high industrial importance. These industries are generally located in rural areas and play a key role in sustainable rural development, providing job opportunities to rural unemployed youth. and The Central and state governments are quite proactive with regards to such village industries as they provide financial back-up to build market chain through different schemes.

1.2.4 Medicine Industry

Incidences of cardiovascular diseases, cancer, diabetes, AIDS, malaria, dengue, tuberculosis, asthma, arthritis etc. are increasing throughout the world with changing life style and food habits. The acceptance for ayurvedic drugs and herbal drugs is at the peak as they have no side effects and these are holistic in nature.

India, being home for a large number of medicinal plants can be a major player in the global pharmaceutical industry. The traditional medicines of India are now being accepted globally. The pharmaceutical industry relies on various plant resources which are in great demand. In fact, there is an acute shortage of herbal drugs for cancer, diabetes, cardiovascular diseases etc.

Anticancer drugs obtained from *Catharanthus roseus* and *Nothopodytes nemonum* are highly priced in the international market. *Digitalis purpurea* which yields digitoxin is also in great demand for the management of cardiovascular diseases. Quinine - the age old drug obtained from the bark, stems and roots of *Cinchona* is used to treat malaria.

Hirda, *Beheda* and *Amla* are used to make Triphala churna, which has great industrial importance. It is not only a powerful laxative; it is also used to treat cardiovascular diseases and helps to rejuvenate and detoxify the liver and blood.

Amla (*Phyllanthus emblica*) fruits are processed to obtain more than a dozen of products such as jams, candy, amla tea, amla supari, etc. At present, amla is in great demand as it has many health benefits. *Adhatoda vasica, Aloe vera, Comifera mukul (Gogool), Rauwolfia serpentina, Dioscorea* and many other plants are used in pharmaceutical industry to produce useful drugs. Aloe gel, juice, powder,is an important raw material for the production of medicines, nutraceuticals and cosmetic products.

1.2.5 Timber Industry

The wood used in building, construction etc. is called as timber.

Timber has been a valuable forest resource from ages. The complete timber industry depends on the following resources:

(i) *Tectona grandis* (Teak wood): It yields the best quality timber which is highly valued throughout the world. Teak wood is the best quality wood for furniture, building, construction, etc. as it is durable and resistant to fungi.

(ii) *Dalbergia sissoo* (Sisam wood): After teak, it is the second most important timber yielding tree. Sisam wood is used for furniture. *Cedrus deodara* (Deodar) the coniferous wood, is light, durable and an important resource for the timber industry. It is in great demand as building material. *Melia azadirachta* (Neem), *Shorea robusta, Adnia cordifolia* also play a significant role in the timber industry. *Melina* timber is an alternative for costly teak wood

1.2.6 Dye Industry

Plant dyes and colours are widely used in the textile industry, food industry etc. because these natural colours are hygienic and non hazardous as compared to synthetic colours and dyes. Herbal dyes, paints, colours are eco friendly, biodegradable and non polluting, hence production of herbal dyes is fast expanding. Plant dyes and colours are environmentally safe and consumer acceptance for them is increasing.

The important resources for plant dyes are

Bixa orellana : Fruits are used to produce orange red dye.

Butea monosperma: It is a source of natural colour as the coloured flowers are used for dying clothes.

Saffron is very often used to add colour and flavour to food products.

Dyes are also derived from lichens and beet roots. Passion fruits as well as the fruits of tomato, yield various colours and pigments like xanthophylls, lycopenes etc. Leaves, woods, barks, seeds of various plants are resources of dyeing industry e.g. Turmeric (halad), *Indigofera* (Neel). *Mallotus philippensis* (kunku) is a source of red colour dye obtained from seeds.

1.2.7 Gum Industry

The mucilaginous, water soluble material obtained from *Acacia* tree is called as gum. *Acacia* sp, Cherry, Peach etc. are the important resources for the gum industry. Gum arabic, is a made of sap taken from two species of the Acacia tree; Senegalia senegal and Vachellia seyal. It is a key ingredient in lithography and is used in paint production, glue, cosmetics, printing and in textile industries. Guar gum, obtained from Guar seeds is commercial important as it has applications in textile, paper, cosmetics and pharmaceutical industry. *Commiphera mukul* is the source of guggul gum-an ayurvedic medicine used to treat disorders of lipid metabolism and to lower weight.

1.2.8 Tannin Industry

In tannery industry, the skin of animals, is treated to convert it into leather. Hides are immersed for several weeks in increasing concentrations of tannin. Tannins bind to the proteins in the hide which makes them less water-soluble, and more resistant to bacterial attack. Tannins occur naturally in the bark and leaves of many plants. The primary barks of chestnut, oak, hemlock, mangroves, wattle and myrobalan are used for the tanning process. Vegetable tanned hide is flexible and is used for luggage and furniture eg. *Acacia* species.

Points to Remember

- The practical and commercial application of botany in our day-to-day life for our well being and welfare is known as industrial botany.
- Food and fodder industry, textile and timber industry, pharmaceuticals, dyes, gum as well as tannin industries depend on botanical resources. There is high potential for industrial botany as India is blessed with the rich phytodiversity.
- When the demand for a particular product or byproduct increases in the market on the basis of consumer acceptance, the producers set up its multiple units at national, and international levels.
- Main resources of food industry are rice (*Oryza sativa*), wheat (*Triticum sp*) *Sorghum sps*, millets like bajara, pulses like *Cicer sp, Cajanus sp*, green gram, black gram etc.
- Fruits and vegetables also contribute on a large scale to food industry.
- Spices and condiments are gradually becoming a part of the food industry.
- In textile industry, cotton, jute and sisal fibre as well as coconut fibre (coir) are the main contributors.
- Fodder industry depends on several fodder crops, grasses etc. e.g *Berseem*, elephant grass, lucerne grass.
- India is one of the leaders in pharmaceutical industries as the country is gifted by rich biodiversity of medicinal plants.
- Herbal drugs are being used to treat cancer, AIDS, cardiovascular disease, diabetes, blood pressure, hyper tension. These drugs have a holistic approach and do not have any side effects.
- In India, forest industries are equally important as they produce and process different products such as timber, dyes, gums and resins, tannins, etc.
- To enjoy and exploit the benefits of industrial botany it is necessary for everyone to conserve phytodiversity as it is the future goldmine.

Exercises

Short Answer Questions

1. Explain what is industrial botany and give any two major plant resources of food, fodder and timber industry.

2. Enlist the botanical resources of following industries - dyes, gums and tannins.
3. Write short notes on plant resources and industries.
4. Describe briefly the resources of food industry.
5. Explain the resources used in fodder industry.

Long Answer Questions

1. Give a brief account of timber and tannin industry.
2. What are dyes? Enlist its major resources.
3. Give the resources of gums and fibre industry.
4. Justify: "To see the glorious progress of industrial botany conservation of biodiversity is a must".

Chapter 2...
Floriculture Industry

Contents ...
2.1 Introduction to Floriculture
2.2 Important Floricultural Crops
2.3 Open Cultivation Practices, Harvesting and Marketing of Tuberose
2.4 Greenhouse Technology, Concepts, Advantages and Limitations
2.5 Cultivation Practices, Harvesting and Marketing of Rose
2.6 Cultivation Practices, Harvesting and Marketing of *Gerbera*
   Points to Remember
   Exercises

2.1 Introduction to Floriculture

Flowers are nature's most beautiful creation. Flowers come in a variety of shapes, sizes and colours and many of them are endowed with sweet and appealing fragrance.

Cultivation of commercially important cut flower producing plants and ornamental plants as well as marketing of cut flowers, live plants, their economic products like essential oils, medicines and preserves is known as **Floriculture.**

Floriculture is an aesthetic branch of horticulture. Earlier, in our country, floriculture was considered only as a gardening activity related to growing of flowers, but now a days, it includes production, marketing and processing of the floral products also.

Due to increasing standard of living, aesthetic sense and awareness about flowers, and use of decorative, ornamental plants, there is a great demand for high quality bloom, seeds and hybrids. Cultivation of fragrant flowers like rose, tuberose, jasmine etc. for extraction of essential oils is a profitable business due to increasing demand in cosmetic and soap industries for the same. Bonsai i.e. mini plants have great importance in landscaping of homes, restaurant, hotels, etc.

In India, flowers and gardens have been associated with our life and culture from ancient times. But with changing life styles and increasing urbanisation, floriculture has assumed a commercial status during the current century. With the declaration by the Planning Commission that floriculture is 'an extreme focus segment'; the floriculture industry in India has got a tremendous boost. Floriculture in India now includes all the activities related to the production and use of flowers, ornamental plants, seeds and bulbs etc. The growth of floriculture is reflected in the number of commercial units being set-up for domestic as well as export markets and in the mushrooming of flower shops all over the country. The business of cut flowers is the most popular segment of floricultural trade in India. A number of exotic flowers now being grown in India meet the high quality standards as required by the international markets.

The following conditions in India favour the growth of floriculture industry.

- We have diverse agro-climatic and geographical conditions so that many of the modern flowers can be grown round the year in one or other part of the country. A variety of potted plants, ornamental nursery plants, bulbs, can be grown in different locations of India without involving expensive devices and methods.
- Geographic location of our country is also quite central in terms of logistics. India can access the highly developed European markets and has an excellent reach over Middle East and Far East markets.
- Skilled and low cost man power favours flower cultivation.

Due to the above advantages, the floriculture industry has been considered by Government of India as a top priority area for export. Floriculture offers good career opportunities for a young graduate.

If floriculture is developed scientifically on an industrial basis, it will be a great source of money and employment.

2.2 Important Floricultural Crops

The important floricultural crops are the flowering plants producing commercially important flowers and decorative, attractive and colourful foliage. The product obtained from such crops is commonly known as cut flowers. Cut flowers are classified according to the plant part used. The main three classes of the cut flowers are as mentioned below

- **Single flower/flower bud as a cut flower:** Ex. Rose, Carnation, Tulip, Lotus etc.
- **An inflorescence as a cut flower:** In this case, entire inflorescence appears as a single flower. In the capitulum and head inflorescence, ray florets are more attractive due to their bright colour. In such an inflorescence, the disc florets as well as the ray florets open centripetally, therefore these cut flowers have longer vase life. E.g. *Aster, Zinna, Gerbera, Dahlia*, Marigold, Sunflower, etc.
- **Flowering shoot as a cut flower:** In this case, the inflorescence is a raceme, spike, umbel or panicle type with many flower buds as well as mature flowers arranged on a flowering shoot. Ex. *Gladiolus, Delphinium,* orchid flower, Golden rod, Blue daisy, *Chrysanthemum*, etc.

In addition to the cut flowers, foliage of the plants is also in great demand.

In this case, colourful and attractive foliage of various sizes, shapes and colour is used. Ex. Ferns, Palms, *Asparagus, Cycas, Thuja, Croton*, etc.

The cut flowers constitute 45% share of the world trade in floricultural products. The flowers which are more important in cut flower trade are Rose, Carnation, *Gladiolus, Chrysanthemum*, Orchids and *Anthurium*. In India, most of these flowers are grown in the open during the winter season and throughout the year in the greenhouses. Major states in which floricultural crops are cultivated are Andhra Pradesh, Gujarat, Haryana, Karnataka, Rajasthan, Himachal Pradesh, Punjab, Tamil Nadu, Uttar Pradesh and West Bengal. Recently, in the states of Maharashtra and Kashmir, floriculture is being increasingly practiced. The important floricultural crops grown in India are as mentioned below:

- Roses: Delhi, Pune, Bangalore and Chandigarh.
- *Gladiolus*: Pune, Srinagar, Nainital and Bangalore.
- Tuberose and Jasmine: Pune, Bangalore, Coimbatore, Madurai, and Chennai.
- Marigold: Delhi, Pune, Satara and some cities in the northern plains.

The cut flowers like rose, carnation, *Gladiolus* and tuberose are preferred for bouquets and flower arrangements. Flowers like marigold, *Chrysanthemum*, loose flowers of tuberose are used for floral decoration, social functions, making garlands and for religious offerings. The flowers like jasmine, *Chrysanthemum*, tuberose, *Crossandra* and *Barleria* are used by ladies for adoring in their hair mainly in South India.

List of Floricultural Plants

1.	Rose	14.	Marigold
2.	Orchids	15.	*lilium*
3.	*Gladiolus*	16.	*Gerbera*
4.	Carnation	17.	Tuberose
5.	*Chrysanthemum*	18.	*Zinnia*
6.	Jasmine	19.	Statice
7.	*Amaryllis*	20.	*Gaillardia*
8.	*Anthurium*	21.	*Gomphrena*
9.	Day-lily	22.	*Crossandra*
10.	Bird of paradise	23.	Corn flower
11.	*Antirrhinum*	24.	Sweet sultan
12.	China-aster	25.	Golden rod
13.	Stock		

2.3 Cultivation Practices, Harvesting and Marketing of Tuberose

    Botanical Name. - *Polyanthes tuberosa Linn.*
    Common Name - Tuberose, gulcheri, gulshabbo, Rajanigandha, Nishigandh
    Family - Amaryllidaceae / Agavaceae

2.3.1 Introduction

Tuberose occupies a very special position among the ornamental bulbous plants due to its beautiful flowers and sweet fragrance. It is native to Mexico in Central America. It is one of the most important commercial flower producing crop. It bears waxy white and fragrant flowers in pairs on a long spike. Flowers can be used as cut flowers, loose flowers and for extraction of essential oils. It has a strong fragrance and prolonged vase life or keeping quality. During the 16th century it spread to the different parts of the world. The *tuberose* plant has a tuberous hyacinth, which are quite different from the bulbous hyacinth due to which it is named as **Tuberose**.

During the 16th century this plant was referred to as hyacinths. In the middle of the 18th century the **Tuberose** was still referred to as **Hyacinths indicus tuberosus**. The Indian tuberose with a double flower, is commonly called the double tuberose. In India, tuberose is known as 'raat ki rani', 'mistress of the night'. Tuberose is pollinated by nocturnal moths. Like jasmine, tuberose continues to produce its scent even after the flower is picked. In 1753, this plant was classified by **Linneaus** on the basis of structure of the flowering parts and he named this plant as Polianthes. Later on, species Plantarum grouped hyacinths indicus tuberosus under the genus *Polianthes* and the species *tuberosa*.

Towards the end of the 16th century, this flower was introduced in Europe. Tuberose is cultivated in countries like France, Italy, South Africa, USA, India and in many tropical and subtropical areas of the world. In Morocco, acres of land are used for the cultivation of the Tuberose. In southern France, commercial production from bulbs begins when the winter is mild so that they can be stored without the fear of freezing. Countries like Belgium, France and United Kingdom are the major importers of Tuberose cut flowers.

In India, the commercial cultivation is restricted mainly to West Bengal, Karnataka, Tamil Nadu and Maharashtra.

2.3.2 Morphology

It is a perennial dwarf herb exceeding 15–20 cm in height. It is partially hard, bulb producing and sprout through the bulblets. Bulbs consist of scales and leaf bases. The flowering spike arises from the centre of the cluster of leaves. Stem arises from a tuberose rhizome and is covered with narrow basal leaves. It is a condensed form of stem, which remains within scales. It produces shallow, adventitious roots. Leaves are long, narrow, linear, grass like, light green and arise in a rosette or are crowded in an arching form. It bears funnel shaped, waxy white, fragrant flowers in pairs on tall and straight spikes. The terminal flower spike that arises from the bulb produces flowers for many days. Stamens are six in number and are sterile. Stigma is trilobed. Style is slender and united with perianth epiphyllus. Inferior ovary produces many ovules. Fruit is capsule type. Perianth are six in number and arranged in two whorls (3 + 3) and united to form a tube bent in the middle. Perianths are white, fleshy, waxy and aromatic. Number of perianths may be more in some hybrid varieties and tissue cultured plants.

2.3.3 Species

Polianthes tuberosa is monotypic genus. The genus consists about a dozen of species. All species were found growing wild with the exception of **P. tuberosa** which is cultivated. On The floret arrangement in tuberose varieties are classified into two types : (1) Single petalled (2) Double petalled.

Single petalled varieties have only one row of petals e.g. Mexican single, Hyderabad single, Calcutta single, Shringar and Prajwal. Double petalled varieties have more than three rows of petals e.g. Pear double, Hyderabad double, Calcutta double, Suvasini and Vaibhav.

NBRI, Lucknow has released two cultivars i.e. Rajat Rekha and Svarna Rekha. Rajat Rekha produces single type of florets with silvery white streaks along the middle of the leaves. Svarna Rekha bears double type of florets and has golden yellow streaks along the margins of the leaves.

2.3.4 Cultivars

1. **Single:** Flower is pure white and has only a single row of corolla segments. Cultivars are Sringar, Calcutta Single, Mexican Single and Suvarna Rekha.
2. **Double:** Flowers are white tinged and pinkish red. Petals are in several whorls. Cultivars are Suvasini, Calcutta Double and Pearl.
3. **Semi Double:** These are similar to Double but with only two to three rows of corolla segments.
4. **Variegated:** This has variegated leaves with yellow margin.
a) **Suvasini:** This was produced by crossing a Mexican single with a pearl double during 1993-97. It flowers in 115 days from the plantation date. The height of its spike measures upto 95cm and there are 59 flowers per spike having a diameter of 49 cm. In vase, they remain fresh for 8 days. This tuberose hybrid is multi-whorled with fragrant, bold, large and pure white florets on long spikes in contrast to dull-white florets of traditional double cultivars. In normal double cultivars, florets open incompletely whereas in these

cultivar florets open regularly and uniformly i.e. number of spikes per bulbs are about 85000 kg. The cut flowers of tuberose are more preferred by consumers.

b) **Prajwal:** This new hybrid bears single type of flowers on tall stiff spikes. The flower buds are slightly pinkish in colour while the flowers are white. The individual flowers are larger in size compared to local variety. It yields 20 % more loose flowers than Shringar.

c) **Vaibhav:** This new hybrid bears double flowers on medium spikes. The flower buds are greenish in colour in contrast to pinkish buds in Suvasini and local double. Flowers have white spikes and yield is 50 % higher as compared to Suvasini.

d) **Shringar:** This was produced by crossing between Mexican single and Double pearl and released during 1993 - 97. It bears flower in 100 days from the date of plantation. Spike height is 72 cm. Number of flowers per spike are 59. Its diameter is 4.3cm and has upto 8 days vase life. Shringar hybrid variety bears single type of fragrant florets on strong spikes of medium height. Flowers are slightly pinkish at maturity instead of the greenish white colour in normal single cultivars. It gives 40% higher flower yield over normal. Flowers are used for different purposes like cut flower, loose flowers, extraction of essential oil, pot flowers, tuberose concentrate, garlands and landscaping. It is resistant to root knot nematodes. For cut flower purposes both single and double petalled types are preferred. For loose flowers only single petalled varieties should be grown.

2.3.5 Open Cultivation Practices

A) Soil

The Tuberose can be cultivated in various types of soils but can be grown best in a light sandy loam or a clay loam soil. Alkaline and salty soil which are almost unproductive for other crops can be undertaken for the cultivation of Tuberose. Porous loam soil and sandy loam soils with good aeration and well drained soils are most preferred for flower cultivation. Crop requires sufficient moisture level in the soil. The soil should be rich in organic matter. Light red soil also can enhance the growth of Tuberose. The soil pH of 6.5 - 7.5 is favourable for the luxuriant growth of crop. For pot cultivation, a mixture of garden soil, farm yard manure and leaf mould can be used in the proportion of 2:1:1. With good agronomical practices the plant can be grown successfully as a commercial crop in highly saline and alkaline soils. Water logged soil can damage the root system and affect the growth, development and flowering. Before one month of planting, well rotten cow dung or farm yard manure should be incorporated with the soil.

B) Climate

Tuberose can be grown luxuriantly under various environmental conditions ranging from tropical to sub-tropical and temperate climate. Temperatures above 40^0C affect spike length and quality of flower. Even low temperature and frost damage the plants and flowers. Warm, humid areas with average temperatures ranging from 20 - 35^{0}C and relatively high humidity ranging from 68 - 86 % are most suitable for the commercial cultivation of crop. Temperature plays an important role in growth, bud initiation and subsequently flower development. Higher temperatures i.e. above 40^{0}C and low temperatures i.e. below 10^{0}C causes reduction in spike length and weight and also affects the quality of Tuberose flowers. Flowers show poor growth in shady places. Flower bud differentiation and its development occurs best at a temperature of 19.3^{0}C. The temperature range of 20 - 30^{0}C is optimum for its proper growth and development.

The bulbs remain dormant during winter season when the temperature is low. In a strict sense, Tuberose is not photosensitive crop. When it is exposed to a long day photoperiod, it`s vegetative growth is enhanced and early emergence of first flower spike is also observed. It also helps to increase in the length of flower spike and flowering. Increase in the light intensity promotes increase in leaf length and production of quality blooms as well. Low light intensity shows adverse effects on flowering. Winter growing crop requires additional supply of light for better growth and blooming.

C) Planting

Commercially, **Tuberose** is vegetatively propagated by means of bulbs and bulblets.

Well–drained soil is optimum. If soil contains undecomposed organic matter it affects bulb production. It also reduces the yield and quality of flowers. The size of bulb decides the growth and flowering of **Tuberose**. The large bulbs enhance early flowering and give higher yield of spikes and flowers. The bulb size decides the number of flowers per spike, flower quality, daughter bulb production, etc. Bulbs having diameter of 2.0 to 3.0 cm are suitable for planting. Weight and size of the bulb determines vegetative growth, flowering and bulb production. Planting bulbs which are of 3.0 to 3.5 cm in diameter increases the yield and quality of flower spike and increases the production of bulbs and bulblets. Depth of planting varies with the size of bulbs, texture of soil as well as the growing region. Generally bigger bulbs are planted at greater depth. Planting of bulbs at the depth of 6.0 cm in sandy loam soil is recommended. Deep planting delays sprouting and reduces bulb production. Planting of bulbs is preferred during July – August. Generally, in the plains planting is undertaken in the month of Feb – March where as in the hilly region, April – May is suitable. Sequential planting provides the flower almost throughout the year.

Distance between plants decides the yield, quality of flowers, quality and quantity of bulbs. Planting distance also varies with various soil types and climatic conditions where plantation is to be carried. Generally plant spacing of 20 to 30 cm between the rows and 10 to 20 cm between bulbs can be maintained. Normally 100,000 to 250,000 bulbs are required for planting in one hectare of land. Close spacing gives maximum yield of flower per unit area.

If plantation of bulb is done at intervals of 10 to 15 days regular supply of flowers can be obtained. On the onset of spring, the plants resume their normal growth and bloom as usual. The type of cultivars, size of bulbs, time of planting, density of planting, nature of crop and other agricultural practices influence the yield of **Tuberose**. Usually 2.0 to 4.0 lakh spikes /ha or 10 to 15 tones loose flowers /ha can be obtained whereas 20-30 tones of bulbs and bulblets /ha can be obtained.

Digging of bulbs: Tuberose bulbs tend to increase in number and size with growth of the plant. It needs a minimum of 7-8 months for proper maturation. To facilitate easier digging, irrigation is withheld a few days prior to uprooting of bulbs. The entire clump is dug out with spade /pickaxe without damaging the bulbs and bulblets. The leaves are clipped, adhered soil is removed and bulbs and bulblets are separated out from the clump. Bulbs are stored under cool, dry and shady conditions. Before they are taken out for planting, storage of bulbs for 3-6 months is essential.

D) Propagation

It is mainly propagated sexually by seeds and vegetatively or asexually by means of bulbs and bulblets. To avoid viral contamination and for rapid multiplication, propagation is done through tissue culture technique or micro propagation.

1) Seeds: Seeds are difficult to germinate. Seeds can be sown at a depth of 1.5cm in well prepared land. Soil mixture containing leaf mould, garden soil and sand in equal proportions is prepared in nursery bed or seed pan. After sowing, the seeds germinate within two to three weeks under conditions of favourable soil temperature (26^0C) and moisture. Sufficiently grown seedlings are transferred to the desired site.

2) Propagation by bulbs: Commercially, this is the most common and preferred method for the multiplication of Tuberose. Bulbs having diameter of 2.0 cm or above should be selected for propagation. The bulbs must be free from diseases. Usually, conical spindle shaped or boat shaped bulbs are used for propagation. To get maximum production of bulbs, the bulbs must be are planted early. Nearly, about 1.25 to 1.50 lakh bulbs (800 to 900 kg) are required for planting in 1 hectare field.

3) By division: Tuberose can also be propagated using bulb segments. The success of propagation depends on the size of the bulbs. It was noted that only the segments from large bulbs having diameter of 2.0 cm are useful. The bulbs are cut into 2-3 vertical sections- each of them having a bud and a part of the basal plate. After treatment with fungicide, the sections are planted vertically in a rooting medium. For rooting, the bulbs should be maintained at a moderately warm temperature. From the basal plate, new bulblets along with the roots are transferred immediately to the ground or somewhere else where cultivation is to be done.

E) Fertigation

Fertiliser requirement for **Tuberose** varies with climatic conditions and soil types.

Leaf mould, farm yard manure or cattle manure applied at the rate of 20 to 50 cartload per acre during soil preparation enhances growth and flowering.

Generally, fertiliser mixture of NPK at 200:50:70 is recommended. Superphosphate at 60 g/m^2 is useful to increase the number of flowers per inflorescence and the life of flowers. Foliar application of NPK, urea, and orthophosphoric acid and potassium citrate in 0.1% solution at 15 days interval reported effective growth, flowering and bulbs production. Apart from FYM, 100 to 250 kg - N, 100 to 150 kg- P, 202 kg and 75-100 kg - k_2O / ha can be added to get increased yield of flowers.

Fertiliser application with excessive nitrogen causes the flower spike to grow tall and soft making them vulnerable to breakage due to wind. Such plants are susceptible to diseases and pests attack. Nitrogen deficiency leads into reduction in number of spikes and number of flowers per spike and foliage becomes pale green. The deficiency of calcium causes cracking of the spike where as Mg deficiency causes interveinal chlorosis of older leaves. Iron deficiency causes internal chlorosis of new leaves. Cracking of leaf margins, deformed leaves and stunted inflorescence is caused by the deficiency of boron.

F) Irrigation

It is better to irrigate the field before and after planting of bulbs. Irrigation could be avoided until the bulbs have sufficiently sprouted. Since underground bulbs have sufficient stored food material for the initial growth of root and leaves, watering of bulbs before sprouting and rooting causes injury. Two months after sprouting of bulbs, the field should be irrigated at an interval of seven days. In order to obtain high yield of flowers, frequency of irrigation should be increased. Excess moisture while sprouting results in rotting of bulbs and also adversely affects the development of spikes and florets. The frequency of irrigation depends upon soil type, stage of growth and pre-existing climatic conditions. During summer, the crop should be irrigated at an interval of 5-7 days and in winter at an interval of 10 – 12 days

Drip irrigation gives the best yield i.e. 30-32 bulbs. Mulching with black polythene reduces the water requirement by preventing evaporation from soil surface.

2.3.6 Harvesting

After 3 months of planting, Tuberose bears flowers. Spikes are mature and ready for harvesting when lower 1 to 2 pairs of florets open. The whole spike is cut from the plant for cut flower purpose, whereas individual florets are cut at full maturity for use as loose flowers and essential oil extraction. On an average, 15 to 25 tonnes per hectare of loose flowers and

2 lakhs to 6 lakhs per hectare of flowering spikes can be obtained. It provides an additional income of 25 to 30 tonnes per hectare in the form of bulbs and bulblets.

For table decoration, Tuberose is harvested by cutting the spikes from the base. Flower spike should be cut when the first pair of flower is fully open. For making garlands and for floral arrangement, individual flowers are picked from the spike. Cool hours of the day either in the morning or evening is suitable for picking of flowers. The flower spikes are cut with a sharp knife and immediately placed in water. The small leaves on the flower stalk prolong the life of the flowers. The flower spike should be harvested at a length of 75 cm and with creamy white bud or one open floret stage for prolonged shelf life. For long distance transport, spikes with green bud or greenish white bud should be harvested. At least 25,000 spikes per hectare can be harvested if proper care is taken.

After the harvest of the main crop, the flower stalks are headed back and the pot is measured and irrigated. 3 to 4 Ratoon crops can be taken from a single planting. If the bulbs are not uprooted and replanted after 3 to 4 Ratoons, the spikes tend to become smaller and unattractive.

After ratooning the average yield of flower is as follows:

Plant crop - 5 to 10 t/h

First ratoon - 9 to 12 t/h

Second ratoon - 4 to 6 t/h

2.3.7 Marketing

After harvesting, spikes of the Tuberose are subjected to the following processes for the purpose of marketing:

1. Grading

Generally straight and strong stems with uniform length and uniform stage of development are preferred. Flowers should be free from diseases, pests and injury. Flowers are graded into different grades on the basis of length of spike, length of their flowering portion (rachis), number of flowers per spike, weight of spike and quality of individual flowers. Spikes are arranged in round bundles, each bundle having 50 to 100 spikes. A wet newspaper is wrapped on the stem portion of the bundle. To avoid damage to the flowers, spike bundles are wrapped with soft tissue paper or polythene film. Such bundles may be packed in the cardboard boxes and transported to the desirable place. Spikes are sold on number or dozen basis.

With plant growth, bulbs increase in their number and size. It is very essential to dig out bulbs from soil at the proper stage of maturity. Clumps are dug out with a spade. Soil is removed and bulbs are separated from the clumps. Bulbs are graded into different grades according to their size (diameter). Bulbs attain their maximum maturity when flowering is over and plant growth has stopped. Drying of old leaves is also an indication of bulb maturity. A few days prior to uprooting, irrigation must be avoided. Bulbs are stored separately in a cool and shady place. During storage, bulbs should be checked every 8-10 days to avoid the spread of mould and rot.

2. Packaging

Loose flowers are packed in bamboo baskets holding about 10–15 kg flowers and are transported to the nearby wholesale market where they are sold by weight. The flower spikes are graded according to the length of the spike, length of the flowering zone and quality of individual flowers and then bunched in round bundles each having about 100 sticks. Packaging of loose flower in 300 guage thick polythene film bags with no ventilation was found effective in maintaining greater freshness. It retained actual colour for longer duration, reduced water loss and extended shelf life to 4-6 days as compared to 1-3 days in case of flowers that are not packed as described above.

3. Vase Life

The optimum storage temperature for double and single spikes is 7^0C and can be stored for 5 to7 days. Vase life of spikes can be increased by 6 to 8 days by keeping them in 2 % sucrose and 200 ppm aluminum sulphate solution. Ascorbic acid and sucrose in appropriate proportion was found useful in maintaining freshness for a longer period of time. 4% sucrose + 200 ppm 8-HQC is very effective to increase post harvest life. Even 4% sucrose and 20 ppm BA improve vase life. To avoid floret abscission, to promote floret opening and to increase vase life 8 % sucrose + Pulsing of spikes with 4 % glucose solution at 10 ^0C for four hours is helpful in prolonging their vase life.

4. The varieties of the Tuberose that are utilised for various purposes are Arati, Apsara, Poonam, Sapna, Sagar, Shakti, Shobha, Nazrana, Meera, Dhiraj, Tilak and Kumkum.

5. Economic Importance

Now a days, Tuberose is grown in gardens for decoration in pots, beds and borders. It is commercially important due to its different uses. It is highly popular because of its sweet fragrant flowers, longer vase life, ability to withstand longer transportation, easy cultivation, low production cost and high profit, easy availablility of planting material at reasonable price and comparatively less infestation by pests and diseases. Flowers are used for garlands, floral ornaments, bouquets, button holes and in bridal make-up. The long flower spikes are excellent as cut flowers for table decoration. Apart from domestic use, Tuberose can earn the country valuable foreign exchange as an export product. **Tuberose** cultivation contributes towards development of wastelands, which have high salt and alkali content.

The flowers are source of Tuberose oil. It is one of the most valuable and expensive raw material used in the perfumes. Oil is a source of geraniol, benzyl alcohol, methyl benzoate, methyl salysilate, eugenol, benzyl benzoate, methyl anthranilate and aromatic sources. The fragrance of flowers is added to beverages prepared from chocolate and also to stimulants and sedatives. Alkaloid lycorine present in the bulbs, causes vomiting. Hecogenin and tigogenin are steroid saponins isolated from the bulbs. Leaves, flowers, bulbs and roots contain sterol, carbohydrates and traces of alkaloids. Enzyme tran fructosidase is also isolated from bulbs. The bulbs are reported as dry, hot, diuretic and emetic. Flowers are used for antiseptic purpose. Along with turmeric and butter, bulbs are applied as a paste over red rash of infants. The bulbs are also rubbed into a paste with juice of **Cynodon dactylon** and applied to babies. Dried tuberose bulbs in the powdered form are used as a remedy for gonorrhoea. Moreover, Tuberose also possesses powerful healing properties - antispasmodic and anti-inflammatary properties. In Ayurvedic, it is also known to stimulate serenity, creativity and psychic powers.

In Java, flowers are used in vegetable soup. In some cases, tuberose oil is used in flavouring candy, beverages and in baked foods items, in various concentrations such as in non-alcoholic beverages- 0.26 ppm, in ice creams - 0.16 ppm, in ice candy- 1.5 ppm and in baked food- 1.7 ppm.

2.4 Green House Technology – Concepts, Advantages & Limitations

Introduction

Flowers are inseparable from the fabric of human life and they are used for all occasions such as festivals, rituals, pooja, house decorations, birthdays, marriages receptions, etc. Green house technology is a fast growing and highly competitive industry. India has the maximum area under ornamental crops (88,600 ha) followed by China (59,527 ha), Indonesia (34,000 ha), Japan (21,218 ha), USA (16,400 ha). Globally, more than 145 countries are involved in cultivation of ornamental crops and the area is steadily increasing. The world demand for cut flowers is increasing by 10 – 15 % per annum.

Indian Scenario

India is bestowed with diverse agro-climatic and ecological conditions which are favourable for the cultivation of all types of commercially important flowers generally found in different parts of the world. It also enjoys the best climate in selected pockets for floriculture during winter months. India is in an enviable position to become a leader in the world floricultural trade because of the prevailing congenial location, overall favourable climate of economic liberalisation and globalisation and also specific incentives by the government and floricultural development.

Flowers are grown under open cultivation and also under protected cultivation. In polyhouses, roses are mainly grown for export. Other exotic flowers like carnations, *Gerbera*, orchids, *Lilium* and other bulbous flowers are now increasingly produced commercially both for export and domestic market. There are more than 300 export oriented units in India. More than 50% of the floriculture units are based in south zone mainly in Karnataka, Andhra Pradesh and Tamil Nadu. The main importing countries of Indian floricultural products in order are the Netherlands, USA, Japan, Germany, Italy, Denmark, Egypt, Singapore, Switzerland, France, Australia, UAE, Belgium and Sri Lanka. During the year 1999-2000, Indian floricultural products were exported to 75 different countries.

An agricultural country like India has a variety of problems in agriculture itself. In spite of the fact that 80% of the population depends on agriculture, our farmers cannot produce sufficient food grains, oil seeds, pulses, vegetables, fruits, etc. Agro industry is the largest industry in India, but still its production is not satisfactory. Majority of the farmers are below the poverty line. The agricultural production cannot match the needs of the growing population. Environmental degradation, global warming, drastic changes in climate, desertification of soil, depletion of ground water, shortage of rainfall, urbanisation, pollution, etc. have created many problems for agricultural in India. To overcome all such problems we have to use modern technology in agriculture like the polyhouse/green house technology.

Due to the recent policy adopted by the State and Central governments, now-a-days farming methods are rapidly changing in India. Farmers are using various advanced techniques such as plant tissue culture technology, greenhouse technology, etc. As India has a great variety of climate and agricultural practices, diverse agro climatic conditions and three main seasons, it is necessary to use greenhouse technology to cultivate certain commercial crops throughout the year. This high-tech cultivation practices include the use of polyhouse, glasshouse (greenhouse) and shading nets. Greenhouse cultivation or plasticulture is becoming very popular in farmers engaged in horticulture business or the farmers cultivating cut flowers like **Roses**, *Gerbera*, **Carnations**, *Anthurium* for export and some exotic vegetables. Raising of seedlings and plant propagation are important commercial aspects of greenhouse technology. Greenhouse cultivation of crops meets the criteria set for the search of alternate technologies for commercial production of food in India. The use of such advanced technologies will help to achieve a breakthrough in yield potentials and productivities of crops.

2.4.1 Concept and Definition

A greenhouse means an area or a house in which plants are grown under artificially controlled climatic conditions, so that light, temperature and humidity are maintained at required level. Effect of this specific microclimate on the growth and productivity of crop is commonly known as effect of greenhouse.

A Greenhouse is a framed structure covered with transparent or translucent material in which crops can be grown under the conditions of partial or fully controlled environment and which are large enough to allow a person to walk within them and carry out agricultural operations.

"A technique of cultivation of plants of commercial value in a polyhouse is known as **plasticulture**". This protected cultivation of plants is also referred to as **greenhouse cultivation**.

Polyhouses are based on the greenhouse concept to let in heat and light, while preventing the heat from getting out. But instead of the glass on a greenhouse roof, polyhouses are made of cheaper polythene or plastic. By reducing evaporation, they also allow farmers to use sprinkler and drip irrigation systems, thus saving water.

Protected cultivation practices can be defined as a cropping technique wherein the micro climate surrounding the plant body is controlled partially/ fully as per the requirement of the plant species grown during their period of growth. With the advancement in agriculture, various types of protected cultivation practices suitable for a specific type of agro-climatic zone have emerged. Among these protective cultivation practices, Green house/poly house cum rain shelter is useful for the hill zones.

2.4.2 Principles Involved in Green House Technology

The green house is generally covered by transparent or translucent material such as glass or plastic. The green house covered with simple plastic sheet is termed as a poly house. The green house generally reflects back 43% of the net solar radiation incident upon it allowing the transmittance of the "photosynthetically active solar radiation" in the range of 400-700 nm wave length.

The sunlight admitted to the green house is absorbed by the crops, floor, and other objects. These objects in turn emit long wave thermal radiation in the infrared region for which the glazing material has lower transparency. As a result, the solar energy remains trapped in the green house, thus raising its temperature. This phenomenon is called the "Green house Effect". This condition of natural rise in green house air temperature is utilised in the cold regions to grow crops successfully. However, in the summer season, due to the above stated phenomenon ventilation and cooling is required to maintain the temperature inside the structure well below 35^0C. The ventilation system can be natural or a forced one.

In the forced system, fans are used which draw out 7-9m^3 of air / sec / unit of power consumed.

However, in cold regions, natural ventilation is sufficient to maintain the desired temperature in the poly house. This can be achieved using the agro-shade net or by providing doors (on opposite sides) in order to facilitate cross ventilation.

2.4.3 Advantages/Benefits of Greenhouse Technology

1. Greenhouse causes greenhouse effect on the plants that increases the rate of photosynthesis by increasing CO_2 concentration around the plant. CO_2 concentration in the atmosphere is 300 ppm while in greenhouse it is up to 1500 ppm. So plants show vigorous growth and productivity of the plant increases 3 to 4 times and the crop yields are at the maximum level per unit area, per unit volume and per unit input basis
2. Maximum production can be obtained in a small area.
3. Agricultural products can be made available during the off season. This may fetch a high price in the market.
4. The control of microorganisms allows the production of higher quality products which are free from insect attack, pathogens and chemical residue. In greenhouse, the plants are protected from attack of pests and other pathogens; hence pesticides and fungicides can be avoided. Due to this, flowers, fruits and vegetables will be free from pesticides and fungicides This will result in the production of crops of international standards which will increase their export value.
5. Greenhouse can be constructed near the city or market, so that expenses and time spent on transport of the agricultural product can be reduced. Fresh and healthy vegetables, fruits and flowers can be made easily available in the market.
6. Greenhouse cultivation helps in modernising agriculture.
7. Hardening and acclimatisation of tissue culture plants are carried out in the greenhouse.
8. Greenhouse provides totally or partially controlled climatic conditions required for potential growth of crop, which in turn results in high quality crop production.
9. In the greenhouse, microclimate around the plants can be manipulated to obtain early flowering and fruiting.
10. By using pollinating insects in the greenhouse, percentage of fruit setting can be increased.
11. Greenhouse technology is useful for cultivating plants in zones like barren and uncultivated land, wasteland, desert which are usually unsuitable for agriculture.
12. Environment control allows raising plants anywhere in the world at any time of the year i.e. crops could be grown under the inclement climatic conditions when it would not be otherwise possible to grow crops under the open field conditions.
13. Greenhouse cultivation of exportable flowers is one of the major sources of foreign exchange.
14. Greenhouse technology is a boon for nursery owners. The seedlings and saplings of various plants can be made available within the shortest possible time.

15. The transgenic or genetically modified plants require controlled environment to grow, sustain and establish. The greenhouse is the only means to provide such an environment.
16. Greenhouse has played an important role in conservation and cultivation of rare and endangered plants.
17. Greenhouse cultivation may be the right option to provide fresh vegetables, fruits and ornamentals throughout the year and even during off-season to metropolitan and other cities.
18. High value and high quality crops can be grown for export markets.
19. Income from the small and the marginal holdings maintained by the farmer can be increased by producing crops meant for the export markets.
20. It can be used to generate self employment for the educated rural youth in the agriculture sector.

2.4.4 Limitations of Greenhouse (Plasticulture) Technology

1. Initial capital investment for the erection of greenhouse (polyhouse) is very high and hence it is beyond the reach of small farmers or poor farmers.
2. It requires trained and skilled labour, as the farmer needs to know the crop cycle as well as technology of greenhouse.
3. The cost of planting material is very high as the plantlets are raised through tissue culture. Similarly, the imported seeds are used for sowing hence the initial cost is also very high as compared to open field cultivation.
4. The maintenance and day-to-day care of greenhouse is difficult task and it is very costly. It requires heavy recurring expenses.
5. The cost of cultivation is quite high and under such conditions if the market prices are low, it will cause tremendous economic loss, which will be very difficult to recover in successive years. Hence, the financial sustainability is very important factor.
6. The material produced in greenhouse is usually for export, hence well established export market or guaranteed export market is the prime need. If the produce is not exported, then such highly priced material can't be sold profitably in the local market.
7. Because of complete automation in the greenhouse, failure or shortage of electricity due to power cut (load shading) will cause the complete destruction of greenhouse plants resulting in severe loss to the growers.
8. The labour requirement per unit cultivation area in case of greenhouse is less as compared to open field cultivation.
9. For exporting flower, fruits and vegetables cooling system is required to transport the material, which is very costly. Greenhouse cultivation requires the best transport facilities linked to big cities, which is not possible at every place.

2.5 Cultivation Practices, Harvesting and Marketing of Roses

2.5.1 Introduction

Rose (*Rosa alba, R. chinensis*) belonging to family Rosaceae is the most beautiful flower and hence known as queen/king of flowers. It is the most popular, cut flower throughout the world. On some special occasions such as "Valentine's day" its demand increases greatly and it fetches a very high price. Green house cultivation of roses is a highly remunerative business.

Selection of the right variety of flowers is an important skill in commercial floriculture. The flower grower backed by strong marketing and financial assistance can get a foothold in the highly competitive international flower market only when the flowers are of high standards.

2.5.2 Selection of Rose types and Varieties

There are five main types of roses grown for cut flower production.
i) Long stemmed – Large flowers – Hybrid
ii) Medium stemmed- Intermediate – Floribunda
iii) Short stemmed – Small flowers – Sweet roses
iv) Spray roses – Spray Floribunda
v) Miniature roses – Small flowered- Sweet heart roses

Long stemmed roses: Produce shoots of 50-120 cm in length and yield 100-150 stems/year/ sq.m. These hybrid roses are difficult to handle and they have shorter vase life.

Medium stemmed roses: Produce shoots of 50-70 cm length and have big flowers. Yield upto 220 blooms/year/sq.m.

Short stemmed roses: Produce shoot length of 30-70 cm and yield 250-300 stems/sq m/year. These are easy to handle and have good vase life.

Spray roses: They produce many blooms per stem. Their yield is very low and stems are heavy, hence expensive to air lift.

Miniature roses: They have shoot length of 20-40 cm. Flowers are smaller, popular as pot roses.

- The varieties selected should be suitable for growing in a particular climatic condition and it should have excellent production quality.
- The varieties selected should be resistant to diseases and pests. A grower should select high yielding and long stemmed variety which command a high price in the domestic and international markets.

2.5.3 Climatic Requirement of Roses

Commercial life cycle (Yrs.)	Day Temp (^{0}C)	Night Temp (^{0}C)	Humidity (%)	Light intensity (Lux)	CO_2 Conc. (ppm)
6.5 – 7	24-28	18.5-20	65-70	60000-70000	800-1000

Basic climatic requirements are
1) Good light throughout the year
2) Important to maintain a balanced light/temperature ratio
3) Well aerated growing medium
4) Nutrition: Basic elements required- N, P,K, Mg, S and C
   Microelements- Fe, Zn, Mn, B, Cu and Mo

2.5.4 Cultivation

Steps in plantation of roses
- Remove pebbles from the bed before plantation.
- Adequate moisture must be available in the soil at the time of plantation.
- The seedlings should be dipped in Bavistin (0.2%) solution and then planted on bed.
- Plantation to be done by making holes or trenches on bed in a zigzag way.
- Planting should be avoided during the hottest period of the day/year and it should be done either in the morning or late in the evening.

Planting Material: Selection of high quality planting material is critical because of the high price of plants and their long productive life. There are two main types of rose plants that are widely used; the first type are the ones with their own roots and second type are ones which are budded or grafted on a root stock.

Top graft of rose

Budded plants and top grafts of rose plants should be 2 -3 months old and should be procured from authorised breeders for plantation, at least 2.5 months before date of plantation. Planting material is available in poly bags and paper plugs.

Procedure for Planting Roses

Bed Size

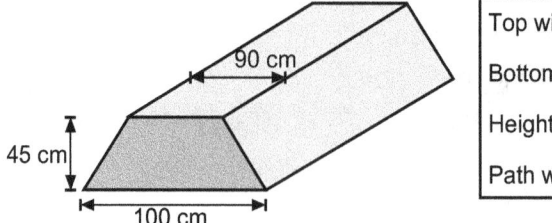

Top width - 90 cm
Bottom width - 100 cm
Height - 45 cm
Path way - 50 cm

Bed preparation for roses
Planting method

Rose plant used for plantation should be 2-3 months old and have minimum of two dark green colour leaves. Bud union of rose plant should not be covered with soil. It should be 2 – 3 cm above the ground level. The sprout coming out of the union should face towards the path at the time of plantation. Rose plants are planted in a zigzag method on the bed. The distance between two plant columns should be 17 cm and between two rows should be 45 cm.

Sr. No.	Area of poly house (m^2)	Planting density	Total plants required
1.	560	7.5 plants/ m^2	4200
2.	1008	7.5 plants/ m^2	7560

Care after plantation

After planting, the soil around the plants must be kept humid and should not be over irrigated. Irrigate the plant with hose pipe immediately after plantation. During periods with strong sunshine or high temperature, the young plants must frequently be given an over head spray with water to allow establishment and reduce post planting losses. For first three weeks, the irrigation should be done only by using hose sprayer and later on irrigation should be done by drip system. Mortality replacement should be done within the week after plantation.

Special cultural practices

For proper growth of rose plant and to ensure high production, special cultural practices are to be carried out which are as follows:

a. **Initial plant development/ mother shoot bending**

   If the young plant is allowed to flower immediately after planting there is serious risk to the important structural frame work of the plant. Various types of plants require different treatments. The first flower is pinched after one month from the date of plantation so that 2 to 3 buds will sprout on the main branch to grow as branches and these branches, in turn, will form buds. When the plant attains this stage of growth, the mother shoot bents towards the direction of path. This cultural operation in rose plants is done to initiate bottom break ground shoot. The maximum leaf area is required to build up a strong root system. The mother shoot is bent nearer to the bud joint.

b. **Plant structure development:** To develop more growing points, plant structure development plays an important role. After planting, the ground shoot will start growing from the crown of the plant. The weak ground shoots should be bent at ground level, for forming a basic and strong frame work of plant structure for production throughout their life cycle. The strong ground shoots should be cut at 5th five pair of leaves after 4$^{1/2}$ months from the date of plantation. The medium ground shoots should be cut at 2nd or 3rd five pairs of leaves.

c. **Bending in roses:** Bending helps in maintaining enough leaf area on the plants. The maximum leaf area is required to build up a strong root system. The leaves of a plant are involved in gaseous exchange. Leaves are important for producing carbohydrates during photosynthesis.

$$6 H_2O + 6 CO_2 \longrightarrow C_6H_{12}O_6 + 6O_2$$

Only weak and blind shoots are selected for bending. Bending breaks apical dominance of the plant. It is a continuous process and hence carried out throughout the life cycle. Bending should be such that most of the stems lay below horizontal. In summer season it is generally advised not to go for bending as it provides favourable condition for mite infestation.

Bending is done on 1st or 2nd five pair of leaves. One can also grow roses in greenhouse without bending by keeping some blind shoots on plants in standing position for extra photosynthesis and uptake of water and nutrients. While bending the stems, care should be taken such that the stem does not break and the leaves do not touch the soil on the bed.

d. **Removal of suckers:** The growing suckers should be removed in order to check new growth on the bent stem. The buds should be removed from the bent stem in order to check the incidence of thrips and bud rot (botrytis).

e. **Disbudding:** Standard varieties are those with one flower on each stem. But as nearly all varieties produce some side buds below the central bud these side buds have to be removed. The removal of these buds is known as disbudding. It should not be done too early or too late. If done too early it may harm leaves and if done too late then it causes large wounds in the upper leaf axil. When bud attain pea size and shows slight colour then it is right time to do disbudding.

For most spray varieties, the center crown bud is to be removed. Disbudding is generally done on weak stem so that it can convert itself to thick stem and in future cuts can be taken. Thick stems produce strong sprouts where as thin stems give out weak sprouts.

f. **Pinching:** Removal of unwanted vegetative growth from the axil of leaf below the terminal bud is called pinching. This helps to produce good quality flowers and buds and avoids wastage of energy in the development of axillary bud if done at right stage and right time. It leads to apical dominance.

g. **Wild shoot (root stock) removal:** Wild shoots are the unwanted growth at the union on the root stock. They should be removed at the earliest as these will deplete nutrients and stunt the growth and development of the plant. They should not be cut but removed from its union by pressing it with thumb in order to check its further sprouting.

h. **Support of the plants:** The support system consists of bamboo/ GI pipes/ 'L' angles inserted on both sides of bed at start and end of the bed. Posts are placed at intervals of 3m on both sides of the bed, along the sides of bed. Fastened at the posts, at 30 cm – 40 cm intervals are 14 gauge GI wires or plastic string to support the plant. Between the wires and across the bed, thin strings can be tied to keep the width of the bed constant.

Support system makes intercultural operation easy and protects the buds from being damaged, by not allowing the stems to bend into the path.

i. **Pruning or under cutting:** Rose plant pruning or under cutting is necessary to decrease the height of the plant. This is done in the month of June-July. Pruning or under cut is practiced to discourage the growth of weak sprouts.

j. **Maintenance of beds:** In green houses roses are grown on raised beds. The fertile soil of the beds has a tendency to collapse into the path due to hosing by pipe, weeding and hoeing, friction with spray pipe, etc. Hence maintenance of bed is to be done by adding fresh soil to bed or by shifting fertile soil from path to bed.

k. **Weeding and loosening of the soil:** This is done with the help of long weeding hook (khurpi). This operation is helpful for removal of weeds, breaking the top layer of algae and to facilitate better aeration of the soil. This is to be done very carefully otherwise it may damage the active roots.

l. **Application of bud caps:** Bud caps are generally placed on the bud when they are of pea size. This helps to increase the bud size and shape to meet customer demand.

m. **Removal of Dieback:** As the crop gets older (aged) dieback appear in the crop due to use of infected secateurs or wrong pruning practices or hard pruning. Because of this the stem starts drying from the cut towards the bottom of the plant.

It should be removed from the crop, from time to time, to keep the crop healthy. The secateurs should be dipped in bavistin solution to disinfect it everyday before starting and after harvest respectively.

Fungicides drenching schedule for rose plants are as follows

Sr. No.	Fungicide	Dose	Time of drenching
1.	Bavistin	1 g/litre	Immediately after plantation
2.	M – 45	1 g/litre	3 days after plantation
3.	Bavistin	1.5 g/litre	7 days after plantation
4.	M – 45	1.5 g/litre	10 days after plantation
5.	Bavistin	2 g/litre	14 days after plantation
6.	M – 45	2 g/litre	17 days after plantation

Harvesting

Sr. No.	Particulars	Place of cutting	Month from date of plantation
1.	Ground shoot cutting	At 5th five pair of leaves from bottom of plant	3 to 3.5
2.	First harvesting	2nd or 3rd five pair of leaves from first cut	4.5 to 5
3.	Second/ Regular harvesting	2nd or 3rd five pair of leaves from first cut	6th month onwards daily harvesting

The rose should be cut with the help of sharp secateurs. Ground shoot cutting should be done on 5th five pair of leaf, one or two eye buds sprout from lower leaves below the cut. These sprouts will grow into flowers within a period of 35 to 50 days. This varies from variety to variety. Later on, the first harvest should be taken from 2nd or 3rd five pair of the leaves above the first cut. During the summer season, or when there is less leaf area on plant, it is always advisable to take cut on 3rd five pair of leaves above the first cut. Always bend thin stems and take cut on thick stems to get strong shoots.

Regular harvesting is done on 2nd five pair of leaves. Some times under cutting is also practiced as it is an important technique to keep rose plants at reasonable height. Harvesting cut should be sharp and inclined in order to avoid the deposition of water or spray solution. When the temperature is low in the green house, harvesting is done only once i.e. during early morning hours. When there is high day temperature, it is necessary to perform a second harvesting in the late afternoon.

Cut stages of roses play an important role in harvesting. Harvesting of rose is a skilled job hence performed by trained personnel. Cut stages of roses for export is stage 0 and 1 where as cut stage 2 and 3 is for domestic market.

Cut stages of Roses for domestic purpose and export

In general 70 – 80 rose cut flowers should be kept in a bucket (50 litre capacity) containing 10 litres of clean chlorinated water or water containing preservatives like Chrysal RVB or Florissant.

The stems should not to be harvested in following cases:
- Disease and pest affected stems.
- Damaged stems.
- Stems below 35 cm stem lengths.
- Too weak and too thick stems.
- Bent stems.
- Bent neck and bull head buds.

The stems not harvested because of above reasons should be bent to increase leaf area on a plant.

Marketing

Farmer should visit the market and study the following points:
- Average selling price
- Varieties in demand
- Preference of colours, peak demand period, major national and international markets for the product.

By exporting flowers to various countries a grower can earn good profits. To capture the export market he must produce good quality and quantity of flowers. He should study the international market by visiting the websites of different auctions in different countries, and websites of main traders and retailers in different countries. This will help him to get ideas about market and the different varieties. Demand season for flowers is generally from October to March. It coincides with marriage season, festivals like Deepawali, Christmas and important events like New Year and Valentine. Trends in prices need to be considered while planning cut flowers productions.

2.6 Cultivation Practices, Harvesting and Marketing of Gerbera

Introduction

Gerbera, commonly known as Transvaal Daisy, Barberton daisy or African Daisy is an important flower grown throughout the world under green house conditions. The flowers are of various colours and are well suited for floral arrangements. The cut blooms also have a long vase life. These flowers occur in wide range of colours such as yellow, orange, pink, brick red and various other intermediate shades. The flower stocks are long, thin and leafless. The gerbera varieties are single, double and semi double. Gerbera consist of about 40 species, of which *Gerbera jamesonii* is under cultivation. Gerbera cultivation in green house conditions produce quality flowers matching export standards. Its cultivation in greenhouse is a profitable venture.

Varieties

Sunset, Nevada, Sangna, Lynx, Macho, YCD-1, YCD-2, Vino, Venturi. etc. are the popular varieties of gerbera.

Soil and Climate

Sandy loam with good drainage capacity having a pH of 5.5 – 6.0 is most suitable. Temperature should be within the range of 25 - 27°C to avoid bud abortion/scorching. It is better to raise the crop under poly/green house.

Climatic requirement of Gerbera

Name of crop	Commercial life cycle (Yrs)	Day Temp (°C)	Night Temp (°C)	Humidity (%)	Light intensity (Lux)	CO_2 Conc. (ppm)
Gerbera	2.5 -3	20-24	18-21	60-65	40000-50000	800-1000

Season

The crop can be cultivated throughout the year.

Propagation and Planting

It can be propagated through suckers and tissue culture plantlets. Raised beds with 4 ft. width and 40 cm height and formed at an interval of 60 cm. Planting is done at a distance of 30 x 30 cm.

Greenhouse cultivation of Gerbera

Before starting *Gerbera* cultivation, disinfection of the soil is absolutely necessary to minimise the infestation of soil borne pathogens like *Phytophthora*, *Fusarium* and *Pythium* which could otherwise destroy the crop completely. The beds should be drenched / fumigated with 2% formaldehyde (100 ml formalin in 5 litres of water / m^2) or methyl bromide (70 g / m^2) and then covered with a plastic sheet for a minimum period of 2 to 3 days. The beds should be subsequently watered thoroughly to drain the chemicals before planting. Well developed tissue culture plants having 4 -6 leaves can be planted firmly without burying the crown.

Irrigation

Drip irrigation is done once in 2 – 3 days @ 3.75 litre/drip/plant for 15 – 20 minutes. Average water requirement is about 500 – 700 ml/day/plant.

Manuring
Basal
Neem cake - 2.5 ton/ha
P - 400 g/100 sq.ft.
$MgSO_4$ - 0.5 kg/100 sq.ft.

Top dressing

Calcium ammonium nitrate and muriate of Potash at the ratio of 5:3 is mixed and applied at 2.5 g/plant/month.

After cultivation

1. Hand weeding is done whenever necessary.

2. Remove the flower buds up to 2 months and then allow for flowering.
3. Rake the soil once in 15 days to facilitate easy absorption of water, fertiliser and to provide air to the roots.
4. Remove older leaves to facilitate new leaf growth and good sanitation.

Plant Protection
1. To control Nematodes – Carbofuran: 7-8 kg/ha is applied at the time of planting.
2. Leaf spot – Carbendazim: 2 g/lit or Mancozeb 2 g/lit is sprayed alternatively.
3. Leaf miner – Chlorpyrifos: 20 EC 2 ml/lit.
4. Glasshouse whitefly – Monocrotophos: 36 WSC 2 ml/lit or Neem oil 3 ml/lit.

Season of flowering and Harvesting

When flowers are completely open, harvesting is done. Flower stalks are soaked in sodium hypochloride solution (5-7 ml/lit of water) for 4-5 hours to improve vase life.

Post harvest handling

Harvesting is done when the outer 2-3 rows of disc florets are perpendicular to the stalk. The heel for the stalk should be cut about 2-3 cm above the base and kept in fresh chlorinated water. Flowers should be graded and sorted out in uniform batches. Flowers are packed individually in poly pouches and then put in carton boxes in two layers.

Bushiness

An abnormality characterised by numerous leaves, short petioles and small laminae, which gives some cultivars of *Gerbera* a bushy appearance is known as bushiness. Nodes are not clearly distinguished and no internode elongation is seen.

Stem break

It is a common post harvest disorder in cut *Gerbera*. This is mainly caused by water imbalances. It could be ethylene controlled and associated with early senescence caused by water stress.

Yellowing and purple margin

Nitrogen deficiency causes yellowing and early senescence of leaves. Phosphorus deficiency causes pale yellow colour with purple margin. Increase in levels of nitrogen and phosphorus were found to promote development of suckers and improve flowering in *Gerbera*.

Yield

The crop yields 2 stems / plant / month. Harvest starts from 3rd month of planting and continues up to two years. Under open conditions, 130 -160 flowers / m^2 / year and under greenhouse condition, 175 - 200 flowers /m^2 / year can be obtained.

Grading

Based on stem length and diameter, flowers are graded as A, B, C and D category.

Marketing

The flower heads are covered with polyethylene bags and wrapped properly to avoid damage and injuries to the petals of flowers during transport. The flowers are sold in the market in bunches of a definite number. The bunch has same coloured flower with equal length of stalks. Sometimes single flower is also sold in the market. For export market, top graded *Gerbera* flowers are selected. The flowers should be transported up to airport in cooling van. Export of *Gerbera* flowers is more remunerative and profitable.

Points to Remember

- Floriculture is an aesthetic branch of horticulture.
- Cultivation of commercially important cut flower producing plants and ornamental plants, their marketing and processing is known as floriculture.
- India has diverse agro climatic and geographical conditions so that many cut flowers can be grown round the year.
- Floricultural product includes cut flowers and decorative, attractive, colourful foliage and economic products like essentials oils medicines and preserves.
- Cut flowers are classified into three groups such as single flowers as a cut flower, inflorescence as cut flower and flowering shoot as cut flower.
- The cut flowers constitute 45% share of the world trade in floricultural products.
- Important cut flowers are Rose, Carnation, *Gladiolus, Chrysanthemum*, Orchids and *Anthurium*.
- Green house/ polyhouse technology is the cultivation of flowers, vegetables and ornamentals under controlled conditions of light, temperature, humidity and CO_2 concentrations.
- Green house technology has several types of advantages over open cultivation such as highest production, export quality, can be grown in any season, maximum profit in minimum area, protection against pest, diseases and insects.
- However, there are many limitations for green house cultivation such as very high production cost, skilled labour, very high capital investment and hi-tech infrastructure.
- Losses after failure are very high and hence difficult to tolerate by farmers.
- Technical constraints for export.

- Cultivation of roses under green house condition is highly profitable as the market is ever increasing and well established. Many varieties of roses are available for selection and hence the growers have abundant choice.
- Cultivation practices are well standardised and highly remunerative.
- Cultivation of *Gerbera* requires highly skilled labour and well developed technique.
- Because of the large choice of varieties to the growers, amazing flower colors to attract the costumers, span of life cycle, well developed harvesting and marketing strategy cultivation of *Gerbera* is highly profitable.
- Botanical name of Tuberose is *Polianthes tuberosa*
- Common names of the tuberose are Gulcheri, Gulchabbo, Rajanigandha and Nishigandh.
- *Polianthes tuberosa* is monotypic genus.
- Tuberose varieties are classified on the basis of floret arrangement.
- Main classes of tuberose varieties are single pettaled and double pettaled.
- Main cultivars of tuberose are Suhasini, Prajwal, Vaibhav and Shringar.
- Tuberose can be cultivated in a light sandy loam or a clay loam soil with pH ranging from 6.5 to 7.5.
- Tuberose is a tropical plant that grows best under optimum climatic conditions of
- 20 - 35°C, relative humidity of 68 - 86%.
- Temperature below 10°C causes reduction in spike length and weight as well as affects the quality of flower. Low intensity of light shows adverse effect on flowering.
- For planting, tuberose bulbs having diameter of 2 - 3 cm are used.
- Recommended spacing for planting tuberose is 20 x 25 cm.
- Tuberose is propagated by bulbs, by bulbs segments and by seeds.
- Super phosphate at 60 gm/m^2 is useful to increase number of flowers per spike.
- During summer, crops should be irrigated at an interval of 5 - 7 days and in winter at an interval of 10 to 12 days.
- Drip irrigation gives best results for tuberose cultivation.
- Tuberose bears flowers after three months of planting.
- Spikes are matured and ready for harvesting when lower one to two pairs of florets open.
- Tuberose is harvested by cutting the spikes from the base.
- Marketing of tuberose includes grading, packaging, transporting and selling.
- Normal vase life of tuberose cut flowers is 6 - 8 days.
- Due to waxy nature of the flowers they remain fresh for longer time.
- The flowers of tuberose yield tuberose oil used in perfumes.

Exercises

Short Answer Questions
1. What is floriculture? Give its scope.
2. What are the floricultural products? Enlist few examples.
3. What are the advantages in India for floriculture industry?
4. What are cut flowers? Give their classification with examples.
5. Give a brief account of floricultural crops cultivated in India.
6. Explain morphological characters of Tuberose and add a note on Tuberose cultivation.
7. Enlist important cultivars of tuberose and mention their important features.
8. Describe open cultivation practices of Tuberose.
9. Write a note on harvesting of Tuberose
10. Describe various steps in marketing of Tuberose.
11. Give economic importance of Tuberose.
12. Write a note on methods for increasing vase life of Tuberose.
13. Write short notes on:
    - Cultivars of Tuberose.
    - Soil and Climate requirements of Tuberose.
    - Propagation of Tuberose.
    - Fertigation of Tuberose.
    - Harvesting of Tuberose.
    - Economic importance of Tuberose.
    - Commercially important varieties of Tuberose.
    - Morphological characters of Tuberose.
    - Packaging of Tuberose.
    - Planting method of Tuberose.
    - Irrigation of Tuberose.

Long Answer Questions
1. Define Green house technology and explain its advantages.
2. Explain the concept of green house technology and add a note on its limitations.
3. Explain principles of green house technology.
4. Enlist the different varieties of roses.
5. Enlist the different varieties of *Gerbera*.
6. Give an account of green house cultivation of roses with reference to climatic requirement.
7. Explain the propagation of roses and *Gerbera*.
8. Explain the harvesting of roses.
9. Explain the harvesting of *Gerbera*.
10. Write in brief on : (i) Marketing of roses (ii) Marketing of *Gerbera*.

Chapter 3...
Plant Nursery Industry

Contents ...
3.1 Introduction
    3.1.1 Concept of Nursery
    3.1.2 Basic Infrastructure of nurseries
    3.1.3 Types of Nurseries
    3.1.4 Brief Account of Nurseries
    3.1.5 Outputs, Commercial Applications and Profitability
3.2 Propagation Methods
    3.2.1 Sexual (Seed) Propagation
    3.2.2 Natural Vegetative Propagation
    3.2.3 Artificial Vegetative Propagation
    Points to Remember
    Exercises

3.1 Introduction

In India, due to the modern developments in the field of agriculture with special reference to horticulture, need for healthy, seedlings/plantlets of desirable plant species in required number is highly demanded. To fulfill this need, the technique of mass production of seedlings is evolved, which is commonly known as nursery technique. The nursery technique involves raising seedlings, sampling, grafting of ornamental plants of economical value, through scientific methods.

3.1.1 Concept of Nursery

Nursery is place where necessary infrastructure facilities, trained man power and required plant material is made available to produce required number of healthy seedlings/plantlets of the desirable plant species. The art of raising larger number of seedlings or plant saplings in a protected area is known as nursery technique and the site where the operation are carried out is known as nursery. Nursery is a better and a more convenient method to manage seedlings under a small or large area. Nursery provides suitable climate to emerging plants for their better growth and development. The raising of seedlings in nursery not only reduces the time span between the sowing and harvesting of the crop but also increases the uniformity of the crops.

3.1.2 Basic Infrastructure of Nursery

The following basic infrastructure is required for commercial nursery.

1. **Nursery entrance:** The entrance should be accessible to the nursery office. The nursery entrance provides the first and most important opportunity to present a good image and impression.
2, **Fence:** Nursery should be well protected by providing walls or barbed wire fences surrounded by thorny hedges to prevent tresspass of animals and people.
3. **Roads and paths:** There should be a proper planning for roads and paths inside the nursery. Each road/path should lead the customer to a point of interest in the nursery area.
4. **Nursery office cum stores:** It is required for effective management of the nursery. The office building should be constructed in a place which is suitable for better supervision and to receive customers. A store room of suitable size is required for storing, packing materials, polybags, tools, implements, pesticides and fertilisers.
5. **Sales area:** The nursery sales area should be located close to the nursery entrance with a representative display of saleable plant materials.
6. **Seed beds:** In a nursery, seed beds are essential to raise the seedlings and rootstocks. Beds of one meter width of any suitable length are to be made. A working area of 60 cm between the beds is required. Sprinkler irrigation system should be provided for watering the seed beds.
7. **Nursery beds:** Nursery beds require more space for raising seedlings/rootstocks in polybags. Nursery bed area should be of a depth of about 30 cm and of a width of about one meter or alternatively of one meter width with 60 cm depth working place. Such beds can be irrigated by overhead micro sprinklers or a flexible hosepipe.
8. **Potting mixture:** Potting mixtures for different purposes can be prepared by mixing fertile red soil, garden poyata soil, well rotten farm yard manure, leaf mold, oil cakes etc.
9. **Compost pit:** The compost pit should be constructed near the potting shed in order to facilitate the collection of compost materials for storage.
10. **Propagation area:** The propagation area is required for the nursery operation and it must be located in an area accessible to the production and potting areas.
11. **Nursery water supply:** The source of water should be within the nursery area. A number of water taps or water reservoirs (well and pond) should be provided inside the nursery area.
12. **Shade net nursery house:** The shade nets are mainly used to protect the nursery plants from direct sunlight. The shade nets are available in desired shading percentage.

13. **Polyhouse:** This is now used commercially for raising seedlings in the off season or in adverse weather conditions. The size of polyhouse varies according to the number of seedlings to be raised.

14. **Site / location:** The nursery should be established on a raised open ground. It should be convenient for transportation of material.

15. **Drainage:** Proper drainage system is required for an ideal nursery.

16. **Packing shed and materials:** Before delivery of the material to the customers they are to be properly packed and labeled. For packing, baskets or boxes are kept in the shed.

17. **Electricity:** There should be separate electricity supply power station (D.P.) for the nursery.

18. **Soil/mixture:** Nursery requires soil mixture i.e. Red soil (poyata garden soil), well decomposed farmyard manure, and river sand.

19. **Containers:** Containers for producing plug seedlings. e.g. earthen pots, seed pans and seed boxes, polythene bags, plastic pots, plug trays, clay pots, block containers etc.

20. **Fumigation in nursery:** Methyl bromide, chloropicrin, 1,3-dichloro-propene, trisodicum phosphate and potassium permanganate etc. are used for fumigation in nursery.

21. **Chemical control in nursery:** The control of pests is brought about with the useof chemical pesticides which includes insecticides like DDT, gammaxine, methoxychlor etc, fungicides like Bordeaux mixture ,herbicides such as 2-4-dichlorophenoxyacetic acid and rodenticides like warfarin, strychnine etc.

22. **Nursery tools:** The following tools are used in nursery. These are khurpi, khasi spade, sabbal, hand fork, water can, hand sprayer, secateur, hedge shear, edging iron, budding knife, sickle.

23. **Media for raising seedlingss in nursery:** Peat, sphagnum peatmoss, hypanaceous peat moss, peat moss, coco soil, coir (coconut fiber) sawdust and wood chips, sludge, rice hulls, cotton gin trash, leaf mold, humus or muck, bagasse, coco peat, etc. are required for nursery production of container grown plants.

24. **Transporting vehicles:** Tempoes and small trucks should be provided to the nursery for transporting the material and implements.

25. **Growth hormones or regulators:** Gibberellin, (GA), Indole acetic acid (IAA), Ethylene and cytokines etc. are used in growth of plants in nurseries.

3.1.3 Types of Nursery

There are various methods to classify nurseries. Classification of a nursery is based on the types of plants grown. The main types of nurseries are mention below

(i) Ornamental plant nursery.

(ii) Fruit plant nursery.

(iii) Medicinal plant nursery.

(iv) Vegetable plant nursery.

(v) Orchid nursery.

(vi) Forest nursery.

3.1.4 Brief Account of Nurseries

1. Ornamental plant nursery

Nursery that produces plant material of ornamental plants which are used for beautification, landscaping and decorative purposes is known as ornamental plant nursery. Ornamental plant nursery business has developed on a large scale in areas near towns and cities. The mother plants are grown for vegetative and seed propagation. The seed propagated plants such as seasonal flowers, seedlingss are raised for cultivation and sale. Varieties of various ornamental plants like shade loving foliage plants, flowering plants, creepers etc. may be propagated in the nursery. Planting materials such as seedlingss of flowers, bulbs and corms may be produced in an ornamental nursery. Common examples of ornamental nursery plants are Crotons, Roses, Tulips, Nephrolepis, etc.

Common ornamental plant species grown in the nurseries for commercial plantation are as below :

(i) Bulbs: *Gladiolus, Tulip, Amaryllis, Canna,* Bird of paradise, *Lilium* etc.

(ii) Annuals: *Antirrhinum,* Carnation, *Petunia, Cosmos, Zinnia, Dianthus Calendula, Chrysanthemum,* etc.

(iii) Foliage plants: *Coleus, Colocasia, Croton, Philodendron, Dracaena, Asparagus, Ficus, Begonia, etc.*

(iv) Flowering plants: *Aster, Jasmine, Chrysanthemum, Gerbera* Marigold, Carnation, *Crossandra, Baleria,* Roses, etc.

(v) Ferns: *Adiantum, Nephrolepis, Asplenium, Pteris,* etc.

(vi) Climbers: *Bougainvillea, Hiptage, Aristolochia.*

(vii) Trees: *Michelia, Bauhinia, Erythrina, Ixora, Jacaranda, Cassia, Delonix.*

(viii) Cacti and succulents: *Agave, Aloe, Euphoria sp., Epiphyllum sp., Opuntia sp., Zygocactus,* etc.

(ix) Palms and cycads: *Phoenix, Areca, Chamaerops, Howea, Cycus sp., Zamia* etc.

The propagation of ornamental plants in nurseries is generally using (i) seeds, (ii) vegetative parts. This is very common method multiplication of ornamental plants. In addition to this, budding, layering and grafting are also used.

2. Fruit plant nursery

This type of nursery particularly deals with production of fruit plants. It is further divided in different categories like production of single fruit nursery, mixed fruit nursery, tropical fruit nursery, sub-tropical fruit nursery, temperate fruit nursery and arid fruit plant nursery etc. Production of fruits yield much more produce per unit of area and certainly more profit than ordinary farm crops. Now farmers are taking interest in planting more fruit plants. Development of fruit nursery is a long term business and requires a lot of planning and is expensive. Soft wood grafting of mango, cashew, grapes and pomegranate plants can be propagated by mass multiplication of fruit plants under modern nursery and these grafts are made available to the farmers for cultivation in the field.

Fruit plants seedlings if prepared from the seeds show segregation of characters and the flowering as well as fruiting require a long time hence majority of fruit plant saplings are prepared by grafting, layering, air layering, cuttings etc. as the fruit plants that develop are true to their mother plants in fruit characters like size and shape, colour, taste, aroma etc. e.g. Air. layering – pomogrante, stone grafting-Mango, Stem cuttings – Grapes. Air-layering – Guava, patch budding – Ber, coconut from selected seed nuts, seedlings – papaya.

Micropropagation is also used for producing tissue culture plantlets of some important fruit plants e.g. Banana.

3. Medicinal plant nursery

Medicinal plant nursery plays a key role in cultivation of various types of medicinal plants. The medicinal plants generally grow in the forest, hence we cannot get guaranteed seedlings of medicinal plants, For healthy and well grown planting material of medicinal and aromatic plants, we have to rely on medicinal plant nursery. The medicinal plant growers are in need of seedlings, saplings, cuttings, of medicinal plants. These can be made available to the farmers through medicinal plant nursery. It is difficult to collect planting material in required quantity from forest only and so medicinal plant nurseries can provide the planting materials.

The infrastructure of medicinal plants nursery is similar to other nurseries. The commercially important medicinal plants. i.e. *Aloe vera, Adathoda vasica, Withania somnifera* (Ashwagandha), *Glycyrrhiza, Chlorophytum* (Safedmusli), Jatamashi, *Rauwolfia serpentine* (Sarpagandha) *Asparagus* (Shatavari), *Saraca indica* (Ashoka), *Senna*, Amala, *Emblica officialis*, Longpapper, Isapgol, Brahmi, Gymnema, Kalmegh, Mentha, Tulsi, Guggul, Stevia are some common examples of medicinal plants required on large scale. Hence their seedlings should be prepared and made available to the growers.

(i) Preparation of seedlings in nursery beds - The viable, healthy and authentic seeds of medicinal plants should be collected when they are available and these seeds are generally sown during favourable season in the nursery beds. The seeds germinated are transplanted into plastic bags and then sold to the growers. Sometimes, naked seedlings(without plastic bags) can be taken for transplantation. e.g. *Withania, Ocimum*, Jatamasi, Liquorice etc.

(ii) The planting material of medicinal plants are also prepared from underground planting materials like Rhizome, tubers, corms, suckers, runners, stolons, offsets etc. e.g. *Rhizome* – Ginger, Turmeric, Tubers – *Dioscorea, Aconites*. Jalap bulb – *Gloriosa*, Garlic, Corm – *Colchicum*, Suffron; Runner – Brahmi, Offset - *Aloe vera*, Stolon – *Glycerrhiza, Jasmine*, Sucker – *Mentha*.

(iii) Artificial method of propagation of medicinal plants. The plant parts like root, stem, leaves are used for propagation of medicinal plants. The cuttings are prepared in nursery beds or in polythene bags and the rooted cuttings are used for plantation at desired place. Stem cutting e.g. *Nathopodities coleus, Stevavia, Clerodendron* etc. Root cuttings, Brahmi, Leaf cutting – *Bryophyllum*.

4. **Vegetable Plant Nursery**

   Vegetable plant nursery is a place where seedlings of various vegetable crops are prepared and made available for cultivation to the farmers. In a vegetable nursery, seedlings of different types of vegetables like cabbage, tomato, brinjal, chillies etc. can be grown in nursery beds or in portrays.

   In vegetable plant nursery, seedlings of common fruit vegetables root vegetables, tuber vegetables, bulb vegetables, can be prepared upto suitable sizes and made available to the customers for further cultivation in field.

   Vegetable plant nursery is becoming more popular because it is a profit oriented business and farmers require readymade seedlings to save the time. Vegetable nurseries prepare the seedlings in a large scale at a common place. They take at most care and prepare healthy seedlings of different vegetable crops. In a vegetable nursery, mostly, the seedlings are prepared from seeds only. These seeds should be viable and healthy to avoid losses and mortality.

5. **Orchid Nursery**

The orchids are the most beautiful and attractive flowering plants, with flowers found in a variety of fragrances, colours, shapes. Orchids can be grown in nursery by providing favourable climatic conditions. Following are the common examples of orchids- *Vanda, Dendrobium, Onicidiam* etc. For germination of seeds of orchid, seed beds can be filled with compost consisting of coconut husk, burnt brick pieces, leaf mould with fern fibre and charcoal. The orchids are also propagated through micro propagation technique. They can be developed through explants from shoots growing on false bulbs or from leaf tips or from flower stalk cuttings. Commercial method of vegetative propagation of hybrids of *Cattleya, Phalaenopsis, Cymbidium* etc. can be done by meristematic culture. *Epidendrum, Dendrobium* and *Vanda* orchids can be propagated by their vegetative organs like offsets, through cuttings and air layerings. Offsets develop from *Dendrobium* and *Epidendrum* can be detached from parent plants and planted in small pots. Air layering technique is used for *Vanda*. This orchids can be grown even by cutting method. Orchids are exportable cut flowers and hence they are in very high demand. Orchid nursery is highly profitable but it requires high-tech facilities and for this capital investment is very high. The orchids highly sensitive and require mainly cold climate. Preparing artificial cold conditions for their growth is a costly one. Very few nurseries of orchids are available in tropical and sub-tropical areas but they are many orchids nurseries in temperate regions where cold climatic conditions are natural available.

6. **Forest Nursery**

Forest nursery is a place where saplings of forest plants are prepared and made available for planting. Forest nursery is specifically meant for conservation of forest plants. This type of nursery is meant for specifically acclimatising and maintaining the exotic forest plant species. Site of the forest nursery is usually in the same forest area or nearby convenient area with a similar environment. Forest nursery is an ideal forest ecosystem for growing desired forest plant species. Methods used for raising plant saplings mainly include common methods used by local people as well as some advanced techniques standardised for propagating the specific forest plant species.

The forest nursery plant species in which the seed germination is very poor and difficult are raised through special techniques. The rare and endangered forest plant species, which are on the verge of extinction are conserved and multiplied in forest nursery. The area of forest nursery is very vast with different sections accessible to nurserymen. The saplings of forest species are prepared on a very large scale so that the plants are provided in bulk quantity. The forest nursery deals with a variety of plants like timber, medicinal plants, fuel and fodder plants, plant with ecological importance e.g. soil conservation, nitrogen fixing trees, soil binders, wind breakers, mulchers (soil covering) e.g. *Azadirachta Indica, Bombax Cieba, Casuarina equisetifolia, Eucalyptus tereticornis*, etc.

3.1.5 Output, Commercial Applications and Profitability

The nursery business is expanding very fast in different states of India including the state of Maharashtra. The nursery business is highly profitable and net profit depends on the skill and techniques of nursery men. The nursery business involves capital investment and creates job opportunities. The commercial nurseries of ornamental plants, orchids is the source of foreign currency for a country like India. The labour cost, consumables, infrastructure, planting material etc. is comparatively cheaper in India. Hence, the cost of production is very low in India as compare to foreign countries. Because of this nursery business is highly profitable in developing countries as compared to developed countries like U.S.A. Europe etc. The demand for nursery plants of Roses, Tulips, Carnations, *Gerbera, Gladiolus,* Tuberose is increasing day by day. As a result of this, the nursery business has became a profit oriented business. Small scale nurseries which are generally run by small farmers, having limited infrastructure and land are able to earn lakhs of rupees through nursery business.

The ornamental nurseries are becoming more popular as it requires minimum infrastructure and earn maximum profit. The seedlings are seasonally sold out and hence sustain period is very less and farmers get their money back within a short span of time.

The saplings of fruit plants nursery require more time to be prepared as compared to seasonal flowers. Because of the horticultural growth in India fruit plant nurseries have increased to an industrial level and the profit is also very high.

The demand for herbal drugs in India and throughout the world is increasing tremendously and hence there is urgent need for commercial cultivation of medical plants. Therefore, nursery of medicinal plants is in very high demand. Medicinal plant nursery is a new concept that has emerged at a commercial level and hence there is less competition in the market. As a result of this, it will be more profitable yielding high economic returns.

A nursery businessman must be prepared to make substantial investment for many years before getting the economic returns. The nursery grower has to invest lot of money for setting any type of nursery. He should be able to handle the ups and downs in profits associated with different types of nurseries. The economic risk in nursery business is very high and the loss should be tolerable by the grower.

Timber in the market is becoming more and more costly. Similarly the major and minor forest produce for e.g. Gums, resins, wild fruits and vegetables are also in great demand. As a result of this, farmers are interested in large scale production of timber yielding plants like Teak, Sisso etc. Because of the commercial value of sandal wood, oil and other commercial products sandal wood plantation has become a very profitable business. The natural dyes and colours are very popular in food industry and textile industry, hence plantation of these plants is increasing. Considering this demand for forest resources forest plant nursery has become crucial. The profit from forest plant nurseries is equally high like that of medicinal plant nursery. At present only forest department is engaged in making forest plant nursery. But the government is encouraging farmers, institutions and. NGO's to start forest plants nurseries to increase the green cover of earth and to fulfill the demand of major and minor forest products mention above.

The different types of nurseries provide job opportunities and help in income generating aspect.. Techniques of nurseries are becoming more and more advanced and hence high technology nurseries have come into limelight. In brief, all types of nurseries have tremendous commercial applications, job potentials, boost economic growth and earn foreign exchange. Because of nursery business, women have become economically empowered and they have developed small saving groups to start nurseries. At present their earnings have increased and they are becoming economically self sufficient.

3.2 Propagation Methods

Introduction

A successful propagation method is one that will transmit all the characteristics of the mother plant to the daughter plants. If the desirable characters are lost during the procedure then, the method is not suitable for that particular type of plant. It is then necessary to try and use another propagation technique that will retain the characteristics. Plants varieties that are grown now a days have particularly desirable characteristics which are derived from wild plant populations through mutations and plant breeding.

Propagation of various economically important plants is practiced since ancient times. Plant propagation technique is the basis of agriculture. The hybrids, transgenic plants, etc. are the outcome of man's knowledge about the different plant varieties and their characteristics.

The basic objective of plant propagation is to produce new offsprings, seedlings or plantlets, which will be exactly similar to the original plants. For cultivation of useful plants man has started to try various methods for plant propagation from original few stock plants.

Propagation is the inherent potential of all living organisms including plants and animals (microscopic or megascopic). They reproduce to continue the perpetuation and multiplication of their own species. Plant propagation takes place by various natural and artificial methods.

Types of Propagations

All plants generally propagate by two basic methods:

(1) Sexual propagation (seed propagation)

(2) Vegetative propagation (Asexual propagation): Vegetative propagation is of two types : (i) Natural vegetative propagation, (ii) Artificial vegetative propagation.

(3) Micropropagation (Tissue culture): It is a recently developed and widely used method of plant propagation for high value cash crops, exotic or exportable floricultural and vegetable crops *in vitro*.

The different methods of plant propagations are summarised in the following chart.

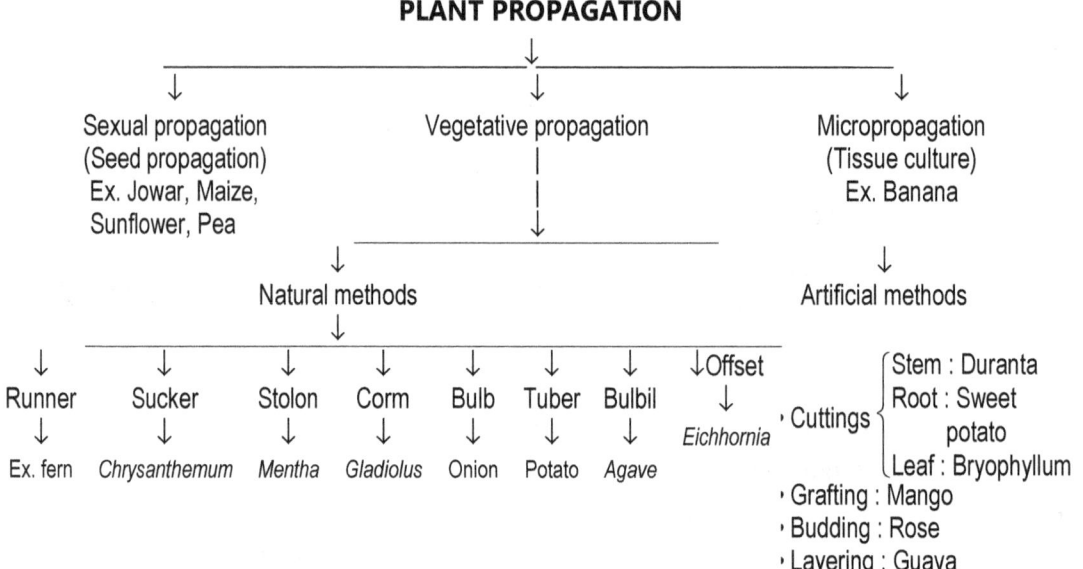

3.2.1 Sexual propagation (Seed Propagation)

Sexual propagation involves the union of the pollen (male) with the egg (female) to produce a seed. When a seed is mature and put in a favourable environment, it will germinate and begin active growth. The seed is made up of three parts:

1. The outer seed coat - protects the seed
2. The endosperm - is a food reserve and
3. The embryo - is the young plant itself.

I. Storage of Seeds

Generally the seeds are stored because it is not possible to sow all seeds in the following season. When the seeds are stored it is necessary to ensure that the seeds are dry, clean and the pulp is carefully removed. Properly stored seeds can remain viable for a very long time. Seeds should be stored in an air tight jar or container with a screw top and this in turn should be placed in a cool, dark place. Excessive variation in temperature should be avoided and should be kept dry. Under such conditions the seeds will retain their viability for two to five years.

II. Viability Testing of Seeds

For seeds that have been stored for several years, it is advisable to test the viability of seed before planting.

(1) One easy way of determining the viability of seed lot cut test. The seed is simply cut into half to see whether there is an embryo inside. Often the embryo is aborted or has been eaten by insects and in such case, the seed would not germinate.

(2) Another simple test is to soak the seeds in water. In this test, the "floaters" are empty seeds and should be removed. The seeds which sink are good and can be used for planting.

These tests are not, strictly speaking, viability tests but are useful to screen out seeds that have no possibility of germinating.

III. Seed Structure

The outer protective covering of seed is called seed coat. The outer coat is called **testa** and inner layer is called **tegmen**. **Testa** is hard and tegmen is thin and membranous. Externally the seed shows scar of detached funicle called hilum. There is a small pore called **micropyle**. Some seeds show origin of seed coats (chalaza) and part of funiculus fused with seed wall (raphe). Embryo is differentiated into radicle, plumule and cotyledons. Radicle gives rise to **primary root** and plumule gives rise to **aerial shoot**. The part of embryonic axis between the radicle and the point of attachment of cotyledons is called **hypocotyl**. Similarly axis between the plumule and the point of attachment of cotyledons is called **epicotyl**.

a. Structure of Dicot seed

1. Embryo of dicot seed possesses two cotyledons.
2. Hilum is present.
3. Small pore micropyle is present which absorb water during germination.
4. There is a short ridge on the other side of hilum called raphe.
5. Testa and tegmen is present.
6. Reserve food is in the form of carbohydrates and proteins.
7. The micropylar end of embryonal axis is called radicle.
8. The other side of embryonal axis is called plumule.
9. The embryo axis between the plumule and cotyledonary node is called epicotyl.
10. The portion of axis between the radicle and cotyledonary node is called hypocotyl e.g. Bean, groundnut etc. (Fig. 3.1 (b))

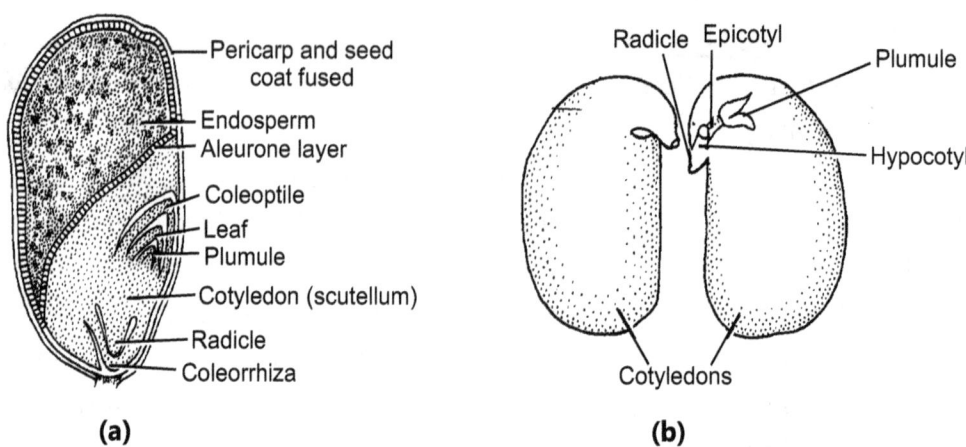

Fig. 3.1: Seed Structure : (a) Monocot seed, (b) Dicot seed

b. Structure of Monocot Seed

1. Monocot seed has one cotyledon.
2. Major portion of grain is occupied by starchy endosperm. It is surrounded by thick layer called aleurone layer.
3. Aleurone layer is proteinaceous, it plays an important role at the time of germination.
4. The embryo is present in the groove at the end of the endosperm.
5. A shield-shaped cotyledon known as scutellum is attached laterally to the embryonal axis.
6. Radicle is present towards the pointed end of the grain.
7. Radicle is covered with coleorrhiza (Protective layer).
8. Plumule is present towards the broader end of the grain covered with coleoptile (protective layer).
9. The germination is hypogeal as during germination, the cotyledon remains underground. e.g. Maize. (Fig. 3.1 (a))

IV. Seed Germination

The fertilised ovule is called as **seed**. Embryo in the seed is a miniature, future plant. It acts as a propagule for multiplication of the species.

The process by which immature embryo develops into mature, independent plant is called germination.

If the viable seeds are placed under proper environmental conditions of moisture, temperature and light, the embryo in the seeds will resume their growth. The food from the endosperm or cotyledons nourish the developing embryo until the new shoot rises above the ground. Seed germination may be epigeal or hypogeal. In **epigeal** germination the cotyledons are pushed above the ground and in **hypogeal** germination the cotyledons remain below the ground. As most of the seedlings are polyembryonic, they produce many seedlings after germination. Out of these one seedling is of sexual origin and the rest are produced vegetatively from the cells of nucellus, which are called as apogamic seedlings. The apogamic seedlings are identical to parent plants in growth and production e.g. *Citrus*, mango. (Fig. 3.2 (a) & (b))

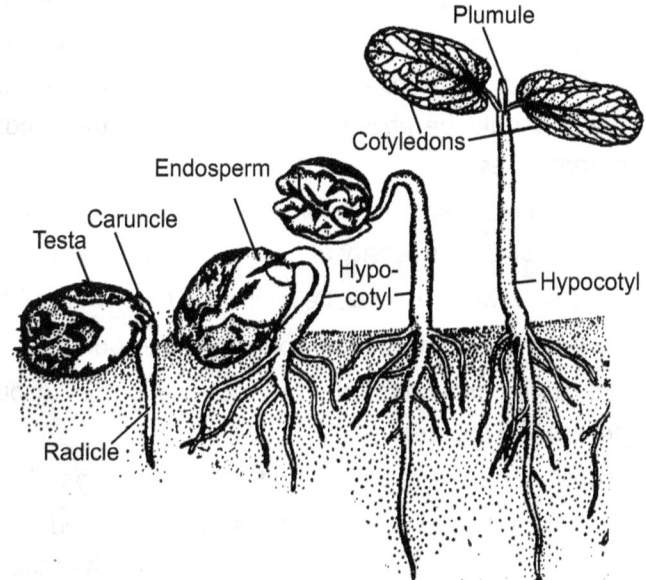

Fig. 3.2 (a): Epigeous germination e.g. Castor

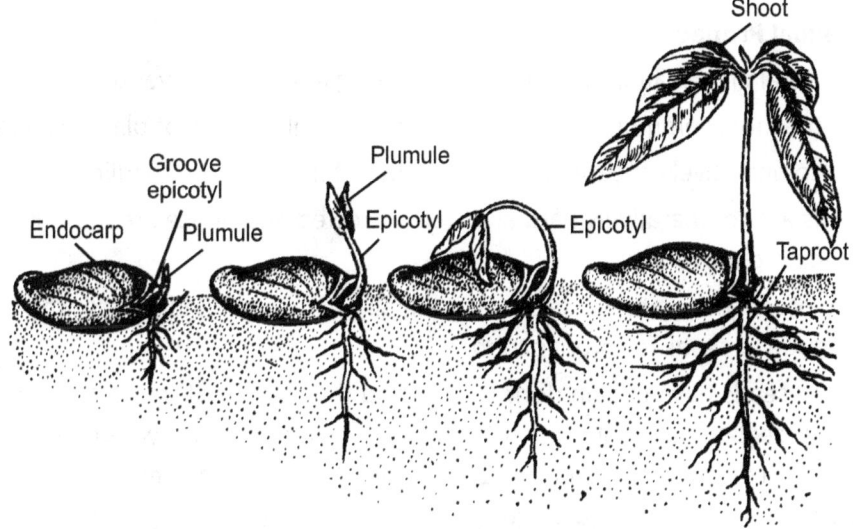

Fig. 3.2 (b): Hypogeal Germination e.g. Mango

Criteria for Selection of Seeds

Before raising the plants from seed, it is necessary to select healthy fruits for collection of seeds. While doing this, the following points should be taken into consideration.

1. The fruits selected should possess the desired characters such as size, shape, colour, flavour, taste and improved keeping quality.
2. The fruits should be fully mature and borne on vigorous and healthy plants.
3. The grower must know the genetic constitution of the plant variety. The genetic makeup of seed is not constant and always changes towards the inferior quality. Therefore, grower should be able screen and discard the seedlings which are of inferior or different types.
4. One should know the climatic requirements of the plants grown for commercial production of seeds such as intensity of light and water requirement.
5. The seeds should be sown in an area/field which is free from soil-borne pathogens.
6. Seed should be purchased or collected from a reliable source.
7. To maintain the purity and uniformity in yield, it is better to purchase new seeds every year from reliable sources.
9. It is better to collect the seeds from the fruits developed from the oldest flowers.
10. It is better to label the plants whose seeds are to be collected. Once the blooming is over, it is difficult to distinguish the superior plants from the others.
11. Only dry seeds should be collected because wet seeds are likely to be infected easily. The infected seeds are damaged and lose their viability.

Merits of Sexual Propagation

Seed or sexual propagation of plants has following advantages over the other methods.

1. It is the most common, easy, simplest and natural method of plant propagation.
2. It is comparatively cheaper and easy method for raising the seedlings.
3. Seeds are comparatively hard and well protected and hence are not damaged easily during propagation.
4. The production rate of seeds is generally very high and hence, there won't be shortage of seeds for propagation.
5. As the seeds have certain dormancy period they can be stored safely for future use. Many seeds remain viable for many years, if stored at very low temperature. e.g. The seeds of Lotus remain viable for 1000 years, if stored at low temperature.
6. Seed germination can be easily controlled or regulated. It is possible to stimulate or inhibit seed germination by using different, easy and cheap methods. This is a great advantage to grower.

7. Seeds are suitable and convenient planting material to handle or to carry during transport or exchange.
8. Without seeds the process of hybridisation is not possible, because the hybrids are generally formed by crossing the parents, raised from seeds.
10. In some plants vegetative propagation is not possible, in such cases, seed propagation is the only way to propagate them e.g. Papaya, Coconut, etc.
11. Seed propagation does not require any special equipments or materials like grafting knife, polyethylene sheet, moss, etc.
12. It does not require special plant material like stock, scion, bud, etc.
13. It does not require special techniques or skills like budding, grafting, layering, etc.
14. The new plants developed from seeds have longer life, bear more fruits and generally they are very robust.
15. These plants act as best stock plants for budding or grafting.
16. During seed propagation chances for transfer of diseases are very less as compared to vegetative propagation.

Demerits of Sexual Propagation

The seed or sexual propagation of plants has the following demerits:

1. The plants produced through seed propagation are not identical to their parents, as the seeds are produced through natural cross pollination, and therefore they show mixture of characters.
2. Due to segregation of characters, the seedlings obtained through sexual propagation show variations in future generations.
3. The plants propagated through seeds require longer time for flowering and fruiting. e.g. Mango tree developed from seeds require 7 to 8 years to bear flowers and fruits. But the grafted plants start bearing fruits from 3rd year after planting.
4. Due to dormancy in the seed the germination rate is very slow or sometimes the seeds may never germinate at all.
5. Due to improper storage, mishandling or over storage, the seeds lose viability and cannot be used for propagation.
6. Some plants produce non viable or sterile seeds, which are not useful for propagation. These plants cannot be propagated through seeds.
7. The seeds sometimes have seed borne pathogens, which are transferred to the developing seedlings.

8. The plants propagated through seeds are not uniform in growth, yielding capacity and quality of produce.
9. The superior, best or novel characters of mother plants cannot be maintained through seed propagation.
10. The genotypes of fruit and ornamental plants are highly heterozygous, hence the characters of such plants are immediately lost, if they are propagated through seeds.

Vegetative Propagation

Many horticultural plants e.g. flowering, fruiting and ornamental plants are usually propagated by asexual or vegetative methods of propagation. The totipotency in plants has enabled them to grow and reproduce through vegetative propagation. Any vegetative part of plants undergoes cell division and differentiation, leading to vegetative propagation. Even from a single vegetative cell the entire plant can be reproduced. Each and every part of the plant has capacity to regenerate the missing part of that plant. e.g. stem cuttings can produce roots, root cuttings can produce stem and the leaf cuttings can produce the roots and stem. In vegetative propagation, genetically identical plant is produced. In brief vegetative propagation can be defined as propagation of plants through vegetative structures (parts) such as root, stem and leaves.

It takes place by two methods: (i) Natural methods, (ii) Artificial methods.

3.2.2 Natural Methods of Vegetative Propagation

Many herbaceous, perennial plants propagate naturally through modified or specialised vegetative structures such as runners, corms, suckers, bulbs, tubers, bulbils, stolon, offsets, etc. which is known as natural vegetative propagation. These structures remain dormant in adverse environmental conditions and store food for developing plant. In addition to propagation they also perform the function of perennation and storage. Some of the natural methods of vegetative propagation are described below :

1. Runners: Runner is a thin, long, slender branch, which arises from the axil of a leaf. It runs along the surface of the soil for some distance and then gives rise to new plant by producing adventitious roots below and shoot above. The runner has long internodes and small scale leaves at the nodes. A bud is present at the tip of the runner. The runner produces new daughter plants, little away from the parent plant, so that competition between the parent and daughter plants is avoided. The daughter plants in turn produce runners which again propagate the plant in a similar manner. Thus, it is very efficient and quick method for multiplication of plants. It is generally observed in herbaceous perennial plants like Doob grass (harali), *Hydrocotyle*, Strawberry, *Oxalis* etc. (Fig. 3.3)

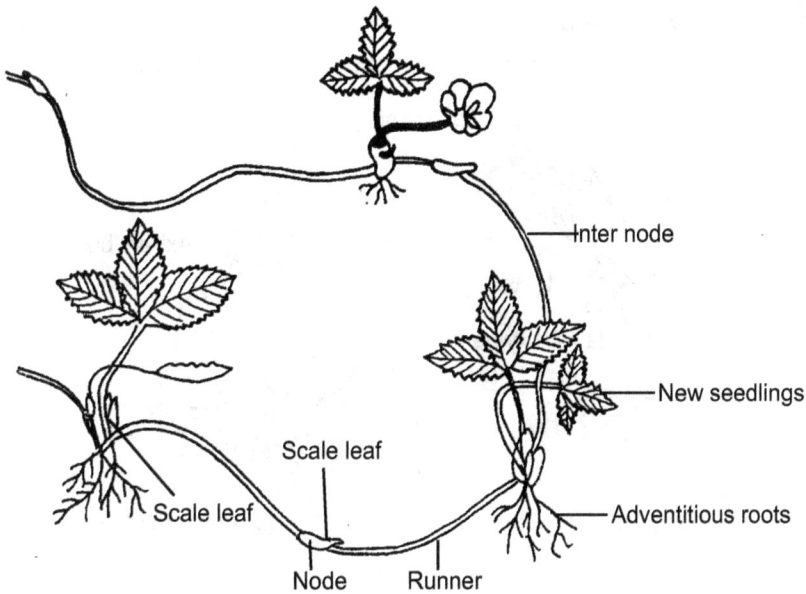

Fig. 3.3: Runner producing plants at the nodes - *Fragaria vesca* (Strawberry)

2. Suckers: It is an underground, slender branch, produced from a meristem from the root at the base. They emerge at a distance from the originating plant and forms a new plant. e.g. *Chrysanthemum, Sansevieria*, mint. (Fig. 3.4)

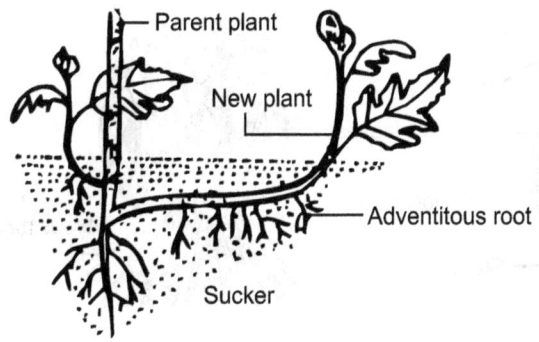

Fig. 3.4: Sucker of *Chrysanthemum*

3. Bulbs: The bulb is a reduced convex disc-like underground stem. Adventitious roots are produced from its lower side. The disc-like stem shows compressed internodes. Leaves arise from the nodes. The terminal bud lies at the centre of the bulb and it develops into aerial shoot bearing flowers. The axillary bud may form small daughter bulbs, from which new plants are formed. There are two types of bulbs. (Fig. 3.5)

(i) Tunicated bulb: Onion is a common example of tunicated bulb. In onion, leaves are arranged concentrically which are thick and fleshy called cataphylls. The bulb is covered by dry, membranous and papery scales. Similarly, in bulbs of Tulip, Tuberose the scale leaves are arranged concentrically on the disc and the whole bulb is covered by dry membranous scale leaves called tunic. Hence, these types of bulbs are known as tunicated bulbs.

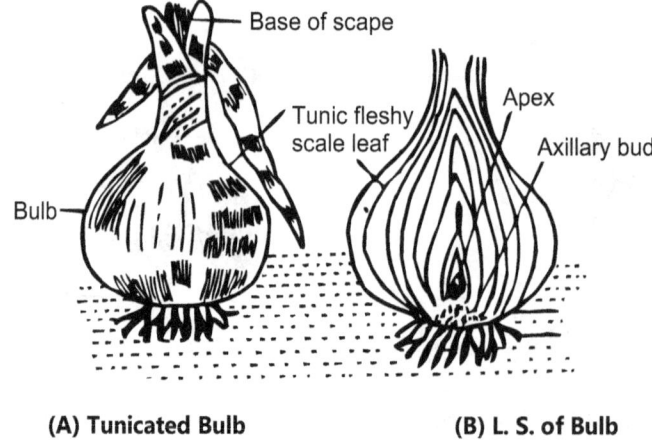

(A) Tunicated Bulb   (B) L. S. of Bulb

Fig. 3.5

(ii) **Scaly bulb:** In this type, the scale leaves are not arranged in concentric manner, but they are loose and overlapping. The bulb is not covered by membranous, dry covering i.e. tunic. Hence they are called non tunicated or scaly bulbs. e.g. Lily, *Oxalis* and Garlic. In garlic, fleshy scale is called clove. These cloves are not arranged concentrically but are separate and overlapping. Each clove is enclosed by whitish skinny tunic. (Fig. 3.6)

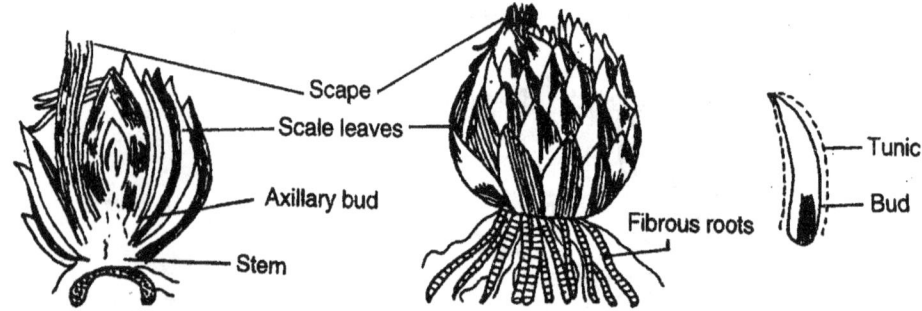

(A) Scaly bulb of Lily   (B) L.S. of scaly bulb of Lily   (C) V. S. of Clove of Garlic

Fig. 3.6

4. **Tubers:** Tuber means any fleshy part of the plant which may store food. When it is a stem it is called stem-tuber; when it is a root it is called root tuber. Common example of stem tuber is potato. In potato the main stem is erect. Axillary buds present in the axils of lower leaves develop into lateral branches. These branches grow down into the soil and swell at their tips into tubers due to accumulation of food and growth is arrested. Tuber shows nodes and internodes which are not distinct due to swelling. At the nodes, there are scale leaves in the axils of which axillary buds called ' eyes ' are present. Under favourable conditions, these

eyes sprout and produce new plants. Tubers are also present in other plants e.g. *Cyperus rotundus* (Nagarmotha). (Fig. 3.7)

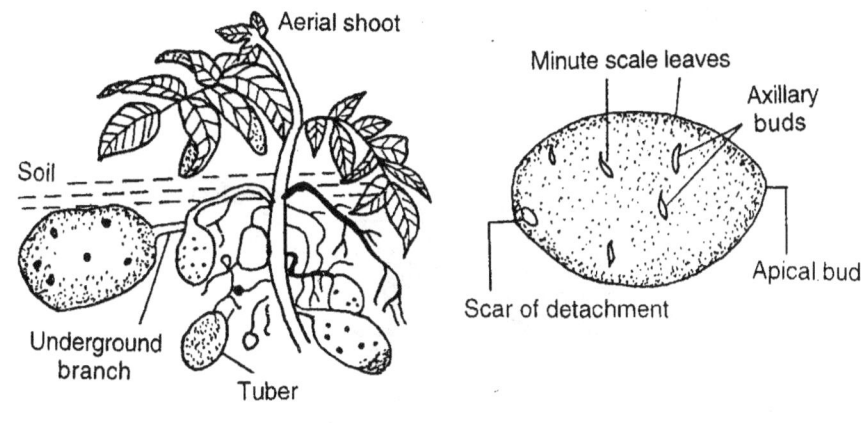

(A) Potato plant showing Tubers   (b) Tuber of potato

Fig. 3.7

5. Corms: The corm is an stout, underground, condensed, swollen base of the main stem. It grows vertically and consists of nodes, internodes and scaly leaves. It has a single large apical bud and many small axillary buds at the nodes and number of adventitious roots at its base. Many a time, three generations of corm can be seen. Towards the base, previous year's old shrivelled corm is present, above which the present year's large swollen corm is present. The terminal or axillary bud on present year corm represents next year's corm. Adventitious buds develop cormils on the present year corm. e.g. *Amorphophallus* (Suran), *Gladiolus, Colocasia*. (Fig. 3.8)

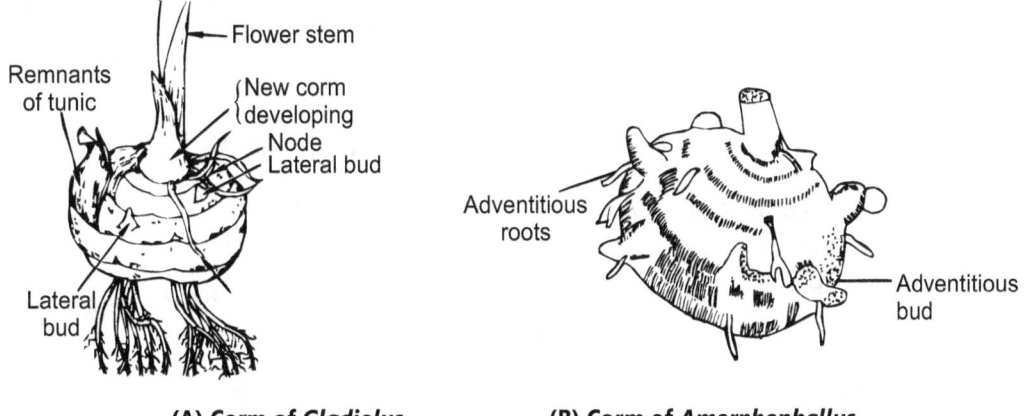

(A) Corm of *Gladiolus*   (B) Corm of *Amorphophallus*

Fig. 3.8

6. Rhizomes: It is an underground stem, growing horizontally under the soil. It is modified for storage of food material (generally starch) and vegetative reproduction. The rhizome shows nodes and internodes on it. The buds present at nodal region produce new sprouting, shoots and roots at the base. The rhizome can be cut into small pieces having at -least a single bud; this after planting gives new plants. e.g. *Canna indica* (Kardal), Banana, Ginger, Sugarcane, ferns etc. (Fig. 3.9)

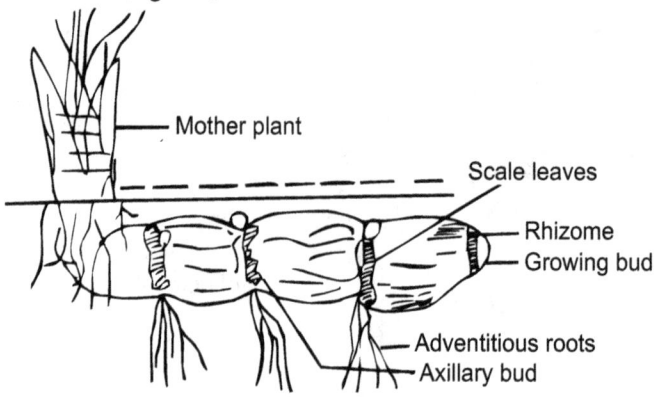

Fig. 3.9 : Rhizome of *Canna indica*

7. **Bulbils :** It is the modification of either vegetative or floral bud. It is a multicellular body specially meant for vegetative reproduction. The bulbil gets detached from the plant, falls down on the soil and after getting favourable conditions develops into a new plant. E.g. *Dioscorea*. In *Dioscorea* the axillary vegetative bud does not develop into

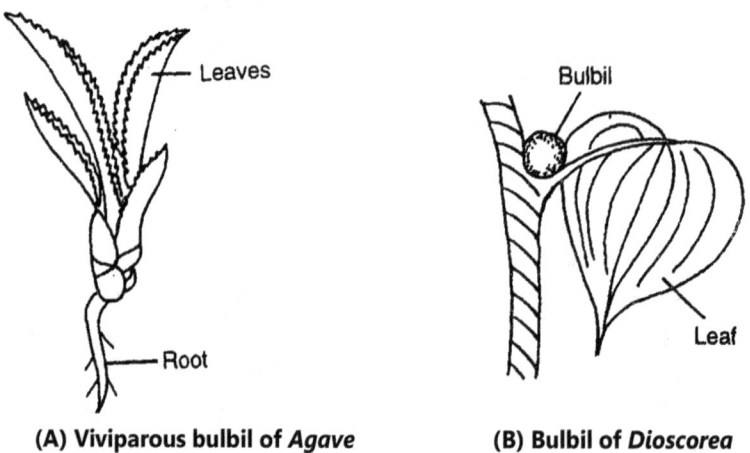

(A) Viviparous bulbil of *Agave*   (B) Bulbil of *Dioscorea*

Fig. 3.10

branch, but it is modified into bulbil. It is round, multicellular and stores food. Another example is *Agave* (Century plant) in which the flower-bud instead of developing into flower, is modified into bulbil. This bulbil does not immediately get detached from the mother plant, but remains attached to it for sometime. It germinates and develops into small plant which then falls down on the soil. Thus it shows vivipary. (Fig. 3.10)

8. Stolons : It is a special type of branch similar to the runner. But it does not grow horizontally from the very beginning. At first, it grows upward aerially like an ordinary branch, then bends downward towards the soil. When it touches the soil, adventitious roots are produced below and shoot above, thus a new plant is developed. e.g. *Nephrolepis* (fern), *Mentha*, Raspberry. (Fig. 3.11)

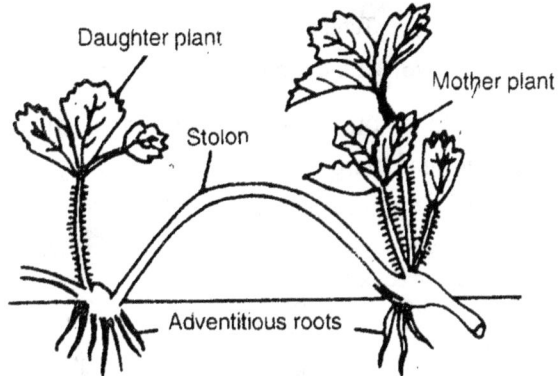

Fig. 3.11 : Stolon of *Mentha*

9. Offsets: It resembles the runner, but it is shorter and thicker as compared to the runner. It is generally found in aquatic plants. It develops from axillary bud of the main stem. e.g. *Pistia* and *Eichhornia*. In these plants, it grows in water for some distance and then produces a new plant. (Fig. 3.11)

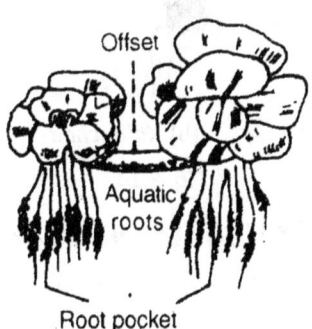

Fig. 3.12 : Offset of *Pistia*

10. Roots: Woody plants like *Dalbergia sissoo*, *Murraya* etc. produce buds on roots which grow into new plants. Tuberous roots of sweet potato (*Ipomoea* batatas), *Asparagus* etc. also produce adventitious buds that develop into new plants. Roots of sweet potato are biennial. They are produced in one season, herbaceous shoots die off. These roots function as storage organs and undergo dormant period. In the following season the adventitious buds grow into new shoots. The tuberous roots that have stored food provide nourishment during the initial shoot growth. (Fig. 3.13)

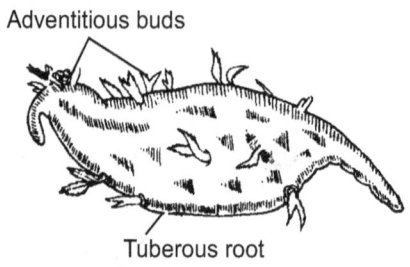

Fig. 3.13: *Ipomoea batatas*

11. Leaves: In some plants, foliar buds are produced which grow into new plants. The foliar buds are produced on the leaf margin and sometimes they are produced on the leaf surface. E.g. *Bryophyllum, Kalanchoe* and *Begonia*. (Fig. 3.14 (a) to (c))

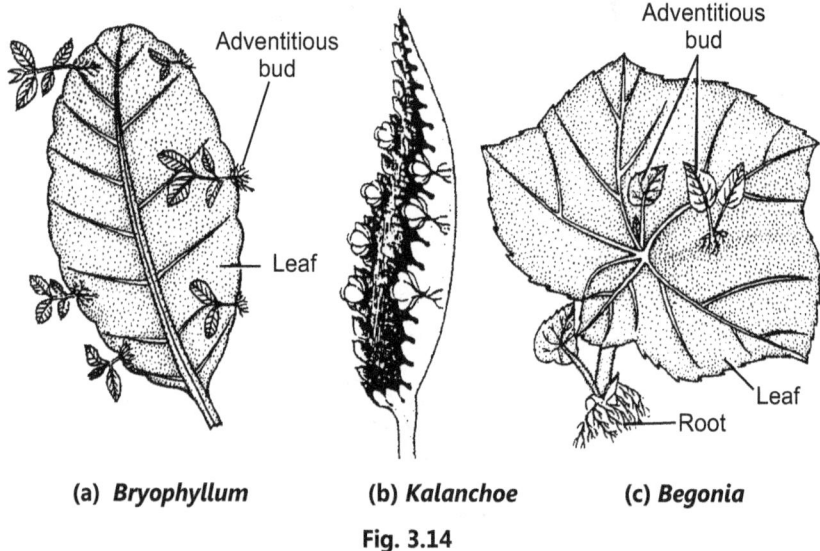

(a) *Bryophyllum* (b) *Kalanchoe* (c) *Begonia*

Fig. 3.14

3.2.3 Artificial Methods of Vegetative Propagation

Artificial vegetative propagation allows us to get desired offspring from a particular plant variety. This type of propagation is carried out in order to get healthier plants, maintaining the desired traits, and to get vigorous and efficient production rate offspring.

The artificial methods of vegetative propagation are as follows : (I) Cuttings, (II) Layering, (III) Grafting and (d) Budding.

I. Cuttings

It is the most commonly used and simple method of vegetative propagation which does not require much of the equivalent or cutting skills.

Cuttings are any vegetative part from the mother plant that is detached (cut) and placed under favourable conditions of soil and climate. It produces new roots and shoot and develops into new plant.

Technique : Take the cuttings early in the morning. Select healthy, single-stemmed shoots and seal them in opaque, plastic bag. Cuttings should be prepared as soon as possible after collection. Insert the cuttings into the compost and water them.

In selecting cutting material, it is important to use stock plants, that are free from diseases, vigorous and fairly productive.

The cutting knife used should be sharp. It should be washed in a fungicide before use. The cut should be made in one stroke.

Types of Cuttings: Cuttings are of four types.

(1) Stem Cuttings (2) Root Cuttings (3) Leaf Cuttings (4) Leaf-bud Cuttings.

Success of cutting mainly depends on the formation of adventitious roots by cuttings. Meristematic cells are responsible to produce roots and shoots(bud). Cutting of some plants produce roots by mere contact with moist soil, while some require rooting hormones.

(1) Stem Cuttings: This is the most important type of cutting, which is divided according to the nature of wood used in the cuttings. (a) Soft wood cuttings (b) Hard wood cuttings.

(a) Soft wood Cuttings: These are taken in spring, when the new shoots of the parent plant just beginning to harden. The young basal shoots of herbaceous perennials are also used. Softwood cuttings often provide the best chance of rooting, in species that are difficult to propagate.

Soft wood cuttings require more attention and equipment. This type of cutting is always made with leaves attached. They must be handled carefully to prevent drying. Temperature should be maintained during rooting at 21^0C to 23^0C. They produce roots within 2 to 4 weeks. Length of the cutting should be 3 to 5 inches with at least two nodes. The leaves on lower portion are removed, while the upper leaves are retained. Flowers should be removed. E.g. *Magnolia*, Barberry, *Hydrangea*. (Fig. 3.15 and 3.16)

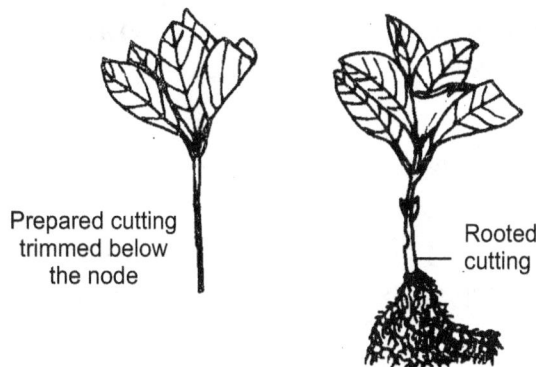

Fig. 3.15 : *Hydrangea macrophylla* **plant**

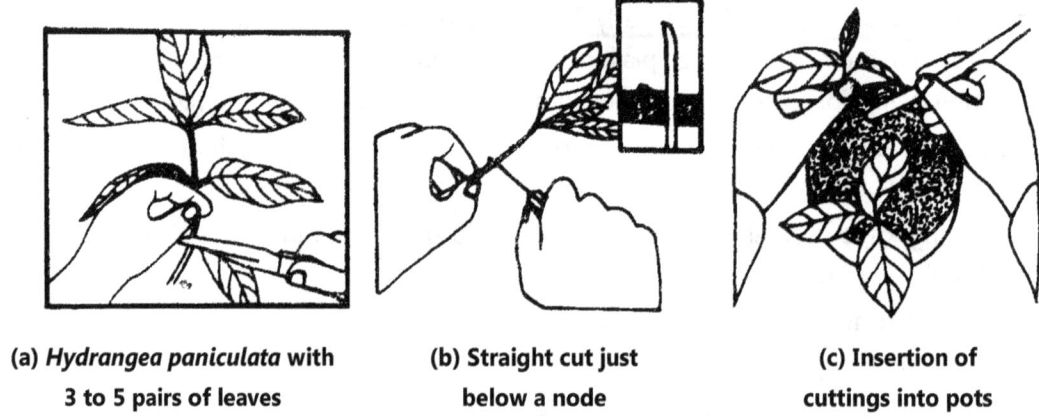

(a) *Hydrangea paniculata* with 3 to 5 pairs of leaves

(b) Straight cut just below a node

(c) Insertion of cuttings into pots

Fig. 3.16: Propagating shrubs by soft wood cuttings

(b) Hard Wood Cuttings: Cuttings made from the past seasons growth or older wood that has shed its leaves and has become well lignified are called hard wood cuttings. It does not require special equipment during rooting. Hard wood cuttings are easily transplanted after rooting. These cuttings are taken during dormant season.

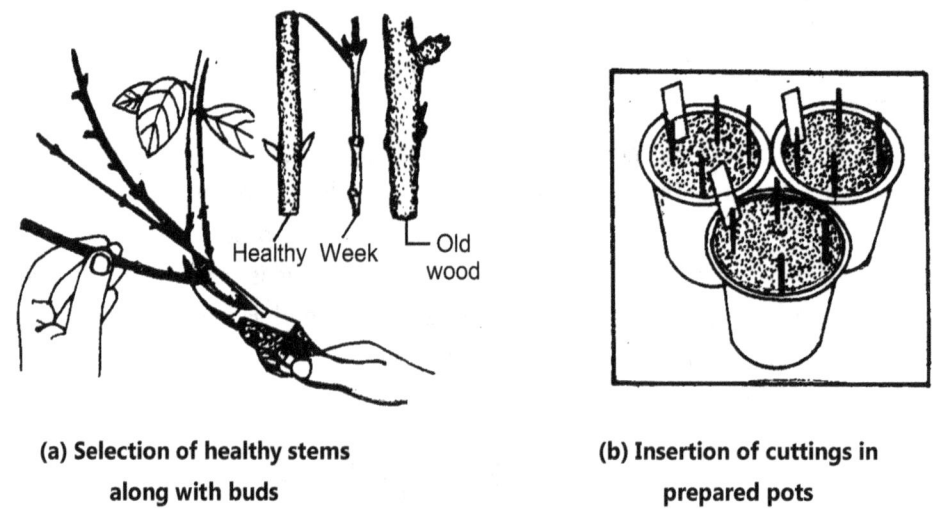

(a) Selection of healthy stems along with buds

(b) Insertion of cuttings in prepared pots

Fig. 3.17

They are not immediately planted but are kept in moist wrapping material like moss and stored at about 40° F till next growing. They are treated with root promoting hormones (e.g. *Keradix*) before planting. Cutting having 4 to 12 inches length and at least two nodes are made from old wood. The top cut is given slightly above a node and the lower cut slightly below the node.

Deciduous, woody, ornamental as well as fruit plants are propagated by this method.

E.g. *Bougainvillea*, Rose, Apple, Pear, Cherry, Plum, Fig, Lemon, Orange *Salix*, etc. (Fig. 3.17)

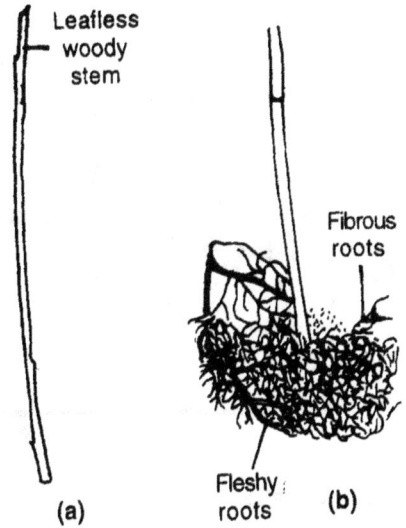

Fig. 3.18 : e.g. *Salix alba*

In hard wood cuttings as the stem used is matured, it contains sufficient quantity of reserved carbohydrates and has very low percentage of water. Hence it is very essential to check the water loss from these cuttings. Thus, all the leaves from these cuttings are removed, keeping a small part of petiole intact to avoid injury to the bud or node.

Nerium, *Juniper* etc. are propagated by this method.

II. Layering

Definition: Layering is a simple method of vegetative propagation in which the rooting of the shoots or branches takes place *in situ*, i.e. adventitious roots develop on the stem or branch which is still attached to the mother plant.

During layering the branch is injured and the suitable conditions are provided to the injured part to produce roots. The rooted branch is detached and a new plant is obtained. The layered branch is known as a layer. In some plants layering occur naturally e.g. in Raspberries, the branches develop roots at nodal region, when their branches touch the soil. In some plants the tendency of producing adventitious roots is induced by giving artificial treatment.

Types of Layering

Layering are of the following types (1) Simple , (2) Serpentine, (3) Air layering, (4) Mound layering, (5) Trench layering, (6) Tip layering.

For all types of layering adequate supply of oxygen and moisture is essential. The light should be avoided and young wood should be selected.

Gootee or air layering: This kind of layering is most commonly practiced in India and has been given various names such as pot layering, air layering, marcottage or gootee. It differs from ordinary layering in that instead of bringing a branch to the soil, the soil is taken to the branch. However, the principle is the same. A ring of bark, about 3 cm long is removed from below the bud portion of the selected shoot. It is covered with soil, moss or other moistening materials. It is then covered and tied with a piece of gunny cloth, or by using plastic wraps which allow aeration but there is no loss of moisture. The wound or exposed portion is treated with the rooting hormones like keradix just before covering it with moist

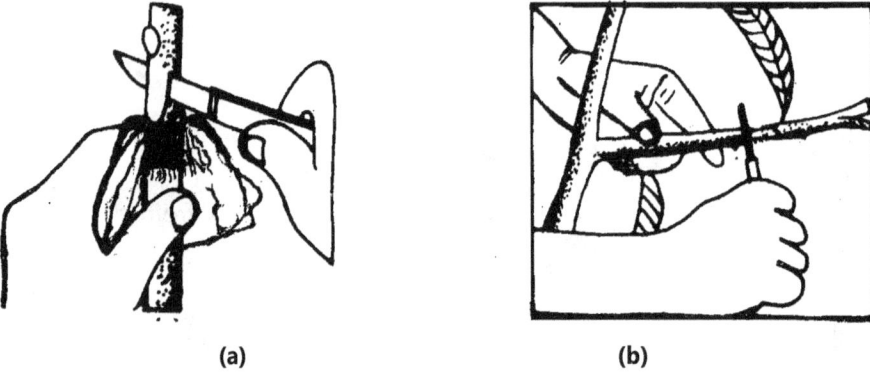

(a)   (b)

Removal of bark and girdle formation

(c) Wrapping of polythene film the moss and tieing at each end   **(d) Roots on air layering observed through the polythene film**

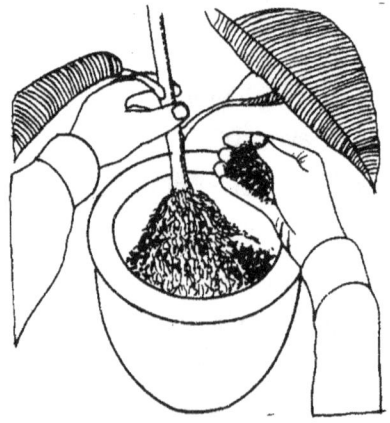

(e) Gootee planted in Pot

Fig. 3.19: Steps in air layering

moss. As soon as enough roots are visible through plastic wrap, the plant is detached from the parent. The ornamental plants like *Dracaena, Boungainvillea, Ficus* as well as fruit trees like litchi, lime, chiku, pomegranate, mango, cashew nut, guava etc. are propagated by this method. (Fig. 3.19 (a) to (e))

III. Grafting

Definition: Grafting refers to connecting a part of one plant to another in such a manner that they will unite and ultimately grow and develop as a one plant.

The terminology used in grafting is -

Root Stock: The plant or part of the plant on which grafting is done is called root stock or stock. It provides root system to the grafted plant.

Scion: The part of the superior and desired plant which is to be grafted on the stock containing several dormant buds is called the scion. It forms the top of the new plant which bears flowers and fruits after successful grafting.

Types of Grafting: The major types of grafting are (i) Whip grafting (ii) Tongue grafting (iii) Side grafting (iv) Approach grafting (v) Stone grafting (vi) Wedge grafting (vii) Cleft grafting.

a. Inarching or approach grafting: This method is commonly used in case of evergreen trees like mango, guava and sapota. Peculiarity of this type of grafting is that both scion and stock are rooted plants and scion remains a part of the parent tree till the union with the stock is complete. The stock and scion plants are raised in pots or in the soil but the height of both should be the same. It is also essential that the thickness of the stock seedling and the scion shoot should be the same.

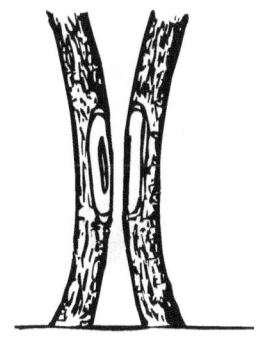  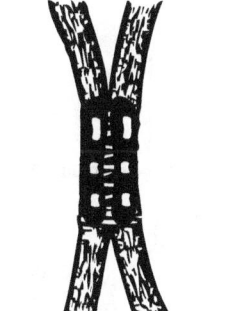

(a) Slicing – cut made both on stock and scion

(b) Tying together

(c) Union

Fig. 3.20: Approach grafting in mango

A slice of bark about 4 cm long on the side of the stock facing the scion shoot is removed. After preparing the stock, the scion is also prepared in the same manner. They are both drawn together, joined and are tightly bound with fibre. After tying, it is sealed with grafting wax. The pot or area around stock seedling is regularly irrigated till complete union takes place. As soon as the union is complete, within 2 to 3 months, the scion is separated just below the point of union through gradual stages. In the first stage a cut is given about half way or slightly less. This cut is made deeper after 10 to 15 days. If the scion shoot does not show any sign of withering, it is completely detached from the parent tree after a week. The plant is now kept under shade of a tree and becomes ready for planting in the field during the next season. (Fig. 3.20)

Inarching is also useful in those trees which are damaged by some diseases or by rodents on the root or lower part of the trunk. In such cases the method of inarching is slightly modified. 2 to 4 seedlings are planted close to the diseased or damaged plant on all sides and they are inarched in the bark of the tree above the point of damage. While performing the operation, the seedlings are sliced at a height which is just above the point of damage of the diseased tree. An inverted ' T ' cut is made in the bark of the tree at that point and the sliced seedling is inserted into this incision. It is the tied. After union the diseased tree will stand on these seedling roots. The original disease affected root system can be removed.

b. Stone grafting: This method is also called epicotyle grafting and commonly used in mango plant. This method is most promising for multiplying plants in large number within short period. The seeds are placed on a sand bed and covered with 50 to 75 cm thick layer of leaf mould for germination. (Fig. 3.21)

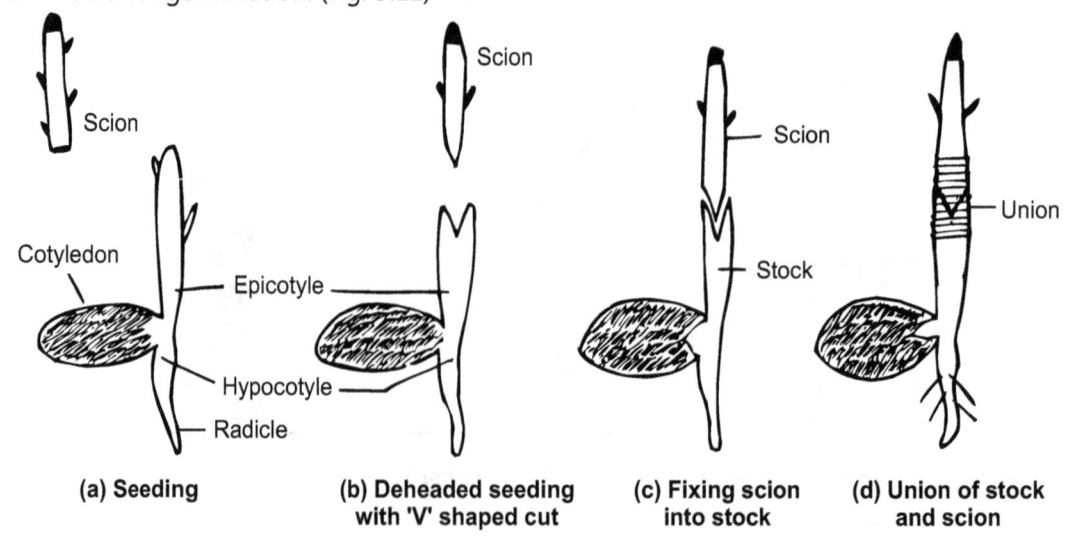

(a) Seeding (b) Deheaded seeding with 'V' shaped cut (c) Fixing scion into stock (d) Union of stock and scion

Fig. 3.21: Stone grafting in mango

Germinated seedlings of 8 to 15 days are grafted by deheading the seedling about 5 cm above the stone and inserting the wedge shaped scion in the vertical slit in the Deheaded root stock. Polythene tape is used for tying the graft. Immediately thereafter the grafts are planted in polythene bags filled with soil and farm yard manure mixture (1 : 1). The grafts are watered and kept in semishade condition to avoid damaging effects of sun and rain.

Stock - Scion Relationship

The root stock supplies water and nutrients to the scion. The amount of water and nutrients supplied by root stock affects the scion and make changes in the form, size, shape and longevity of scion. It also has an effect on the time and amount of flowering, as well as time of maturity, size, colour and quality of the fruit. Similarly, the scion also influences the stock, which is not easily noticed. Vigorously growing scion supplies more food material to the root system. The branching nature of scion causes the vigorous growth of root system.

Most important factor of compatibility is the union between stock and scion with success. Grafting is possible between varieties in a species or between species of a genus or between genera of a family. The plants belonging to different families are incompatible. Sometimes the graftage is apparently successful but the union is not complete or satisfactory. In such cases, after a few years the tree becomes dwarf, unhealthy and ultimately dies off. The difference in the relative vigour of stock and scion causes larger development of the stem above the union and vice-versa. The causes of incompatibility are not completely understood. In some cases it may be the formation of an imperfect union between root stock and scion or some inhibition of the transport of material across the union in phloem.

IV Budding

Definition: When the scion is a small piece of bark or a wood containing a single bud, the process is called *budding*.

Budding can be defined as a special form of grafting in which instead of a branch, a bud is grafted on the stock.

Types of budding

There are two types of budding

(A) ' T ' or shield budding and (B) Patch budding

(A) ' T ' or shield budding

This type of budding is commonly used by gardeners for the propagation of many ornamental, flowering plants as well as some fruit trees. It is regularly applied to propagate roses. Budding is a form of grafting in which instead of a branch with many buds, only one bud along with or without wood is grafted on the stock. All side branches and suckers near the budding point are removed. There are three steps in budding operation (a) Preparation of stock (b) Preparation of scion (c) Insertion of scion or bud.

(a) Preparation of stock: The stock is prepared only when the bark of the stock separates easily from the wood. At first a vertical cut, about an inch long is made in the stock. A horizontal cut is then made at the top of the vertical cut so as to form a ' T ' shaped incision. Then the knife is twisted slightly to open the two flaps of bark for the insertions of the scion i.e. bud. The cut is extended only through the bark and should not go deep into the wood.

(b) Preparation of scion: Usually bud is removed after preparing the stock to avoid drying of the scion.

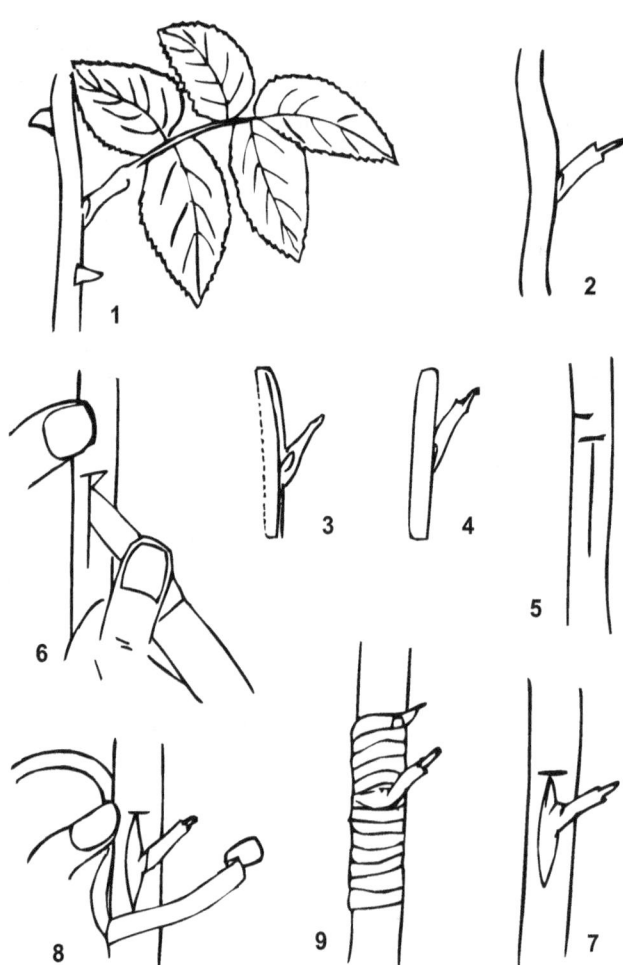

Fig. 3.22: ' T ' or shield budding technique In rose

1. Part of the scion with ' bud ' and leaf; 2. The leaf cut off and thorns removed, 3. Shield-shaped bark with the 'eye'; 4. "Budding eye' with Candle'; 5. T-shaped cut on stock cleared on thorns and leaves; 6. 'T' shaped cut being loosened for inserting the 'budding eye'; 7. 'budding eye' inserted; 8. tying the 'eye' with a polythelene strip; 9. The 'eye' securely tied.

A clear sloping cut is made about half an inch below the bud which passes about an inch above the bud. As a result of this a shield shaped piece of bark with a bud in its middle is detached from the stem. The part of wood attached to the bark is then removed carefully without injuring the bud. (Fig. 3.22)

(c) Insertion of bud or scion: The shield shaped piece of bark containing a bud is inserted into T shaped cut made on the stock. The shield is pushed under the two raised flaps of bark and is properly covered by two flaps of bark keeping the bud exposed. The graft is then tied with polythene tape keeping the bud uncovered. The whole operation should be done quickly to avoid drying of the bud.

When the bud develops into a shoot the wrapped polythene tape is removed and the stock is cut off 2 to 3 inches above the bud.

Due to ' T ' shaped cut made on the root stock it is called ' T ' budding and shield shaped bark of scion, it is called shield budding.

Advantages of vegetative propagation

In horticultural practices vegetative methods of propagation are more preferred to sexual methods of propagation because it has following advantages:

1. The asexual or vegetatively propagated plants are of true type. They are uniform in their growth, yielding capacity, fruit and flower quality. The cultivator can thus be sure about the type of flower, fruit that he is going to expect from the vegetatively propagated plants, which is not possible through seed propagation.
2. Some fruit varieties are seedless. Such varieties can only be propagated vegetatively e.g. Banana, Pineapple, Grape, Guava, etc.
3. Vegetatively propagated plants produce fruits earlier than seedling plants (sexual propagation).
4. It is rapid and simple method of propagation through which large number of new plants can be obtained.
5. Some fruit plants and ornamental plants having unusual habitat for growth or have unusual colouration. These unique characters of such plants are immediately lost if they are propagated by seeds. Therefore, to continue and maintain the unique characters, vegetative propagation is highly essential.
6. Methods of vegetative propagation are useful for enhancing vigour of exhausted plants.
7. Parent plants produce new plants without genetic change.

8. Some fruit varieties are susceptible to certain diseases. By budding or grafting them on to resistant root-stocks, those varieties can be grown without pest or disease. E.g. some diseases in case of *Citrus* and Grapes, can be avoided by this method.
9. It is possible to take advantage of modifying influence of root stock on the scion. In some cases, variety may be otherwise very suitable but may not grow in particular type of soil and climatic conditions. Then this is possible by grafting the variety on the suitable root stock. In extreme cold region Apples are grown on Russian stock or Crabapple.
10. By vegetative propagation it is possible to regulate the plant size, fruit quality, maturity etc. according to the grower by using different root stocks.
11. Cross pollination is made possible by grafting shoots of other suitable varieties, called pollinizers on some branches of the self- unfruitful variety. Some varieties of fruits like Almond and Plum which are self unfruitful can be made fruitful by this method.
12. Grafting helps in healing of wounds caused by rodents, or implements.
13. Composite plants can be raised by grafting. This type of plants bear several varieties or types of fruits or flowers. e.g. on one root stock different citrus fruits like grapefruit, pummelo, mandarin and sweet orange can be grown. Similarly, on single root stock flowers of different colours can be obtained by bud grafting in roses.
14. On the wild inferior species of the plant, superior varieties can be grafted so as to convert wild plant into productive one.
15. Some plants produce seed which germinate with difficulty or even after special treatment, seedling are small and susceptible to diseases e.g. Potato and Sweet potato. Therefore for commercial production, vegetative propagation is the only method in these plants.

Disadvantages or Demerits of Vegetative Propagation

1. The vegetatively propagated plants, particularly the budded and grafted ones are generally not as vigorous and long lived as the seedling plants.
2. For vegetative propagation skill labour is required.
3. New varieties cannot be developed by the natural means of vegetative propagation.
4. Grafted or budded plants are comparatively costly.
5. Artificial methods of vegetative propagation are restricted to dicotyledons and gymnosperms.
6. Many diseases can get transmitted to new plants through the infected vegetative plant parts used.

Points to Remember

- There are six types of nurseries like (i) ornamental, (ii) plant nursery, (iii) fruit plant nursery, (iv) medicinal plant nursery, (v) vegetable plant nursery, (vi) orchid nursery and (vii) forest nursery.
- Nursery is place where seedlings are raised for planting purpose.
- The art of raising a larger number of seedings or saplings in a protected area is known as nursery technique.
- The plants propagated by grafting or budding require raising of rootstocks.
- Propagation of plants are of three types
  a. Seed propagation
  b. Natural vegetative propagation
  c. Artificial vegetative propagation
- Ovary, ovule, integuments and nucellus are the parts of the seed.
- Storage of seeds is important in the process of plant propagation by seeds.
- Viability testing of seeds is important for propagation by seeds.
- Environmental conditions play an important role in seed germination.
- Vegetative propagation is of two types: (a) Natural and (b) Artificial.
- Natural vegetative propagation takes place by modification of root, stem and leaf.
- Artificial vegetative propagation can be done by different ways and means. Some major types are as follows:
  a. Stem cutting
  b. Air layering
  c. Grafting
  d. Budding

Exercises

Short Answer Questions

1. Write short notes on the following :
   (i) Types of nurseries
   (ii) Ornamental plant nursery
   (iii) Fruit plant nursery
   (iv) Medicinal plant nursery
   (v) Vegetable plant nursery
   (vi) Orchid nursery
   (vii) Forest nursery

2. Write short notes on:
   (i) Seed viability testing
   (ii) Storage of seeds
   (iii) Seed germination
   (iv) Natural vegetative propagation by tubers
   (v) Natural vegetative propagation by leaves
   (vi) Suckers
   (vii) Runners
   (viii) Bulbils
   (ix) Bulbs
   (x) Stock-scion relationship
   (xi) 'T' layering
   (xii) Air layering
   (xiii) Approach grafting
   (xiv) Stone grafting

Long Answer Questions
1. Describe the concept and types of nurseries.
2. Describe the infrastructure required for the ornamental plant nursery.
3. Give commercial applications of orchid nursery.
4. Give an account of infrastructure required for vegetable plant nursery.
5. Describe commercial applications and profitability in forest nursery.
6. Give commercial applications, output and profitability in medicinal plant nursery.
7. Explain merits of sexual propagation.
8. Explain natural vegetative propagation by stem.
9. Explain artificial vegetative propagation by stem cutting.
10. Describe artificial vegetative propagation by air layering.
11. What is grafting? Explain stone and approach grafting.
12 Describe the structure of dicot and monocot seed?
13. Explain merits and demerits of vegetative propagation.
14. Describe the demerits of sexual propagation?
15. What is propagation? Briefly outline the various method of plant propagation.
16. Define vegetative propagation and give its merits.
17. Give an account of demerits of vegetative propagation.
18. Describe any two of the natural methods of vegetative propagation with suitable examples.
19. Give merits and demerits of vegetative propagation.
20. Enlist the artificial methods of vegetative propagation and write a note on soft wood stem cutting.
21. Describe in brief layering with suitable example.
22. Explain the steps involved in approach grafting.

Chapter 4...
Plant Tissue Culture Industry

Contents ...
4.1 Concept of Tissue Culture
4.2 Culture Techniques
    4.2.1 Types of Explants
    4.2.2 Preparation of Media
    4.2.3 Methods of Sterilisation,
    4.2.4 Inoculation Techniques,
    4.2.5 Incubation
    4.2.6 Hardening of Plantlets
4.3 Commercial Significance
    Points to Remember
    Exercises

4.1 Concept of Tissue Culture

The conventional methods of plant breeding were most widely used for crop improvement. However, these conventional methods have some limitations. To overcome these problems, conventional methods are being replaced with plant tissue culture techniques for increasing the disease resistance, yield, durability, etc. These objectives are difficult to achieve through conventional methods. The term *tissue culture* is commonly used in a very wide sense to include *in vitro* culture of plant cells, tissues as well as organs. Tissue culture is also called as *in vitro* growth, which literally means growth in the glass containers such as test tubes, bottles, conical flasks, etc. It is based on the phenomenon of totipotency, which is defined as the ability of isolated plant cells to divide, redivide and regenerate into whole plant on artificial nutrient medium under controlled conditions. This technique is also called micro propagation; especially when it is used for plant propagation. The prefix 'micro' generally refers to the small size of the plant part used for propagation, but it could equally refer to the size of the plantlets which are produced as a result. Micro propagation results in the production of a large number of plants from small parts of a stock plant in a relatively short period of time. Micropropagation is defined as the *controlled, in vitro propagation of plants under aseptic conditions*. It can also be defined as a *method of large scale, in vitro propagation of plants, in which plant cells, tissues or organs are cultured on artificial nutrient medium, under aseptic and controlled environmental condition.* The technique in which organised structures like root tips, shoot tips, embryos, etc. are cultured *in vitro* to obtain them as organised structures, is called organ culture. In this chapter, the term tissue culture is used in its broad sense to denote aseptic culture of plant cells, tissues and organs.

4.2 Culture Techniques

The *in vitro* techniques were developed initially to demonstrate the totipotency of plant cells predicted by Haberlandt in 1902. *Totipotency* is the ability of a plant cell to perform all the functions of development, which are characteristic of zygote, i.e., ability to regenerate into a complete plant. In 1902, Haberlandt reported culture of isolated single palisade cells from leaves in Knop's salt solution enriched with sucrose. The cells remained alive up to 1 month, increased in size, accumulated starch but failed to divide. Efforts to demonstrate totipotency led to the development of techniques for cultivation of plant cells under defined conditions. This was made possible by the amazing contributions from R. J. Gautheret in France and P.R. White in U.S.A. during the third and the fourth decades of 20th century. Most of the modern tissue culture media has been derived from the work of Skoog and coworkers during 1950s and 1960s.

The technique of *in vitro* cultivation of plant cells and organs is primarily devoted to solve two basic problems: (1) to keep the plant cells and organs free from microbes, and (2) to ensure the desired development in the cells and organs by providing suitable nutrient media and other environmental conditions. The first problem can be eliminated by using modern equipments and careful handling during various operations. The second problem remains the area of active research and is likely to be so for quite some time in the future. At present, it relies mainly on the manipulation of culture medium, especially growth regulators, and, to a much lesser extent, on other factors, including environmental conditions.

4.2.1 Types of Explants

An explant is the plant part used for tissue culture experiment. Mostly apical and axillary buds are used as explants. It may include portions of shoots, leaves, stems, flowers, roots and single, undifferentiated cell, tissues or organs.

The pathways through which whole plants are regenerated from cells and tissues or explants such as meristem broadly fall into three types:

1. The method in which explants that include a meristem (viz. the shoot tips or nodes) are grown on appropriate media supplemented with plant growth regulators to induce proliferation of multiple shoots, followed by rooting of the excised shoots to regenerate whole plants

2. The method in which totipotency of cells is realised in the form of *de novo* organogenesis, either directly in the form of induction of shoot meristem on the explants

or indirectly via a callus (unorganised mass of cells resulting from proliferation of cells of the explants) and plants are regenerated through induction of roots on the resultant shoots

3. Somatic embryogenesis, in which asexual adventive embryos (comparable to zygotic embryos in their structure and development) are induced directly on explants or indirectly through a callus phase.

4.2.2 Preparation of Media

Before preparing medium for tissue culture, concentrated stock solutions of macronutrients, micronutrients, vitamins and growth hormones are prepared and stored in the refrigerator. Use of already prepared stock solutions makes preparation of medium easy. Stock solutions of macronutrients, micronutrients and vitamins are prepared in 10X, 20X, 50X or 100 X concentrations, which means the ingredients are taken respectively in 10, 20, 50 or 100 times more than the recommended quantities.

During medium preparation, calculated quantities of different stock solutions are used. Stock solutions of growth hormones are separately prepared in concentrations of 10 mg / 100 ml, 50 mg / 100 ml or 100 mg /100 ml depending upon the requirement. Most of the growth hormones are first dissolved in a few drops of 0.1 N NaOH and then diluted with distilled water, as these are not directly soluble in water.

Different scientists have standardised nutrient media for *in vitro* plant growth. Composition of the nutrient media standardised by White (1953), Murashige and Skoog (1962), Gamborg et. al. (1968) and Nitsch (1969).

The stock solutions are prepared as per the ingredients of the desired medium. All the macronutrients are dissolved in distilled water to make common stock solution. A stock solution of micronutrients is prepared by dissolving all the micronutrients except iron.

The characteristic of iron is its capacity to be oxidised easily from ferrous (Fe^{++}) to ferric (Fe^{+++}) state, and readily reduced back from ferric to the ferrous form. In order to stabilise iron in ionic form, iron compounds should be dissolved along with chelating agents like Na_2EDTA (ethylene diamine tetra acetic acid disodium salt). In absence of a chelating agent, Fe^{++} or Fe^{+++} ions are liable to be precipitated and thus not available to the growing plant tissues.

Therefore, iron stock solution is separately prepared by dissolving $FeSO_4$ and Na_2 EDTA in boiled or hot distilled water. Vitamins as per selected medium can be dissolved together to make common vitamin stock solution.

Table 4.1: Nutritional composition of some plant tissue culture media (mg per Liter)

Medium Components	MS (Murashige and Skoog 1962)	B5 (Gamborg et al (1968)	White (1953)	Lloyd and McCown (1981)
Macronutrients				
NH_4NO_3	1650.0	-	-	400.0
KNO_3	1900.0	2500.0	80.0	-
$CaCl_2.2H_2O$	440.0	150.0	-	96.0
$MgSO_4.7H_2O$	370.0	250.0	720.0	370.0
KH_2PO_4	170.0	-	-	170.0
$(NH_4)_2SO_4$	-	134.0	-	-
$NaH_2PO_4.H_2O$	-	150.0	16.5	-
$CaNO_3.4H_2O$	-	-	300.0	556.0
Na_2SO_4	-	-	200.0	-
KCl	-	-	65.0	-
K_2SO_4	-	-	-	990.0
Micronutrients				
KI	0.83	0.75	0.75	-
H_3BO_3	6.20	3.0	1.5	6.2
$MnSO_4.4H_2O$	22.30	-	7.0	-
$MnSO_4.H_2O$	-	10.0	-	29.43
$ZnSO_4.7H_2O$	8.6	2.0	2.6	8.6
$Na_2MoO_4.2H_2O$	0.25	0.25	-	0.25
$CuSO_4.5H_2O$	0.025	0.025	-	0.25
$CoCl_2.6H_2O$	0.025	0.025	-	-
Na_2EDTA	37.3	37.3	-	37.3
$FeSO_4.7H_2O$	27.8	27.8	-	27.8

Contd...

Vitamins and other supplements				
Inositol	100.0	100.0		100.0
Glycine	2.0	2.0	3.0	2.0
Thiamine HCl	0.1	10.0	0.1	1.0
Pyridoxine HCl	0.5	-	0.1	0.5
Nicotinic acid	0.5	-	0.5	0.5
Ca-panthothenate	-	-	1.0	-
Cysteine HCl	-	-	1.0	-
Sucrose (g)	30	20	20	20
pH	5.8	5.8	5.5	5.8

The preparation of media is done after making all the stock solutions. A few of the steps of media preparation vary depending upon the type of nutrient medium and the method of its sterilisation. Sucrose is the most commonly used sugar in plant tissue culture media. Generally, 30 g sucrose is used for preparation of one litre of medium. Initially, it is dissolved in a suitable volume of distilled water and then exact required volumes of macronutriens, micronutrients, iron, vitamins and growth hormone stock solutions are added. After making up the final volume to the desired level by addition of distilled water, pH of the medium is adjusted to 5.8 by using 0.1 N HCl or 0.1 N NaOH solutions. Gelling agents like agar 8 g /l or phytagel 2g /l is added to the medium followed by its digestion on either a gas burner or on hot plate. It is then poured into washed and sterilised culture vessels like test tubes or bottles. Generally, 10 -15 ml medium is poured in each test tube and 30 to 50 ml in a bottle depending upon the size. Suitable closers like cotton plugs or polypropylene caps are used to close the culture vessels. Some times, aluminium foil or a polythene film called 'cling film' is wrapped around the closers before the vessels are kept in an autoclave for medium sterilisation.

4.2.3 Methods of Sterilisation

Test tubes, bottles and conical flasks which are commonly used as tissue culture vessels are first soaked in dilute detergent solution for a few hours and then washed thoroughly with tap water and finally rinsed with distilled water. The glasswares are then dried in oven and sterilised by autoclaving at 121°C temperature (15 lb / inch^2 pressure) for 20 minutes.

Sterilisation of the medium in an autoclave is done at 121°C temperature and 15lb / inch^2 pressure for 20 minutes. Sterilised media bottles and test tubes are kept in dust free area until they are used for inoculation. Method of preparation of liquid medium is similar to that of semisolid medium. However, liquid medium does not contain gelling agent like agar or phytagel. Therefore, after making the final volume up to the desired level and adjusting its pH, the medium is directly poured into culture vessels and sterilised.

Some of the chemical components of nutrient media are thermo labile and therefore non-autoclavable - gibberellic acid is one of them. If the medium contains gibberellic acid it should be sterilised by filter sterilisation method. Liquid medium can be sterilised by allowing it to pass through 0.3 μ membrane filters. When semisolid medium with thermo liable component is to be sterilised, the medium is autoclaved without that component and then the filter sterilised solution of thermo labile component is added in the medium, under aseptic conditions.

The explants are treated with dilute dettol solution for 5 minutes. This is followed by treatment with 0.05 % to 0.1 % $HgCl_2$ (mercuric chloride) for 2 to 5 minutes. One should standardise suitable concentration and duration of $HgCl_2$ treatment for the type of explants under consideration. Treatment with $HgCl_2$ solution is followed by thorough washing with sterilised distilled water at least three times. This is done under aseptic conditions inside the laminar flow cabinet. Other methods of surface sterilisation include treatment with dilute NaOCl (sodium hypochlorite solution for 10 to 30 minutes). Several times, surface sterilisation involves combination of $HgCl_2$ and NaOCl treatment. In some cases, explants are treated with 70% ethanol for 30 to 45 seconds, before giving $HgCl_2$ or NaOCl treatment. Surface sterilised explants are then inoculated on a suitable nutrient medium.

4.2.4 Inoculation Techniques

Inoculation refers to placing of surface sterilised explants on suitable nutrient medium, under aseptic conditions in the laminar flow cabinet. Before surface sterilisation, required materials should be sterilised and arranged in the laminar flow cabinet including bottles or test tubes with media, coupling jar containing ethanol, cotton, sterilised distilled water, empty beakers, gas burner, tools like forceps, blade holders, surgical blades etc. Sterile airflow of the laminar flow cabinet is switched on and the working surface is wiped with ethanol before arranging the required materials in it. UV tube installed in the laminar flow cabinet is kept on for 20 to 30 minutes before inoculation. Aseptic conditions must be strictly followed during inoculation. Operator's hands should be clean. The operator should wash hands with soap and then wipe with ethanol before starting inoculation. Operator should wear laboratory clothes like apron, cap and mask. If aseptic conditions are not properly maintained, fungal or bacterial contaminations set in and spoil the inoculated explant.

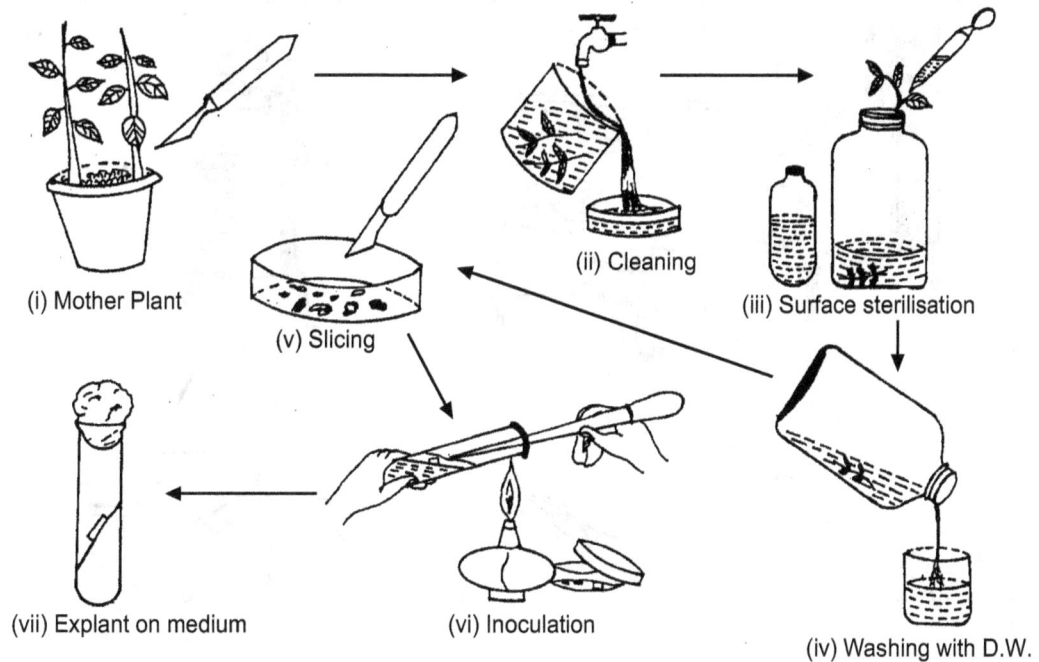

Fig. 4.1: Plant tissue culture technique

4.2.5 Incubation

Culture vessels, after inoculation, are maintained under controlled environmental conditions in the growth room or culture room. This is known as incubation. Constant temperature at 25 ± 2°C is maintained by installation of air conditioner in the growth room. Light intensity provided to the cultures is 1000 to 3000 Lux. One or two fluorescent tube arcs are installed on each shelf of the culture rack. Cleanliness is strictly maintained in the growth room. Cultures are observed every day for their growth as well as contaminations if any. Contaminated cultures are immediately isolated and discarded in order to prevent spreading of contaminants. Generally, photoperiod of 12 hours is provided to the cultures. Cultures in incubation room are generally sub cultured after 4 to 5 weeks.

Aseptic transfer of growing plant parts from one medium to another freshly prepared medium is known as sub culture. It provides fresh dose of nutrients to the growing plant parts. It also facilitates isolation of growing plant tissues from the exudates like polyphenols leached out from the plant parts in a period of 4 to 5 weeks. Necessary processing namely cutting, trimming, scrapping, etc. of the growing plant parts is possible at the time of subculture. Multiple shoot formation is mostly dependent on the way of processing of the plant parts, in addition to the chemical composition of the nutrient medium. If sub culturing is not done on time, growing plant parts show deficiency symptoms and they may even die.

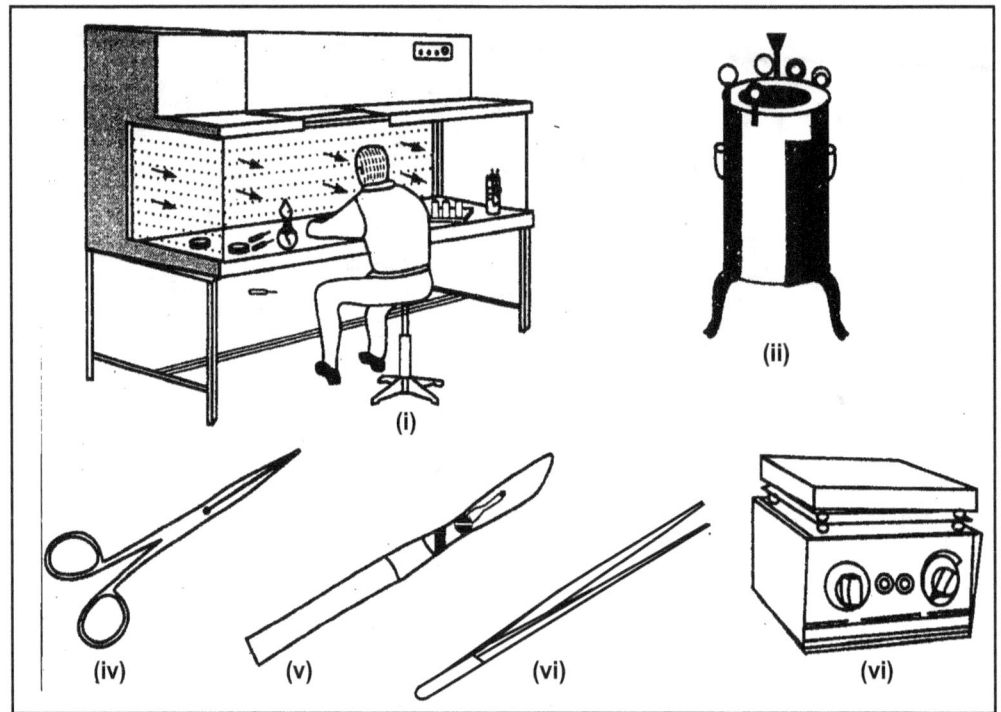

Fig. 4.2: Some instruments used in plant tissue culture laboratory : (i) Laminar air flow, (ii) Vertical autoclave, (iii) Magnetic stirrer, (iv) Scissor, (v) Cutting knife, (vi) Forcep

For *in vitro* rooting, auxin containing media are used. Indole butyric acid (IBA) and naphthalene acetic acid (NAA) are commonly used for this purpose. Individual shoots are isolated from the clumps of multiple shoots. This is done in an aseptic environment in the laminar flow cabinet. Isolated shoots are then transferred (sub cultured) onto the rooting medium. Generally, root formation takes place within a period of 2 - 4 weeks. Some times, *in vivo* rooting of shoots is also tried, in which *in vitro* grown shoots are isolated from the clumps, treated with rooting hormones, planted in appropriate substrates and then grown in the green house.

4.2.6 Hardening of Plantlets

Growing of tissue culture raised plantlets in green house, for a period of 6- 12 weeks to make them sturdy enough to survive in field conditions is known as hardening. It is carried out in two main phases namely primary hardening and secondary hardening. Primary hardening is done in the mist chamber or humidity tunnels for a period of 3 - 6 weeks. Tissue culture raised plantlets are washed with water to remove traces of nutrient medium in contact with their roots. They are then treated with an anti-fungal solution like 0.1 % bavistin and planted in a suitable substrate. Generally, coco peat, vermiculite, soil rite or rice husk are used either individually or in combinations as substrates for primary hardening. Liquid fertilizers are provided to these plantlets once in a week. About 70 - 80% relative humidity and 10,000- 25000 Lux light intensity is provided to the plantlets during primary hardening.

Secondary hardening of the plantlets is done outside the mist chambers but in the green house. About 50 - 60 % relative humidity and 40,000 - 50,000 Lux light intensity is provided to the plantlets. Liquid fertilizer dose once in a week is continued. Substrate used for secondary hardening is generally a combination of soil and sand in 2:1 or 3: 1 proportion. Sometimes rice husk or coco peat is also used in combination with other substrates. Period of secondary hardening is also 3 - 6 weeks. After completion of secondary hardening, plantlets are taken out of green house and cultivated in the fields.

4.3 Commercial Significance

Plant tissue culture is used widely in plant sciences, agriculture, horticulture and forestry. The commercial significance of plant tissue culture is as follows.

1. The plants raised by tissue culture technique are disease free.
2. The growth of the plants is uniform.
3. All plants are identical and high yielding and ready to be harvested at the same time.
4. The limitations of plant breeding can be overcome by tissue culture technique.
5. High yielding varieties can be produced by tissue culture technique.
6. Tissue culture technique can produce a large number of plants within a small time span and place.
7. Plant tissue culture is useful in conservation of rare or endangered plant species.
8. A plant breeder may use tissue culture to screen cells rather than plants for advantageous characters, e.g. herbicide resistance or tolerance.
9. The production of valuable compounds, like plant derived secondary metabolites and recombinant proteins which are used as biopharmaceuticals has become possible due to bioreactors.
10. Distantly related species can be cross pollinated and the resulting embryo is tissue cultured which leads to the growth of the embryo that would have otherwise died. This technique is known as **Embryo Rescue.**
11. For production of doubled monoploid (dihaploid) plants from haploid cultures to achieve homozygous lines more rapidly in breeding programmes, usually by treatment with colchicine which causes doubling of the chromosome number.

12. As a tissue for transformation, followed by either short-term testing of genetic constructs or regeneration of transgenic plants.
13. Certain techniques such as meristem tip culture can be used to produce virus free plant material from stock, such as potatoes, orchids and many species of soft fruit.
14. Production of identical sterile hybrid species can be achieved.

Table 4.2: Plant Tissue Culture Industries in Maharashtra

S. No.	Name and address	Plant production
1.	A-one Biotech and Tissue Culture Pvt Ltd Plot No. N - 3, Floriculture Park, Ambi M. I. D. C. Talegaon Dabhade, Taluka Maval, Pune - 411 033, Maharashtra, India	Banana, Marigold
2.	Ajeet Seeds Ltd. A/P Chitegaon Tal. Paithan, Dist Aurangabad.	Banana
3.	H.U.Gugle Agro Biotech Karmala Road, Jamkhed, Dist Ahmednagar.	Banana
4.	Prime Industries 93, Dadisheth Agiary Lane, Kalbadevi, Mumbai, Maharashtra, 400002	Banana
5.	Reliance Life Sciences Dhirubhai Ambani Life Sciences Center, R-282, TTC Industrial Area of MIDC, Thane-Belapur Road, Rabale, Navi Mumbai 400 701	Banana, Date palm, Pomegranate, Potato, Bamboo, *Jatropha*
6.	Scientific Seedlings India Private limited. Urulikanchan, Pune.	Sugarcane, Banana.
7.	KF Bioplants Pvt. Ltd. Sr. No. 178, Kirtane Baug, Mundhwa Road, Magarpatta, Hadapsar, Pune 411 036	*Gerbera*, Carnation, Strawberry
8.	Nirmal Seeds Pvt. Ltd. Bhadagaon Road, Pachora, Jalgaon, Maharashtra Jalgaon 424201 Maharashtra	Vegetables

Contd...

9.	Krishi Mitra Biotech and research Centre Pvt. Ltd. Near Chandur Railway Station Arvi, Dist. Wardha Maharashtra.	Banana
10.	EPC Industries Ltd. B-20, MIDC Ambad, Nashik 422010	*Eucalyptus*, Banana, Sugarcane.
11.	National Chemical Laboratory, Dr. Homi Bhabha Road, Pune- 411008.	Banana, Teak, Vanilla *Eucalyptus*, Bamboo, Cardamom.
12.	Vasantdada Sugar Institute Manjari Budruk, Tal.: Haveli, Dist.: Pune 412307	Sugarcane.

Points to Remember

- Tissue culture technique is also called as micropropagation.
- It is a much advanced technique than the traditional breeding methods of crop improvement.
- The tissue culture technique is based on totipotency of plant cells predicted by Haberlandt in 1902.
- Totipotency is the ability of a plant cell to regenerate into entire plant.
- Explants are the plant parts used for tissue culture experiment.
- Explants include portions of shoots, leaves, stems, flowers, roots and cells, tissues or organs.
- Stock solutions are prepared before preparing medium for tissue culture.
- Murashige and Skoog (MS) 1962, medium is the most common medium used for plant tissue culture.
- Glasswares are sterilised by autoclaving at 121°C temperature and 15 lb /inch^2 pressure for 20 minutes.
- Sterilisation of media in autoclave is done at 121°C temperature and 15 lb / inch^2 pressure for 20 minutes.
- The explants are treated with dilute dettol solution for 5 minutes before treating with 0.1 % $HgCl_2$.
- Explant is finally surface sterilised with 0.05 % to 0.1 % $HgCl_2$.
- Inoculation means placing of surface sterilised explants, on suitable nutrient medium, under aseptic conditions in the laminar air flow cabinet.

- After inoculation, culture tubes are incubated at constant temperature at $25 \pm 2°C$ in incubation room.
- During incubation, light intensity provided to the cultures is 1000 - 3000 Lux for shoots.
- Aseptic transfer of growing plant parts from one medium to another freshly prepared medium is known as sub culture.
- Hardening is done to make plants sturdy enough to survive under field condition.
- After hardening, the plants are cultivated in the field.
- Tissue culture raised plants are disease and insect free, high yielding, durable and uniform in growth.

Exercises

Short Answer Questions

1. What is plant tissue culture? Explain the concept of plant tissue culture.
2. Define explants and enlist the types of explants.
3. What is a culture medium? Explain the procedure of media preparation in brief.
4. Write a note on sterilisation technique.
5. Write a short note on inoculation and the safety measures involved.
6. Describe the process of incubation.
7. What is hardening? Explain its types and necessity.

Long Answer Questions

1. What is plant tissue culture? Give a brief account of tissue culture technique and discuss the nutritional requirements for the same.
2. Explain types of explants, media preparation, and methods of sterilisation, incubation and hardening.

Chapter 5...
Agri Industries

Contents ...

5.1 Organic Farming

    5.1.1 Concept

    5.1.2 Need of Organic Farming

    5.1.3 Types of Organic Fertilisers

    5.1.4 Advantages and Limitations

5.2 Seed Industries

    5.2.1 Importance of Seed Industries

    5.2.2 Seed Production

    5.2.3 Cotton Seed Processing and Seed Marketing

    5.2.5 Major Seed Industries and Corporations of India.

    Points to Remember

    Exercises

5.1 Organic Farming

Introduction

Organic farming works in harmony with nature rather than against it. This involves using techniques to achieve good crop yields without harming the natural environment or the people who live and work in it. It is one of the best management systems which promotes and enhances health of an agro-ecosystem, including biodiversity, biological cycles and biological activity of the soil. It emphasises the use of management practices in preference to the use of off farm inputs, taking into account that regional conditions require locally adapted systems. This is accomplished by using possible agronomic, biological, and mechanical methods, as opposed to using synthetic materials to fulfill any specific function within the system.

Organic farming began early in the twentieth century, primarily in Europe, and United States. The pioneers of the early organic movement were motivated by a desire to reverse the perennial problems of agriculture e.g. erosion, soil depletion, decline of crop varieties, low quality food and livestock feed, and rural poverty. They embraced a holistic notion that the health of a nation built on agriculture is dependent on the long-term vitality of its soil. The soil's health and vitality were believed to be embodied in its biology and in the organic soil fraction called *humus*.

5.1.1 Concept

Organic farming is very much native to this land. It is simply based on "feed the soil" which means feeding the soil food web. The soil food web is the living fraction of the soil, composed of bacteria, fungi, earthworms, insects, and a host of other organisms that digest organic matter and provide nutrition to growing crop plants. The concept of organic farming is mainly based on the following principles.

- Nature is the best role model for farming, since it does not use any inputs nor demand unreasonable quantities of water.
- The entire system is based on intimate understanding of nature's ways. The system does not believe in mining of the soil for its nutrients and does not degrade it in any way for today's needs.
- The soil in this system is a living entity.
- The soil's living population of microbes and other organisms are significant contributors to its fertility on a sustained basis and must be protected and nurtured at all cost.
- The total environment of the soil, from soil structure to soil cover is most important.

Thus organic farming is defined as a farming system which primarily aims at cultivating the land and raising crops in such a way, so as to keep the soil alive and in good health by use of organic wastes. Food and Agriculture Organisation (FAO) defined organic farming as *"Organic agriculture is a unique production management system which promotes and enhances agro-ecosystem health, including biodiversity, biological cycles and soil biological activity, and this is accomplished by using on farm agronomic, biological and mechanical methods in exclusion of all synthetic off-farm inputs"*.

5.1.2 Need of Organic Farming

The relevance and need for an eco-friendly alternative farming system arose from the ill effects of the chemical farming practices adopted worldwide during the second half of the last century. The methods of farming evolved and adopted by our forefathers for centuries were less injurious to the environment. People began to think of various alternative farming systems based on the protection of environment which in turn would increase the welfare of the mankind by various ways like clean and healthy foods, low use of the non-renewable energy sources, etc. Many systems of farming came out of the efforts of many experts and laymen. However, organic farming is considered to be the best among all of them because of its scientific approach and wider acceptance all over the world. Modern, intensive agriculture practices have caused many problems, related with soil, water environment, and health.

- Artificial fertilisers and herbicides are easily washed from the soil and pollute rivers, lakes and water courses.
- The prolonged use of artificial fertilisers results in soils with a low organic matter content which is easily eroded by wind and rain.
- Greater amounts are needed every year to produce the same yields of crops.
- Artificial pesticides can stay in the soil for a long period and enter the food chain where they begin to accumulate in animals and humans, causing health problems.
- Artificial chemicals destroy soil micro-organisms resulting in poor soil structure and aeration and decrease in the nutrient availability.
- Pests and diseases become more difficult to control as they become resistant to artificial pesticides. The numbers of natural enemies decrease because of pesticide use and habitat loss.

Organic farming provides long-term benefits to people and the environment as follows.

- Increase long-term soil fertility.
- Control pests and diseases without harming the environment.
- Ensure that water stays clean and safe.
- Use resources which the farmer already has, so the farmer needs less
- Money to buy farm inputs.
- Produce nutritious food, feed for animals and high quality crops to sell at a good price.

5.1.3 Types of organic fertilisers

Any substance that contains one or more essential plant nutrient elements has the potential to be used as a fertiliser. Fertilisers are broadly classified as either organic or inorganic. According to the Minnesota Department of Agriculture, a natural organic fertiliser has to be derived from either plant or animal materials containing one or more elements (other than carbon, hydrogen, and oxygen) that are essential for plant growth. Thus, *organic fertilisers are defined as the materials used as fertiliser that occur regularly in nature, usually as a byproduct or end product of a naturally occurring processes.*

The types of organic fertilisers are as under

a) Compost

Compost is organic matter (plant and animal residues) which has been degraded by the action of bacteria and other organisms, over a period of time. Materials such as leaves, fruit skins and animal manure can also be used to make compost. Compost is cheap, easy to make and is a very effective material that can be added to the soil, to improve soil and crop quality. Compost has following advantages.

- Compost improves the structure of the soil. This allows more air into the soil, improves drainage and reduces erosion.
- Compost improves soil fertility by adding nutrients and by making it easier for plants to take up the nutrients present in the soil. This produces better yields.
- Compost improves the soil's ability to hold water. This stops the soil from drying out in times of drought.
- Compost can reduce pests and diseases in the soil and on the crop.

b) Green manures

Green manures, often known as cover crops, are plants which are grown to improve the structure, organic matter content and nutrient content of the soil. They are a cheap alternative to artificial fertilisers and can be used to complement animal manures. Growing green manure is not the same as simply growing a legume crop, such as beans, in a rotation. Green manures are usually dug into the soil when the plants are still young, before they produce any crop and often before they flower. They are grown for their green leafy material which is high in nutrients and provides soil cover. They can be grown together with crops or alone. Green manures have the following advantages.

- Increase and recycle plant nutrients and organic matter.
- Improve soil fertility and soil structure.
- Improve the ability of the soil to hold water.
- Control soil erosion and prevent weed growth.
- Stop nutrients being washed out of the soil, for example, when the ground is not used between main crops.

c) Blood Meal

It is an excellent source of nitrogen. It is used to side-dress leafy vegetables.

d) Bone Meal

It is one of the best sources of phosphorus. It is applied in the bottom of planting holes of bulbs, shrubs and trees.

e) Fish Meal (Liquid)

It is a good source of micronutrients. It is used to feed container-grown plants every two weeks.

f) Poultry manure

The waste products from the chicken industry contain all three macronutrients i.e. N, P and K which are used all over the world.

5.1.4 Advantages and Limitations

Advantages

- Organic fertilisers are made from naturally occurring sources.
- They lower the amount of greenhouse gases that are released into the atmosphere.
- Nutrients are released only when media is warm and moist.
- The slow-release nature of most organic fertilisers may slightly decrease the runoff of nutrients into local water systems when compared to some quick-release synthetic sources that release nutrients regardless of media conditions.
- Organic fertilisers not only provide essential nutrients to plants, they also improve soil structure.
- Organic matter helps to break up heavy clay soil, improve air circulation and drainage, and it increases the capacity for sandy soils to retain moisture. It maintains good soil structure.
- Makes it easier for the roots of plants to reach moisture and to absorb the nutrients in the soil.
- In terms of the end product, such as the quality of plant produced by a commercial greenhouse, organic fertilisers can be quite competitive with traditional synthetic sources for a detailed study comparing products of organic and inorganic fertilisers.
- When used over a long period of time during in-ground production, organic fertilisers may increase the quality of the soil, including an increase in the efficiency of nutrient utilisation.

Limitations

- Generally costs significantly more than synthetic fertiliser.
- Organic certification requires documentation and regular inspections.
- Organic fertilisers, despite the advantages discussed above, still release nutrients into their surroundings; these nutrients can find their way into local streams, rivers, and estuaries just as nutrients from synthetic sources do.
- Motivations for using organic fertiliser vary from user to user. Businesses may want to go organic in order to sell product, and members of the general public might be interested in organic fertiliser for home use because of environmental concerns. This would increase the cost of the final product.

5.2 Seed Industries

Seed is one of the most important components for agriculture. The quality of seed is very important for sustainable agriculture. It is estimated that the good quality seed alone increases the production. The developments in the seed industry in India, particularly in the last 30 years, are very significant. Introduction of New Seed Development Policy (1988 – 1989) was a significant milestone in the Indian Seed Industry, which transformed the very character of the seed industry. This policy gave access to Indian farmers to the best of seeds and planting material available anywhere on the world. The policy stimulated appreciable investments by private individuals, Indian Corporates and MNCs in the Indian seed sector with strong research and development base for product development gave more emphasis on high value hybrids of cereals and vegetables and hi-tech products such as Bt. Cotton. As a result, farmer has a wide product choice and seed industry today is set to work with a 'farmer centric' approach and is market driven. However, there is an urgent need for the State Seed Corporations also to transform themselves in tune with the industry in terms of infrastructure, technologies, approach and the management culture to be able to survive in the competitive market and to enhance their contribution in the national endeavour of increasing food production to attain food and nutritional security.

5.2.1 Importance of Seed Industries

There is a need for well developed seed industries to fulfill the demand of increasing population. Food is the basic need of life but for a comfortable life we need clothes, shelter, electricity, machinery and numerous other things. Agriculture is dependent on industry for its own development. Tractors, threshers, electric motors are all industrial products. In fact, in our daily lives we all are dependent on manufactured goods. After independence very few industries existed in India like textiles, steel, cement, machine tools and sugar etc. Such Industries contributed only ten per cent to the national income in 1950-51 while agriculture had a share of 52 per cent because all the basic needs were fulfilled from agriculture. The agriculture field can progress only when there are well developed and advanced seed industries. Seed industries are important for the hybrid seed production, quality assurance, seed distribution and marketing, infrastructure facilities, transgenic seed (plant) production and import of seeds etc.

5.2.2 Seed Production

Cotton is a major fibre crop throughout the world. It is grown in tropical and sub-tropical regions of more than 80 countries. The major cotton producing countries are China, India,

USA, Pakistan, Uzbekistan, Turkey, Brazil, Greece, Argentina, Australia and Egypt contributing about 85% of the global production. India has the largest area under cotton cultivation in the world and grows all four cultivated species namely, *G. hirsutum, G. barbadense, G. herbaceum and G. arboreum* on a commercial scale. The major cotton growing states are Punjab, Haryana, Rajasthan, Madhya Pradesh, Maharashtra, Gujarat, Andhra Pradesh, Tamil Nadu and Karnataka. However, the productivity of cotton in India is low due to its rainfed cultivation.

In cotton, hybrid seed production is done either by conventional hand emasculation and pollination or by nonconventional (male sterility based) method.

Limitations of hybrid seed production

There are four main problems of hybrid seed production in cotton such as high cost of hybrid seed (conventional and male sterile hybrids), high cost of cultivation, difficulty in seed production (diploid hybrids) due to very poor seed setting (about 25%) and presence of neps and mots especially in interspecific hybrids. The availability of pure hybrid seeds in time is also a major limitation due to the requirement of grow-out test for genetic purity which does not fit in the period between seed production and planting in the next season. The high cost of conventional hybrid seeds is due to requirement of emasculation and pollination which can be reduced to some extent through use of male sterility. But the yield of male sterility based hybrids is 10-15% lower than conventional hybrids since restoration of sterility is again a problem. Whichever method is selected for hybrid seed production, its commercial production depends on the development of an economical and reliable method to ensure adequate pollen transfer from fertile flower to sterile flower. Since cotton pollen is very heavy and sticky, it is not easily transferred by wind and requires insects especially honeybees for pollen transfer.

5.2.3 Cotton Seed Processing

The processing of cotton seed includes the following steps:

Ginning

'Ginning' means separation of cotton fibres (lint) from the cotton seed. It also removes foreign material like leaves from the lint, and combs - the finished fibres. The machine that carries out this process is called a 'gin'. Before the gin was invented, the lint and seed had to be separated by hand.

The ginning process includes following steps

1. Opening the bolls

A machine called a 'moon buggy' picks up the modules of cotton and loads them onto semi-trailers which transport them from the farm to the gin. The modules are stored at the gin in large specially drained area called 'gin yards'. The modules remain here until they are ready for ginning, the moon buggy again picks them up and places them onto a chain which feeds them into the gin. From there, the cotton is fed into the first part of the gin machinery which opens up the cotton and takes out any green bolls, rocks and sticks which may damage machinery. The gin is operated centrally from a sound proofed control room with computers, control panels and various other technologies to monitor the machinery. If you were walking around the gin you would need to be wearing earmuffs to protect your ears from the noise of the machinery and a face mask to avoid inhaling the fine dust particles.

2. Drying out

Moisture levels are very important for successful ginning. If the cotton gets too moist it forms small lumpy balls called neps. If it is too dry, the fibres break or can cause static electricity. Ideally, cotton is ginned at a moisture level of 5%. If the moisture is too low, water is added. If it is too high, the cotton is heated up in order to dry it out.

3. Pre-cleaning

During the whole process, the seed cotton is transported through the machinery by being blown along by warm air currents. The next step in the process is the pre-cleaning centre. At this stage many different sized and shaped cleaners go into action to try and get rid of all the 'trash' i.e. the dirt, stalks, leaves etc. Horizontal cleaners with metal spikes spin around and drag the cotton over screens. Stick machines spin the cotton around cylinders and impact cleaners beat the cotton between rows of spiked rollers. The extract-feeder then feeds cotton into the gin stand (which is where the actual separation occurs) and finally, after all of this cleaning, the cotton moves along a conveyer belt to the top of the gin stand.

4. Seed separation

Separating the seed from the lint is completed by a saw gin located inside the gin stand. The saw gin consists of a series of circular saws rotating at high speed. The teeth on the saw blades pull the fibre away from the seeds. High-speed brushes then take the lint off the saw blades and the seeds drop out of sight and into storage. The few remaining lint fibres on the seeds are removed in a later process and are used to make low-grade yarn and paper.

5. **Final clean and wrap**

After separation from the seed, there is still some trash remaining in the lint. To remove this trash, the lint goes through another cleaning process which involves blow dry, cleaning through the air jet cleaner, some more rolling through a lint cleaner, and finally, one more pass through the saw gin. At the end of the ginning process the clean lint is pressed into bales (weighing 227 kilos each). Samples are taken from each bale at this stage for grading the cotton. Bales are lastly wrapped in hessian to help protect the lint. From here it is taken to a warehouse to be put into shipping containers for travel by train or road to a spinning mill or a port for export overseas.

5.2.4 Seed Marketing

Cotton is the single most important textile fibre in the world, accounting for about 35 percent of all fibers produced. The United States is a major producer of cotton for the international market, ranking third after China and India. The United States also remains the leading cotton exporter in the world. Six countries Brazil, China, India, Pakistan, Turkey and the United States are the top consumers of the world's cotton.

Cotton is ready for sale after instrument classing establishes the quality parameters for each bale. The marketing of cotton is a complex operation that includes all transactions involving buying, selling or reselling from the time the cotton is ginned until it reaches the textile mill. Growers usually sell their cotton to a local buyer or merchant after it has been ginned and baled, but if they decide against immediate sale they can store it and borrow money against it. Since it is a non-perishable crop, cotton stored in a government-approved warehouse provides a secure basis for a monetary loan.

5.2.5 Major Seed Industries and Corporations in India

Seed Industries

- **Maharashtra Hybrid Seeds Company Limited:**
  Dawalwadi, PO Box 76, Jalna (MS) 431203, India.

- **Maharashtra State Seeds Corporation Limited:**
  'Mahabeej Bhavan', Krishi Nagar, Akola 444 104 (M.S.) India.

- **Krishidhan Seeds Pvt. Limited:**
  'Krishidhan Bhavan' D3 to D6, MIDC, Aurangabad Road, Jalna – 431213 Maharashtra, India.

- **Ajeet Seeds Limited:**
  Chitegaon, Dist Aurangabad Pin 431105, Maharashtra, India.

- **Century Seeds Pvt Ltd:**
  BA-22, Mangolpuri Industrial Area Phase 2, Delhi – 110083, India

- **Eagle Seeds and Biotech Ltd:**
  117, Silver Sanchora Castle, 7, R.N.T. Marg, Indore (M.P.) Pin - 452008 INDIA

- **Indo-American Hybrid Seeds (India) Pvt. Ltd:**
  7th Km, Banashankari-Kengeri Link Road, Channasandra Village, Bangalore South Taluk.

- **JK Agri Genetics Ltd:**
  1-10-177,4th floor,Varun Towers, Begumpet, Hyderbad- 500016

- **Stanagro Seeds Pvt Ltd:**
  No. 339 (Old No. 211) Poonamallee High Road Ist Floor Aminjikarai, Chennai, 600 029

- **Sungro Seeds:**
  IIIrd Floor, Sungro Chamber, B.N.Block, Local Shopping Centre, Shalimar Bagh, Delhi-110088 (INDIA)

- **Syngenta Seeds Ltd:**
  Amar Paragigam, Baner road, opp Sadanad Hotel, Pune – 411025, Maharashtra India

- **Advanta Seeds:**
  8-2-418, 3rd Floor, Krishnama House, Road No.7, Banjara Hills, Hyderabad - 500 034. Andhra Pradesh, INDIA.

- **Nirmal Seeds:**
  Bhadgoan road, Pachora, Dist – Jalgoan, Pin 424201, India.

- **Mansanto India Limited :**
  Ahura Centre, 5th Floor, 96, Mahakali Caves Road, Andheri (East) Mumbai 400 093, India.

Seed Corporation

- **National seed corporation of India:**
  Beej Bhavan, Pusa Complex, New Delhi110012 India

- **Haryana Seed Development Corporation India:**
  Beej Bhavan, Bays 3-6, Sector 2, Panchkula Haryana.

- **Punjab State Seeds Corporation Ltd. :**
  S.C.O. 835-836, Sector 22 – A, Chandigadh

- **Andhra Pradesh State Seeds Development Corporation Limited. :**
  Regd. Office 5-10-193 2nd Floor, HACA Bhavan, Opp Public Gardens Hyderabad 500004.

- **Gujarat State Seed Corporations Limited:**
  BeejBhavan, Sector 10 A, Gandhinagar, Gujrat 382010.

- **Rajasthan State Seed Corporations Limited :**
  Pant KrishiBhavan, Janpath, Jaipur 05.

- **Karnataka State Seed Corpration Limited :**
  BeejBhavan, Bellari Road, Hebbal, Bangalore, 560024.

- **Uttarakhand Seed and Tarai Development Corporation Limited:**
  Pantnagar, P.O. Haldi, Dist. Udham Singh Nagar263146, India.

Points to Remember

- Organic farming is defined as a farming system which primarily aims at cultivating the land and raising crops in such a way so as to keep the soil alive and in good health by use of organic wastes.
- Organic farming is considered to be the best because of its scientific approach and wider acceptance all over the world.
- Organic farming provides long-term benefits to people and the environment.
- Compost, green manure, bone meal, poultry manure are most common organic fertilisers.
- Seed is one of the most important components of agriculture.
- Cotton is a major fibre crop throughout the world.
- 'Ginning' means separation of cotton fibres (lint) from the cotton seed.
- The ginning process includes five steps - opening the bolls, drying out, pre-cleaning, seed separation and final clean and wrap.

Exercises

Short Answer Questions

- What is organic farming?
- Give the need of organic farming.

- Enlist different types of organic fertilisers.
- State advantages of organic fertilisers.
- Give the limitations of organic fertilisers.
- What is ginning?
- What is compost?
- What is green manure?
- Give importance of seed industries.
- Name any two steps involved in ginning.
- Enlist seed corporations of India.

Long Answer Questions
- Define organic fertilisers. Describe any two most common organic fertilisers with their advantages.
- Discuss importance of seed industries.
- Explain cotton seed processing in detail.

Chapter 6...
Mushroom Industries & Cultivation

Contents ...
6.1 Introduction
6.2 Plant Resources
6.3 Cultivation Practices of Oyster Mushroom
6.4 Uses of Mushrooms
6.5 Value added Products of Mushroom
6.6 Commercial Significance of Oyster Mushroom Cultivation
   Points to Remember
   Exercises

6.1 Introduction

Mushrooms belong to Kingdom fungi. Mushrooms do not possess chlorophyll, so cannot prepare their own food and have to depend on dead organic matter or parasitically with other living organisms. Mushrooms are large reproductive structures of fungi. All fungi start their life cycle from a spore, which germinates on a suitable medium and produce vegetative mycelium. The vegetative mycelium derive nutrition and produce fruiting bodies after maturation.

In Latin, "fungo" means to flourish. The term was used to refer to mushroom. In Greek, the term "mushroom" was derived from the word "sphonggos" or "aphoggos" which meant "sponge". The word mushroom is usually thought to be derived from the French "mousseron" or "moss" but it is not used in quite the same sense. Other versions are "muscheron" and "mouscheron"; from these it is easy to understand how the name "mushroom" originated.

The cultivation of mushroom was first started with the cultivation of white button mushroom in France during 1630. Apart from button mushroom, three other mushrooms, like oyster mushroom (*Pleurotus sajor – caju*), paddy straw mushroom (*Volvariella volvacea*) and milky mushroom (*Calocybe indica*) are commercially cultivated in India.

Oyster mushroom has gained popularity due to its easy method of cultivation and ability to grow on various waste materials with high production efficiency. This mushroom is suitable to grow in tropical and subtropical areas.

The term mushroom is mostly used to denote any kind of large fruiting structure of macro-fungi. Mushrooms can be found growing in nature as saprophytes on any kind of organic matter or on fresh or dead wood.

6.2 Plant Resources

Present scenario of Mushroom Production

Agaricus bisporus and *pleurotus spp.* (oyster) are commercially cultivated world wide due to to their acceptability while other edible mushrooms like *Auricularia* spp. *Valvariella* spp. are popular in China and *Grifola* and *Hypsizygus* in Japan. The total world production of all the mushrooms is estimated to be around 4.9 million tones during 1994 and 3.76 million tones during the year 1996.

The mushrooms that are most commonly cultivated are

1. *Agaricus bisporus*(white button mushroom)
2. *Lentinus edodes*
3. *Auricularia spp.*
4. *Volvariella volvacea*(Paddy straw mushroom)
5. *Flammulina velutipes*
6. *Tremella fuciformis*
7. *Agaricus bitorquis*
8. *Pleurotus ostreatus*
9. *P. flabellatus*
10. *P. sajor caju* (Oyster mushroom)
11. *P. eryngii*
12. *P. sapidus*
13. *P. cornucopiae*
14. *Agaricus campestris*
15. *Armillaria mellea*
16. *Bovista plumbea*

Pleurotus or oyster mushroom is a fungal member included in class basidiomycetes. It is locally known as "Dhingri". Pleurotus is the Greek word "Plecura" which means formed laterally referring to the lateral positon of the stipe. The oyster mushroom (species of *Pleurotus*) grows under natural conditions, on trees or dead woody branches of trees as saprophyte and primary decomposer. It is basically a wood deteriorating fungus, well known as tropical edible mushroom. Oyster is easily identified by its eccentric and lateral stipe although it may be absent sometimes. The nutritive value of *Pleurotus* (oyster) on dry weight basis are as follows

Protein	-	47.93%
Fat	-	12.26%
Reducing sugars	-	0.285%
Starch	-	0.120%
Ascorbic acid	-	0.06%
Nitrogen	-	72%

Oyster mushroom is cultivated on a commercial basis in 25 different countries all over the world. It is the 3rd largest cultivated mushroom in the world. It is also cultivated on fresh as well as fermented substrates. It is generally cultivated on any type of agricultural wastes like the straw of wheat, paddy, jowar etc.

MORPHOLOGY

Structure of mycelium

The mycelium of *Pleurotus* is of two types.

(i) Monokaryotic mycelium

It is produced by the germination of basidiospores. It is made up of simple, filamentous and septate hyphae. The cells are uninucleate (monokaryotic), contain granular, vacuoloated protoplasm and oil globules.

(ii) Dikaryotic mycelium

The hyphae of + and − strains come in contact, fuse and a nucleus from one hypha passes into the nearest cell of the other hypha. This mycelium with binucleate cells is known as secondary or dikaryotic mycelium. It remains binucleated till the fruiting bodies are formed.

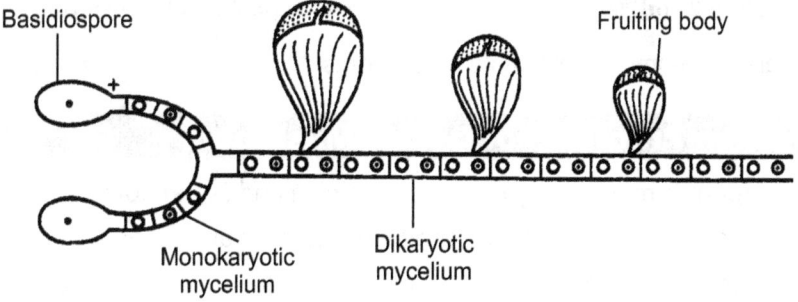

Fig. 6.1: Diagrammatic representation showing basidiospores, monokaryotic mycelium, somatogamy, diakaryotic mycelium and fruiting bodies

Rhizomorph: Some of the hyphae are interwoven into thick cords called as rhizomorph. It functions as roots. This cord-like 'spawn' bears the fruiting bodies.

Pleurotus fruiting body is differentiated into stipe, pileus (cap), gills (lamellae), basidia and basidiospores.

Stipe: The stalk supporting the pileus is known as stipe. It is short, cylindrical and eccentric (attached laterally). Its presence or absence and mode of its attachment to the cap is an important character for identification. Stipe in *Pleurotus* is mostly lateral or may be absent; when present it is continuous with the cap.

Pileus (cap): Pileus is the expanded portion of the stipe. It is fleshy in the larger species and membraneous in the smaller forms. It never becomes woody. It differs greatly in shape, size and colour. The pileus may be two to six inches broad. It is soft, fleshy, smooth and moist. It has involute margin.

Gills (lamellae): Gills are situated on the underside of the pileus. They emerge from the apex of the stalk and radiate out towards the margin. Gills bear basidia and basidiospores.

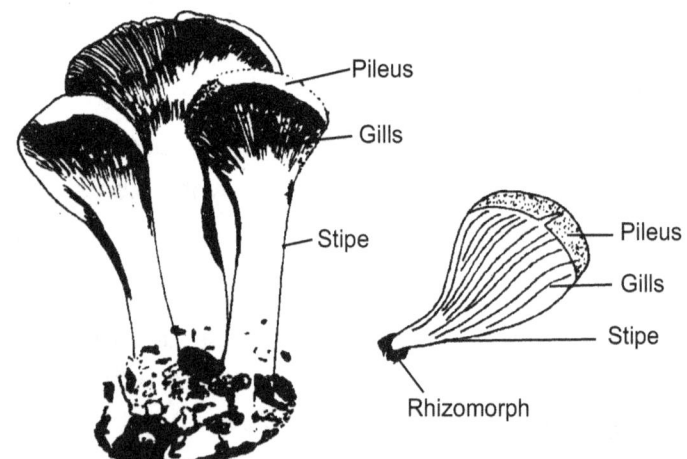

Fig. 6.2 : *(a)Pleurotus ostreatus* fruiting body *(b) Pleurotus sajor caju*

Following are some important edible mushrooms:

6.3 Cultivation Practices of Oyster Mushroom

Oyster mushroom is most widely cultivated in China and South Korea. In India it is mainly cultivated in the eastern and southern provinces. Rice straw or wheat straw is used for cultivation of oyster mushroom. In India, the mushroom is cultivated mainly in small farms or in farmer's houses as a cottage industry. However, now-a-days, it has gained much popularity due to its easy method of cultivation. Thus, mushroom cultivator offers good prospects of its commercialisation due to long shelf-life, pleasant flavour and excellent nutritional value.

Oyster mushroom is cultivated in 25 countries and it is the 3rd largest cultivated mushroom in the world. It can be cultivated on fresh as well as fermented substrate. It can be grown on any kind of agricultural waste like wheat, paddy, jowar or bajra straw, maize cobs or cotton waste or agro industrial wastes of tea, coffee, cotton, tobacco or fruit processing industry. Oyster mushroom is the most suitable mushroom for Indian conditions. It has several advantages over other mushrooms which are responsible for its popularity.

(a) It has a wide substrate range and can be cultivated on any kind of fresh or fermented lignocellulolytic matter.

(b) The cultivation technology is very simple and it does not require temperature controlled growing conditions.

(c) There are mainly two types of species depending upon their growth requirements - summer varieties and winter varieties. The summer varieties are suitable for growing between 22 to 30°C and winter varieties have optimum temperature of 15 to 20 °C. So one can cultivate oyster mushroom round the year in any part of India in very simple growing rooms.

(d) They are very tolerant to environmental conditions and fructifications appear on a wide temperature range. Moreover harvesting or spraying delayed by a day or two, does not affect produce or productivity.

(e) Oyster mushroom basidiocarp can be easily sun-dried for afterwards consumption; moreover the spores are white in colour which does not spoil the produce when kept in freezer for 2 to 4 days.

(f) The inital investment as well as cost of production is very low. The cropping cycle is very short (60 days) so the expenses as well as profit is accrued back in two months time.

(g) It has the largest number of commercially cultivated species world wide which includes *P. flabellatus, P. ostreatus, P. sajor-caju, P. sapidus, P.o florida, P. pultnonarius, P. cystidiosus, P. ervngii, P. eons* and *P. citrinopileatus*.

Mushroom Species

Oyster mushrooms are so named, owing to its shape which resembles the oyster shells. It is also called as "dhingri" mushroom. These are white wood rotting fungi. Several species of *Pleurotus* are cultivated such as *Pleurotus sajor-caju, P. flabellatus, P. florida, P.ostreatus, P. sapidus*, etc. all of which have varied growth requiremenst.

Fig. 6.3 : Different species of oyster mushrooms. (a) *Pleurotus* sajor-caju, (b) and (d) *P. florida*, (c) *P. flabellatus*

Table 6.1: Temperature requirement of different oyster mushroom sp. for their growth

Oyster mushroom sp.	Temperature Required for Growth	
	Mycelial growth (Vegetative)	Fruit body formation (Reproductive)
Pleurotus eous	25 – 30	22 – 26
Pleurotus sajor-caju	25 – 30	18 – 25
Pleurotus flabellatus	25 – 30	22 – 26
Pleurotus florida	25 – 30	15 – 25
Pleurotus ostreatus	25 – 30	10 – 17
Pleurotus sapidus	25 – 30	22 – 26

The facilities and materials required for Mushroom cultivation are listed below

1. Mushroom house or shed
2. Substrate store or shed
3. Cemented water tank for soaking straw
4. Wooden, bamboo or steel racks
5. Hand chopper for cutting substrate i.e. Straw

6. Metallic drum for boiling (for disinfection)
7. Plastic buckets
8. Sprayer and gunny bags
9. Polypropylene bags (16" × 20")
10. Transparent polythene sheet
11. Nylon thread and mosquito net
12. Substrates - paddy or wheat straw
13. Spawn
14. Fungicide – Carbendazim (Bavistin), mancozeb and zineb.
15. Antibiotics: Streptomycin sulphate and tetracycline hydrochloride mixture.
16. Insecticides: Malathion or endosulfan for preventing rat and fly attacks
17. Disinfectant: Bleaching powder, formalin.
18. Good ventilation, light and sanitation

Commercial Cultivation of *Pleurotus-sajor - caju* (fr)

Pleurotus sajor caju is mainly cultivated in India. It is cellulose loving fungus. It grows very well at 20^0–30^0C temperature. Its cultivation is simple and economical. It does not require sophisticated technology or skilled labour.

Spawn: Spawn required for the cultivation of *Pleurotus* which is commonly known as mushroom seed is the propagating material. (white mycelium) used for the cultivation of *Pleurotus* by the mushroom growers for planting beds. It is also known as mushroom bed. Quality of spawn is the basic parameter for successful mushroom cultivation. Pure culture is required for the preparation of spawn, which is obtained from spores or through tissue culture. Under sterile conditions, pieces of the interior tissues of pileus or stipe are cut. With the help of an inoculating needle it is transfered to a suitable nutritive medium. for e.g. Potato dextrose agar or Malt extract agar. The mycelium growing on the culture medium is then used for spawn preparation.

Spawn production: The grains of paddy, wheat, sorghum or maize are washed in fresh water. This washed material is boiled for half an hour to bring the moisture content of grains to 40–50%. The excess water is drained. The boiled grains are allowed to surface dry, by spreading them in shade for few hours. The grains are then mixed with calcium carbonate (lime) and calcium sulphate (Gypsum) at 2% and 0.5% respectively. This mixture is filled up to $3/4^{th}$ of the glass bottles.

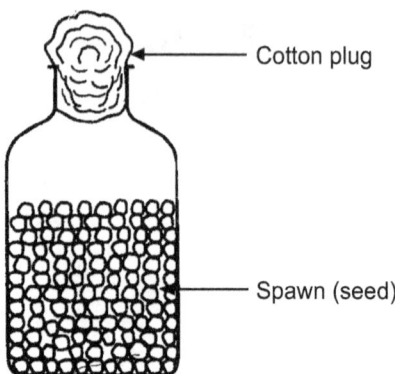

Fig. 6.4: Spawn bottle

Now a days, instead of bottles, polythene bags are also used. These spawn bottles or polythene bags are autoclaved for 30 minutes at 15 lbs pressure. After this, the bottles are allowed to cool at room temperature. Then the grains are then inoculated with pure culture of *Pleurotus sajor caju* mycelium under aseptic conditions. Inoculated spawn bottles or polythene bags are kept in the incubator for 10 to 15 days at 20^0C to 25^0C to multiply and grow. The spawn is ready for use after full development of mycelium in spawn bottles or bags.

Methods of substrate preparation

The substrates e.g. wheat, paddy, jowar, bajra, maize, cotton, sugarcane and jute straws are used. Other materials like dehulled corn cobs, sunflower stalks, discarded waste papers can also be used for its cultivation. However, out of these dried, cereal straw is the best and simplest substrate for the cultivation of *Pleurotus sajor caju*.

Dried paddy straw is chopped into 1 to 2 cm long bits. It is washed and soaked in cold water for about 8 to 12 hours. Then the excess water is drained out. The pre-wetted straw is used by subjecting it to any one of the following treatments.

(a) Hot water treatment

The substrate (pre wetted straw) is directly put in hot water or it can be filled in jute bags and immersed in hot water at 60^0C – 80^0C for half an hour. The excess water is drained off and substrate is spawned after cooling under aseptic conditions.

(b) Sterile technique

The wet substrate (pre wetted straw) is sterilised at 15 lbs pressure for 60 to 90 minutes, followed by spawning under aseptic conditions.

(c) Steam pasteurisation

In this method, pre-wetted straw (wheat or paddy straw) is sterilised by steam pasteurization. The straw is kept in a boiler for half an hour. After cooling, the substrate is spawned.

(d) Chemical sterilisation

The substrate is soaked in Bavistin and formaldehyde for 10 to 12 hours. For 10 kg of substrate approximately 7.00 gms of Bavistin and 125 ml formaldehyde is used. Drain out the excess water. There should not be any trace of chemicals used in the straw, at the time of spawning.

The mycelial growth of oyster mushroom can also take place on fermented lignocellulosic substrates like agro-industrial wastes e.g. tea leaf wastes, malt industry wastes etc. The substrates used for mushroom cultivation should always be fresh and free from any type of infections (viral, bacterial, fungal). In oyster mushroom cultivation, infestation due to various molds is the most common problem. Sometimes these molds completely inhibit the growth of mushroom mycelium. To over come this problem Carbendazim is used to kill the molds present in the substrate.

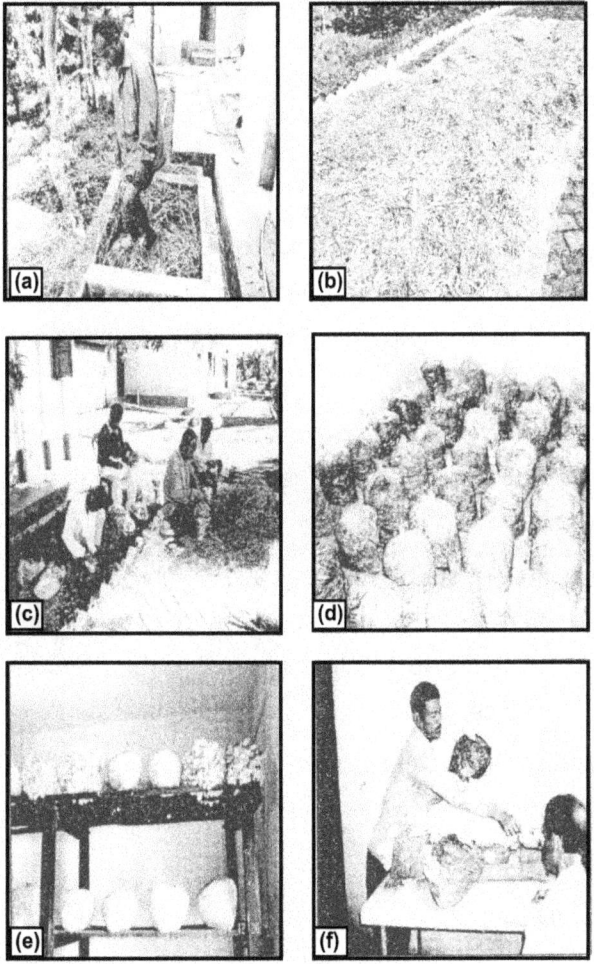

Fig. 6.5 : Cultivation of oyster mushrooms in bas. (a) Disinfection, (b) Drying, (c) Poly bag filling, (d) Spawn running, (e) Fruit body production, (f) Harvesting and weighing

Inoculation on substrate (Spawning)

The polythene bags of size 26 - 38 cm are selected. These bags are sterilised with 2% formalin. The polythene bags are tied at the bottom with thread. These bags are filled with the substrate to about 5–8 cm height to form the bottom layer. Then the spawn is spread on the substrate towards the periphery.

Besan (chana flour) can also be spread over it. It acts as a additional nutrient surface for growth of mycelium. These polythene bags are filled with repeated layers of substrate and spawn. Press the layers every time after filling with wooden log. It gives cylindrical shape to the bed. After filling 4 to 5 layers, the mouth of the bag is tied with the thread. About 40-50 holes are made on the bed for aeration with needle.

The filled polythene bags are kept on the sterilised shelves of the rack. The distance between two beds should be about 6 inches. For 10 kg of paddy straw, 200 gms of spawn and 20 gms of gram flour is used. The beds are kept in well ventilated room at 25^0C temperature and relative humidity should be around 80–90%.

It takes 12 to 15 days for the completion of mycelial ramification through out the substrate bed. The young fruiting bodies appear through the holes of the polythene sheets. At this stage the polythene sheets are cut open, removed and the beds are watered 2 to 3 times a day. Watering also helps in maintaining the humidity around 80–90% during cropping period.

The pin head primordia are observed for 7 days. From this primordia, fruit bodies of mushrooms develop from all over the bed. The fruiting bodies (basidiocarps) are harvested after maturation.

The mushroom beds are not sprinkled with water before harvesting. The second crop will be ready for harvesting after another 7 days. One can get 3 to 4 crops from each bed. Total yield of the crop is about 500 gms to 1500 gms from each bed. First two flushes gives about 80% of the total crop and hence are economical.

Mushrooms are used fresh or may be sundried. These dehydrated mushrooms are stored in airtight polythene bags or bottles.

Alternative methods for *Pleurotus* cultivation are as follows

1. Dustbin basket method
2. Gunny bag method
3. Open tray method

(a) Chopped Paddy Straw mixed with Spawn of *Pleurotus* sp. in Polyethene Bag
(b) Compact bed after stripping off the polythene bag

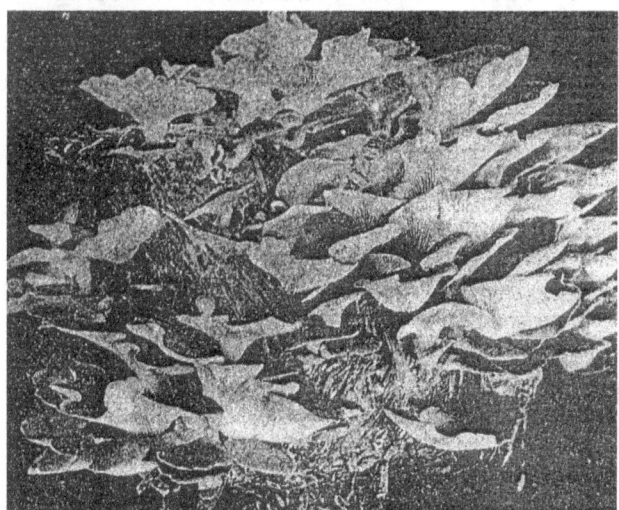

(c) Mature *Pleurotus* grown on bed

Fig. 6.6: Cultivation of *Pleurotus-sajor - caju* (fr)

Do's and Dont's of Mushroom Cultivation

1. Make compost with proper care. At the time of spawning, the compost should not emit the foul smell of ammonia.

2. At the time of filling the trays the compost should not be too wet.

3. A good compost is a key to success. Therefore, make a good compost for mushroom cultivation.
4. The trays should be filled to the rim with compost.
5. Collect the spawn from reliable sources.
6. Contaminated seeds should not be used for mushroom cultivation.
7. The trays filled with compost should be covered with the newspaper. Sprinkle water on the paper, not directly on the compost to increase the moisture of the compost.
8. The casing material should be sterilised before using for casing. It should be used immediately after making it germ-free. If left for few days it may again be infected.
9. The casing materials must be very fine or it will not effect aeration readily.
10. After spawning and before casing the compost should be watered as needed.

6.4 Uses of Mushrooms

1. The most important use of mushroom is as an article of food.
2. It is a good appetizer and adds great flavour to food.
3. The forest mushrooms are nature's most active agents in disposal of the forest's waste material.
4. They are wood rotting fungi and provide food for living trees.
5. They also maintain the ecological balance in the forests.
6. The fruit bodies of **Ganoderma** are used to make hats, various articles of dress, hand bags and picture frames.
7. Bottle corks are made from **Polyporus squamosus**.
8. Fruiting body of **Daedalea** is sometimes used as comb for brushing down horses.
9. **Polyporus nigricans** when dried and pounded, is an ingredient in snuff.
11. **Polyporus bispidus** gives a brown dye which is used for colouring silk, cotton, wool and furniture.
12. Fruit body of **Polyporus fomentarius** are used for flower pots.
13. Many fungi are luminescent; **Pleurotus janapicus** also emits light.
14. **P. officinalis** is used as to stop bleeding.
15. It was also used for diseases of the breast and lungs, as remedy for nigh sweating in tuberculosis.
16. It is also used in treating rheumatism, gout, jaundice and intestinal worms.
17. *Boletus laricis* is frequently used for inflamed eyes and as a gargle for inflammation of the throat.

18. ***Fomes igniarius*** is used for rapid coagulation of blood.
19. ***Clavatia gigantea*** shows anaesthetic.
20. Anticancerous extract of shritake is known to control some cancers and it's properties inhibit the growth of some viruses like influenza.

Following are some of the major constituents of mushrooms

a. **Protein:** Proteins are very essential in our daily diet. In mushrooms, the percentage of proteins is about 18 to 30 per cent on dry weight basis. About 80 per cent of the mushroom proteins are digestible. In oyster mushroom 84.1 per cent of the protein is digestible. It contains essential amino acids, lysine and tryptophan. Mushroom protein is ranked just below the proteins of animal milk and soybean.

b. **Vitamins:** Mushrooms is reported to be an excellent source of thiamine (B1) riboflavin (B2), nicotinic acid and biotin. It also contains vitamin C, A, D and E. These vitamins remain unaffected during the heating or canning of mushrooms.

c. **Minerals:** The high ash contents indicate that these are rich sources of minerals. The minerals, like potassium, phosphorus and sodium are predominant. Potassium and phosphorus are the main constituents of ash in *Pleurotus* sp.

d. **Carbohydrate:** It forms the major constituent of the dry matter of mushrooms. These carbohydrates consists of large number of compounds such as chitin, hemicellulose, amino sugar, sugar alcohols and glycogen. Starch is absent. Carbohydrate content in mushrooms ranges from 39.5 to 93.4 per cent on dry weight basis.

e. **Fat:** Mushrooms contain very low fat. It is about 2 to 8 per cent on dry weight basis. In *Pleurotus sp.* the fat content is 2.85 per cent. The crude fat content of *Volvariella volvacea* is reported to be 5 per cent of the dry weight. In mushrooms at least 70 per cent of total fatty acids are unsaturated which are desirable in human diet. Mushrooms contain high amount of sterols and ergosterol, cholesterol is absent. Ergosterols are useful to produce vitamin D in human body in presence of sun light.

6.5 Value added Products of Mushroom

Mushrooms are used to prevent illnesses thought their use as immune stimulants, antioxidants and immune modulators.

(A) Fresh products / Recipes.
(B) Processed Products.

(A) Fresh products: *Pleurotus sajor caju* is highly nutritious and delicious. Following are the most popular recipes of fresh *Pleurotus* mushroom.

1. **Mushroom pulao:** Wash and chop (50 gm) mushroom, clean and soak the rice for 10 minutes. Heat ghee and fry mushroom lightly. Fry, chopped onion in ghee and add cumin, cardamom, clover, black pepper and bay leaves (Tamalpatra). After the onion and spices becomes brownish, add rice and double the quantity of hot water. Add salt to taste. After rice begins to boil, add fried mushroom to the rice. Cook on a slow fire, till the pulao is ready.

2. **Mushroom paneer:** Cut mushroom (400 g), paneer (20 g) and tomato (50 g) into small pieces. Heat oil in a pan and add chopped onions. Fry until golden brown, add tomatoes to it. Simmer it for 5 minutes. Add mushroom, paneer and salt. Cook it at slow flame till water of mushroom dries up. Add garam masala and serve hot.

3. **Mushroom soup:** Chopped onion is fried until it becomes golden brown; add a little amount (25 g) of flour (maida), stir it, add salt to taste. Add required quantity of hot water, simmer for 5 minutes, add sliced mushroom (500 g) season with spices, cook it for 5 minutes and serve hot.

4. **Mushroom Omelette:** Chop mushrooms and place them in a pan. Add butter, a little salt and pepper and sauté the mushrooms. Fry the omelette mixture and when ready add the sauted mushrooms, fold over and cook for few seconds, serve hot.

5. **Salted mushroom:** Heat the refined oil and add sliced onions. When half cooked, add mushrooms, cover and cook over slow heat. Add a tablespoon of water and if necessary add another tablespoon of water and cook till done. Sprinkle salt and pepper and serve hot with chapaties or sliced bread.

6. **Mushroom samosa:** Cut mushrooms in small pieces, chop onion. Heat ghee in a pan and add mushrooms, chopped onion, green chillies and salt, put off the flame and when water dries up add coriander leaves. Use this for stuffing.

    Sieve white flour, add ghee and make a soft dough by adding water. Make a ball with dough and role them into small chapaties. Cut each into two halves and take one part of it. Fill the samosa with the stuffing. Heat ghee and deep fry, serve hot with tomato sauce or green chutney.

7. **Stuffed capsicum mushroom:** Wash and chop mushroom. Wash and cut capsicums to stuff with mushroom. Trim and remove seeds from capsicums cups. Replace caps and steam in a perforated vessel, about ten minutes, sprinkle salt and keep aside.

    Heat oil, add chillies, onions, and fenugreek leaves, when half done add chopped mushroom cook till mushrooms are done. When still hot, place mushroom stuffing into capsicum cups. Replace caps and steam for two minutes. Remove, add salt to taste and serve.

8. **Mushroom salad:** Boil shelled peas, diced carrots and cubed potatoes in just enough water, cook mushroom in oil and add a table spoon of water. When cooked, add the cooked peas, carrots, potatoes, salt and pepper. French dressing could also be used as an alternate to salt and pepper. Add two table spoons of salad oil or refined oil, two table spoons of vinegar, salt and pepper and half a spoon of sugar and toss them completely before serving.

9. **Mushroom eggs:** Heat cooking oil in a shallow pan. Add chopped onions and a pinch of turmeric and a little curry powder. Add methi leaves and when half done add cut mushrooms, cover with lid and cook mushrooms in milk for 6 to 7 minutes till done. Beat eggs and gently pour over simmering mushrooms covering them completely. Cover with lid and cook till eggs get set. Lift edges with spatulla and carefully slide down pan eggs on mushrooms to a flat plate with egg side up. Serve hot.

(B) Processed Mushrooms

1. **Mushroom Instant-soup:** Contains mushroom powder, dehydrated milk, corn flour and other ingredients. Add 1 teaspoon of soup-powder to boiled water and stir to dissolve throughly for preparing two bowls of hot mushroom soup. Addition of steamed vegetables yields a pleasant taste and makes it more nutritious. Prepare cold soup by pouring soup-powder and ice-cubes in ordinary water. Serve mushroom soup hot or cold with or without steamed vegetables.

2. **Mushroom chips (Vegetarian):** Contains mushroom, soyabean, maize and other cereals, pulses, ground nut, salt and spices. It is fried in refined groundnut oil. It serves as a good crunchy and tasty snack.

3. **Mushroom garlic sauce:** Contains mushroom, garlic, onion and other ingredients. Used an effective taste maker.

4. **Mushroom pickle:**

Fresh mushrooms	125 gms
Mustard powder	Half teaspoon
Turmeric powder	Half teaspoon
Chilli powder	Half teaspoon
Salt	(According to taste)
Sesame oil	30 ml.

Boil mushrooms for ten minutes, drain water and dry in sunlight for two to three hours. Oil, spices and mushrooms are mixed well and then stored in a dry place at room temperature.

5. **Sweet Mushroom Chutney**

    Mushrooms – 1kg, garlic 10 gms, sugar 550 gms, ginger 100 gms, salt 1½ tsp., onion 50 gms, vinegar 80 ml. til oil 50 ml, pepper corn 1 tsp, green chillies – 10 gms, mixed spices 30 gms.

    Wash and slice mushrooms. Chop onion, chilli, garlic, ginger finely. Heat oil in kadai add ginger, garlic, green chilli and cook for about 2 minutes. Add sliced mushrooms and ½ cup water and cook till tender. Add sugar and stir till it leaves water. Add salt, vinegar and red chilli powder and cook for 5 to 7 minutes. Add roasted, powdered spices and cook for 2 min. Let it cool and store in sterilised bottle.

6.6 Commercial Significance of Oyster Mushroom Cultivation

Cultivation of oyster mushroom is mostly done by the seasonal growers without installing any environment controlling device. The methodology of its cultivation is very simple, but different technologies for substrate preparation and its pasteurisation or disinfection are used. In many cases, discarded wastes are used. Thus, there is no uniform method to cultivate the oyster mushroom throughout the country.

The economics of oyster mushroom cultivation for large farm, (India) suggested by Dr. R. C. Upadhyay, Principal Scientist Directorate of Mushroom Research, Chambaghat, Solan (H.P.) during a training in Agartala, October 2010 is presented below

Economics of a Large Farm

a) **Non-recurring expenditure**
   i) 1. Cost of land is Rs. 39,761
       2. Cost of building is Rs. 103,013
       3. Cost of machineries Rs. 16,459
       4. Infrastructure facilities Rs. 159,233
   ii) Total interest and depreciation is Rs. 29,886

b) **Recurring expenditure**

    Cost of raw material, straw, spawn etc.

    Labour wages and interest on working capital is Rs. 117,571.

c) **Cost of Production**

    Total cost of production excluding depreciation is Rs. 147,457.

d) Production of Mushroom

10,732 poly bags per annum i.e. 7235 kg. Price of mushroom @ Rs. 33.48 per kg is Rs. 242,302.

e) Profit calculations

Income on selling Rs. 242,302

Total cost of production Rs. 147,457

Hence, Profit is Rs. 94,845.

Points to Remember

- Mushrooms are large reproductive structures of fungi.
- The cultivation of mushroom was first started with the white button mushroom in France.
- Oyster is the most important and popular mushroom.
- The oyster mushroom (*Pleurotus*) grows under natural conditions as a saprophyte.
- It is cultivated on a commercial basis in 25 different countries all over the world.
- It is cultivated on agricultural wastes.
- ***Pleurotus*** fruiting body is differentiated into stipe, pileus (cap), gills (lamellae), basidia and basidiospores.
- Some important edible mushrooms are species of *Agaricus* and *Pleurotus*.
- Protein, vitamins, minerals, carbohydrate and fat are some of the important resources of edible mushrooms.
- Oyster mushroom is mainly cultivated in small farms as a cottage industry.
- Cultivation practice of oyster mushroom is very simple.
- Oyster mushroom is used as food, medicine, ornamental, in dye industry etc.
- Value added products of oyster mushroom are recipes and processed products.
- There is no uniform method to cultivate the oyster mushroom.
- Commercially production of oyster mushroom is profitable.

Exercises

Short Answer Questions

1. Give nutritive values of *Pleurotus* (oyster) on dry weight basis in tabular form.
2. Enlist any five genera of edible mushrooms.
3. Write a note on "Plant Resources" with respect to protein.
4. Write a note on "Plant Resources" with respect to carbohydrates.
5. Enlist facilities and materials required for mushroom cultivation.

6. Write a note on spawn production.
7. Give an account of methods of substrate preparation in brief.
8. Write any ten uses of mushroom.
9. Give any two recipes of mushroom.
10. Give the process of mushroom pickle production.
11. Write a note on commercial significance of oyster mushroom production.

Long Answer Questions
1. Describe plant resources in oyster mushroom.
2. Describe cultivation practices of oyster mushroom.
3. What is spawn ? Describe spawn production.
4. Explain methods of substrate preparation.
5. Give an account of uses of mushrooms.
6. Explain any five value added products of mushroom studied by you.
7. Explain any four value added products for processed mushrooms.
8. Write Short Notes on
    (i) Facilities and materials required for mushroom cultivation.
    (ii) Spawn production.
    (iii) Do's and dont's of mushroom cultivation.
    (iv) Economic importance of Mushrooms.
    (v) Constituents of Mushroom.

BIBLIOGRAPHY

1. **Krishnamurthy V.** (2000). Algae of India and neighboring countries I. Chlorophycota, Oxford & IBH, New Delhi.
2. **Prescott G.W.** (1969). The algae.
3. **Smith G.M.** (1950). The fresh water algae of the United States, Mc-graw Hill New York.
4. **Das Dutta and Gangulee.** College Botany Vol I, Central Book Depot.
5. **Vashista B.R, Sinha A.K and Singh V.P.** (2005). Botany for degree students – Algae, S.Chand's Publication.
6. **Ainsworth, Sussman and Sparrow (1973).** The fungi. Vol IV A & IV B. Academic Press.
7. **Alexopolous C.J., Minms C.W. and Blackwell M.** (1999). (4th edn) Introductory Mycology. Willey, New York, Alford R.A.
8. **Mehrotra R.S. and Aneja K.R.** (1990). An introduction to mycology. New Age Publishers, ISBN 8122400892
9. **Dube H.C.** (2004). An Introduction to fungi. Vikas Publishers.
10. **Sharma O.P.** (2010). A text book of fungi. S.Chand's Publication.
11. **Vashista B.R and Sinha A.K** (2008). Botany for degree students – Fungi, S.Chand's Publication.
12. **Chopra R.N. and Kumar P.K.** (1988). Biology of Bryophytes. John Wiley & Sons, New York, NY.
13. **Parihar N.S.** (1980). Bryophytes: An Introduction to Embryophyta. Vol I. Central Book Depot, Allahabad.
14. **Prem Puri** (1981). Bryophytes: Morphology, Growth and Differentiation. Atma Ram and Sons, New Delhi.
15. **Watson E.V.** (1971). Structure and Life of Bryophytes. 3rd Edn. Hutchinson University Library, London.
16. **Vashista B.R., Sinha A.K., Kumar A.** (2008). Botany for degree students – Bryophyta, S.Chands Publication.
17. **Eames E.J.** (1983). Morphology of Vascular Plants. Standard University Press
18. **Rashid A.** (1999). An Introduction to Pteridophyta. Vikas Publishing House Pvt. Ltd. New Delhi
19. **Sharma O.P.** (1990). Textbook of Pteridophyta. MacMillan India Ltd. Dehi.
20. **Smith G.M.** (1955). Cryptogamic Botany Vol II. McGraw Hill.

21. **Sporne K.R.** (1986). The morphology of Pteridophytes. Hutchinson University Library, London
22. **Vashista B.R., Sinha A.K., Kumar A.** (2008). Botany for degree students – Pteridophyta, S.Chand Publication.
23. **Gangulee and Kar** (2006). College Botany. New Central Book Agency.
24. **Sundar Rajan S.** (1999). Introduction to Pteridophyta. New Age International Publishers, New Delhi.
25. **Surange K.R.** (1966). Indian Fossil Pteridophytes. CSIR., New Delhi.
26. **Parihar N.S.** (1976). Biology and Morphology of Pteridophytes. Central Book Depot.
27. **Verma V.** Textbook of Economic Botany, Ane Books Pvt. Ltd.
28. **Kochhar**, Economic Botany in the Tropics, Macmillan Publisher.
29. **Gerald E. Wickens**, Economic Botany: Principles and Practices, Springer Publication.
30. **Gurcharan Singh Randhawa and Amitabha Mukhopadhyay**, Floriculture in India, Allied Publishers.
31. **Debashish Sengupta and Raj Kamal**, Floriculture Marketing in India, Excel Books.
32. **Eiri**, Floriculture Hand Book, Engineers India Research in Publication.
33. **John Mason**, Nursery Management, Landlinks Press Publisher.
34. **Ray, P.K.**, Plant Nursery Management: How to Start and Operate a Plant Nursery, Scientific Publishers.
35. **M. K. Razdan**, Introduction to Plant Tissue Culture (2/e), Science Publishers.
36. **Indra K. Vasil, (Eds. - Indra K. Vasil, Trevor A. Thorpe)**, Plant Cell and Tissue Culture, Springer Publication.
37. **NPCS Board of Consultants & Engineers**, The Complete Book on Organic Farming and Production of Organic Compost, Asia Pacific Business Press Inc.
38. **Ann Larkin Hansen**, The Organic Farming Manual: A Comprehensive Guide to Starting and Running a Certified Organic Farm, Storey Publications.
39. Hand Book of Mushroom Cultivation, Processing and Packaging, Engineers India Research In Publishers
40. **Paul Stamets**, Growing Gourmet and Medicinal Mushrooms, Ten Speed Press Publishers
41. **Amarjit S. Basra**, Handbook of Seed Science And Technology: Seed biology, Production, and Technology, Food Products Press publishers

www.ingramcontent.com/pod-product-compliance
Lightning Source LLC
Chambersburg PA
CBHW080243170426

43192CB00014BA/2544